The Colonial Origins
of Ethnic Violence in India

APARC
STANFORD
IIS

THE WALTER H. SHORENSTEIN
ASIA-PACIFIC RESEARCH CENTER

Studies of the Walter H. Shorenstein Asia-Pacific Research Center

Andrew G. Walder, General Editor

The Walter H. Shorenstein Asia-Pacific Research Center in the Freeman Spogli Institute for International Studies at Stanford University sponsors interdisciplinary research on the politics, economies, and societies of contemporary Asia. This monograph series features academic and policy-oriented research by Stanford faculty and other scholars associated with the Center.

The Colonial Origins
of Ethnic Violence in India

Ajay Verghese

Stanford University Press

Stanford, California

Stanford University Press
Stanford, California

Printed on acid-free, archival-quality paper

Printed and bound in Great Britain by
Marston Book Services Ltd, Oxfordshire

Library of Congress Cataloging-in-Publication Data

Verghese, Ajay, author.
 The colonial origins of ethnic violence in India / Ajay Verghese.
 pages cm—(Studies of the Walter H. Shorenstein Asia-Pacific Research Center)
 Includes bibliographical references and index.
 ISBN 978-0-8047-9562-3 (cloth : alk. paper)—
 ISBN 978-0-8047-9813-6 (pbk. : alk. paper)—
 ISBN 978-0-8047-9817-4 (electronic)
 1. Ethnic conflict—India. 2. Political violence—India. 3. India—Ethnic relations.
4. India—Colonial influence. I. Title. II. Series: Studies of the Walter H. Shoren-
stein Asia-Pacific Research Center.
 HN690.Z9S6284 2016
 305.800954—dc23

                              2015028115

Typeset by Bruce Lundquist in 11/14 Adobe Garamond

Contents

*Appendix 3 and Appendix 4 can be found online at http://sites.google.com/site/ajayaverghese/home/data.

List of Illustrations

Tables

Acknowledgments

There are so many people who assisted in the process of writing this book and I am glad to have the opportunity finally to thank them. The project began at The George Washington University (GW) under the supervision of several great teachers. Most of what I know about being a scholar I learned from Manny Teitelbaum. He was never afraid to spare the criticism, and this book wouldn't be the same without his tough love. Henry Hale's brilliant feedback was outdone only by his lightning-fast e-mail turnaround. Henry Farrell was always there to cite just the right book or article when I needed guidance. Dane Kennedy, Irfan Nooruddin, and Kanchan Chandra served as outside readers for the project and helped push my thinking on a number of important issues. I also owe thanks for various reasons to GW Professors Robert Adcock, Eric Lawrence, Harvey Feigenbaum, Shawn McHale, and Kimberly Morgan. In addition, I made many good friends at GW, among them Colm Fox, Enze Han, Brian Karlsson, Craig Kauffman, J. J. Mikulec, Joseph O'Mahoney, and Mike Schroeder. Colm deserves special thanks for creating several of the maps in this book.

A number of scholars provided feedback on various incarnations of this project over the years, including Victoria Farmer, Michael Fisher, Ron Herring, Michael Hechter, Karen Leonard, James Mahoney, and Thomas Rosin. Roberto Foa read the entire manuscript at a very late stage and offered some terrific feedback and much-needed encouragement.

I owe thanks to more people in India than I can possibly recall. My greatest debt is to Asha Sarangi at Jawaharlal Nehru University, who helped me navigate the Indian bureaucracy. I thank in Rajasthan the many fine teachers at the American Institute of Indian Studies' Hindi Language Program, Panjak Sharma and staff at the Jaipur City Palace Archives, the staff of the Institute of Development Studies, and Anupam Sharma. I must thank George and Rekha Varghese, Ronn Mathew, and George Varkey in New Delhi for opening their home to me countless times over the years. My work was also assisted by Radhakrishna Nair, Jaya Prabha Ravindran, and the staff of the National Archives of India. I owe thanks to Thomas Punnose, Jacob Punnose, Premu Philips, Zareena Parveen, and V. Rangaraj at the Andhra Pradesh State Archives and Research Institute, and to the staff of the Nehru Centenary Museum, both in Hyderabad. I must thank Prabha Taunk and the staff of the Deshbandhu Press Library in Raipur, as well as Philip and Mary Cherian, Cecil George, and the staff of the Directorate of Archives in Kerala, especially Reji Kumar, Prakash B., and Pauvabhy. In London, the staff of the British Library were very helpful while I conducted research, and I must thank Frank Verano for generously giving me a place to stay. I also thank Adam Auerbach, Peter Samuels, Julia Kowalski, Patton Burchett, and Lion König for help and camaraderie while I was conducting my fieldwork.

Several institutions provided generous funding for my research, including the Sigur Center for Asian Studies, the Loughran Foundation Endowment, the Konosuke Matsushita Memorial Foundation, and the Cosmos Club. Parts of the book were written while I was a postdoctoral fellow at the Shorenstein Asia-Pacific Research Center at Stanford University, to which I owe a great debt of gratitude. I completed the manuscript while a professor at the University of South Florida St. Petersburg, so I must thank Ray Arsenault, Erica Heinsen-Roach, Hugh LaFollette, Larissa Kopytoff, Adrian O'Connor, Felipe Mantilla, and Thomas Smith for their tireless support. I must also thank the editorial team at Stanford University Press, including Geoffrey Burn, Andrew Walder, James Holt, Anne Fuzellier Jain, Jenny Gavacs, Alice Rowan, and two anonymous reviewers.

I have too many people close to me who deserve my gratitude to list all their names here, but I need to single out two. Travis Valentine has put up with me as a friend for twenty-five years and counting. And without Jenn Ortegren's constant love, care, and support, I am certain I would have gone crazy while writing this book. Last but not least, I need to thank my family. My *ammachi*, Mary Verghese, was very supportive of my research—reminding me before I went to India in 2008 that New Delhi is the capital—and I wish she was here to see the final product. My brother, Ashwin, deserves special thanks for all his support over the years. Finally, my father, Abraham, filled the house with books and gave me a great love of history and politics while I was growing up; and my mother, Anila, always made sure that I did my homework. This book is dedicated to the two of them.

List of Abbreviations

BEIC	British East India Company
BJP	Bharatiya Janata Party
CDR	Centre for Dalit Rights (Jaipur)
CPI	Communist Party of India
CPI-M	Communist Party of India (Marxist)
CPI-ML	Communist Party of India (Marxist-Leninist)
FMS	Federated Malay States
IAS	Indian Administrative Service (formerly ICS—Indian Civil Service)
INC	Indian National Congress
MHA	Ministry of Home Affairs
OBC	Other Backward Class
RSMC	Rajasthan State Minorities Commission
RSS	Rashtriya Swayamsevak Sangh
SCs	Scheduled Castes
STs	Scheduled Tribes
SCST	Scheduled Castes and Scheduled Tribes
UMS	Unfederated Malay States
VHP	Vishva Hindu Parishad
WITS	Worldwide Incidents Tracking System

Glossary of Key Terms

adivasi: "original inhabitant," member of an indigenous tribe

dalit: member of an untouchable caste

darbar: the princely court, used to refer to the government of a princely state

dargah: a shrine, used in this book to refer to the tomb of a Sufi saint in Ajmer

diwan: Chief Minister of a princely state, also spelled *dewan*

istimradars: landlords of Ajmer

jagirdari: an area of land controlled by a Rajput nobleman

jenmi: Hindu landlords in Malabar, also spelled *janmi*

kanamdars: land supervisors in Malabar

khalsa: an area of land controlled directly by the state (British or princely)

Khilafat: an Islamic movement in India to preserve the caliphate of the Ottoman Empire

mansab: ranking in the Mughal political system

Mappillas: Muslims of Malabar

Marathas: Hindu warrior caste in Maharashtra

nawab: a Mughal regional governor

Naxalites: various Maoist guerrilla groups in India

pandaravaka: land controlled by the Travancore princely government *puravaka*: private land in Travancore

raj: rule, or government; India was known as the British Raj

raja, maharaja: king or great king; Hindu ruler of a princely state

rajpramukh: governor of an Indian state between 1948 and 1956

Rajputs: Hindu warrior caste in Rajasthan

reservations: affirmative action quotas

ryotwari: land in which the tribute was collected directly from the peasant

verumpattamdars: cultivators in Malabar

zamindari: a landlord area, usually in British India; a *zamindar* is a
    landlord

The Colonial Origins
of Ethnic Violence in India

Introduction

> Men make their own history, but they do not make it just as they
> please; they do not make it under circumstances chosen by themselves,
> but under circumstances directly encountered, given and transmitted
> from the past. The tradition of all the dead generations weighs like a
> nightmare on the brain of the living.
>
> —*Karl Marx*[1]

In the north Indian state of Rajasthan there are two neighboring districts named Jaipur and Ajmer. To a traveler they would seem almost indistinguishable. Both districts have desert terrain. The people in both areas speak the same language, share a common culture, and work in the same kinds of jobs. The demography of both territories is also similar: they have roughly the same percentage of Hindus and Muslims, as well as members of high castes, low castes, and indigenous tribal groups.[2] Yet these two identical districts responded very differently to a pair of notable political events that occurred in India over the past several decades.

In 1992, a huge mob of Hindu extremists destroyed the Babri Masjid (Mosque) in the northern city of Ayodhya. For years this holy site had attracted the ire of various Hindu nationalist groups who believed it had been built by Muslim invaders on the site of an ancient temple marking the birthplace of the god Ram, the hero of the epic poem Ramayana. The destruction of the Babri Masjid triggered massive Hindu-Muslim riots throughout India. In Jaipur, serious riots gripped the city and led to twenty-eight deaths.[3] Right next door in Ajmer, however, there was no religious rioting.

About a decade and a half later, in 2008, these two districts became sites of another political controversy when huge clashes broke out over the Indian government's policy of reservations, or affirmative action quotas. In India, certain low castes and tribal groups are guaranteed a number of reserved spots in higher education and government jobs. A dispute over the specific allotment in 2008 led to major protests throughout Rajasthan. This time Ajmer was the city embroiled in violence—the government's Rapid Action Force was dispatched there and the entire city was briefly shut down[4]—whereas Jaipur largely remained peaceful.

Contemporary social science research tells us that all individuals have multiple, often crosscutting (or overlapping) ethnic identities, and they can adopt different identities within different societal contexts. Why, therefore, does ethnic conflict in multiethnic states revolve around one particular identity rather than another? Why do people in Jaipur tend to fight over religion whereas people in Ajmer tend to fight over caste and tribal identities? What explains *patterns of ethnic violence* in multiethnic states?

Answering these questions has important implications for India, a violent country wracked by endless Hindu-Muslim riots, caste atrocities, and tribal uprisings (Iyer 2009). But it is also a central question for a number of plural states in Europe, Africa, Asia, and elsewhere. In the broadest sense, the twentieth century witnessed a remarkable amount of political violence based on ethnic identities. The Rwandan genocide, breakup of Yugoslavia, and long-running civil war in Sri Lanka are all emblematic of the brutal ethnic bloodshed that occurs around the world. Beyond this larger point, there are also three additional reasons to understand the genesis of patterns of ethnic conflict. First, not all forms of ethnic violence are equal. Many social scientists argue, for example, that religious identities may be uniquely salient (Wald, Silverman, and Fridy 2005; Grzymala-Busse 2012), and that the fusion of politics and religion is inherently more dangerous than other kinds of ethnic politics (Stark 2001; Vanaik 2007; Wilkinson 2008). A second and related point is that most scholars believe that states have some ability to manipulate the salience of ethnic identities. Policymakers might therefore benefit from de-emphasizing a salient identity—such as religion—in order to lessen the chances of conflict. Finally, understanding how patterns of violence arise can also provide insight into the construction and persistence of ethnic identities over time.

India is an ideal site for this research because it is one of the most ethnically diverse countries in the world—the birthplace of several of the world's major religions and home to thousands of distinct castes, indigenous tribes, and more than twenty official language groups. As Lloyd and Susanne Rudolph (1987: 64) put it, "India is the state Europe would have become had the Holy Roman Empire embodied itself in a modern polity." Table I.1

TABLE I.1
India's Ethnic Demography, 2001

Groups	Percentage
Hindus	80.5
Muslims	13.4
Christians	2.3
Scheduled Castes	16.2
Scheduled Tribes	8.2

SOURCE: Data from 2001 Census.

highlights some of the main ethnic groups studied in this book. This striking pluralism within India has also been implicated in a variety of conflicts throughout the country.

Different regions of multiethnic states tend to experience different kinds of ethnic violence.[5] Northern Ireland has a long history of conflict between Protestants and Catholics, but the rest of the country has been relatively immune from this sectarian violence. In some parts of Nigeria, ethnic conflict centers on religious identity, but in other areas it centers on ancestral city membership. Across Iraq, violence between tribes has engulfed some regions, but tribal politics is conspicuously absent in others. India is no exception: scholars have noted that specific parts of the country contain a "master narrative" that dictates how ethnic conflicts unfold.[6] In the city of Hyderabad, for example, Hindu-Muslim riots have become endemic, but in northern Kerala, caste conflict has long defined the region's politics. These varied conflicts are puzzling because they do not seem to be based on the sizes of the ethnic groups in a particular region (Posner 2005). Almost every district in India is Hindu-majority, yet the Hindu-Muslim divide forms the axis of conflict only in specific parts of the country. In other areas, caste, tribal, or linguistic violence constitutes the dominant narrative of conflict.[7]

Understanding patterns of ethnic violence in India begins with recognizing that the country is one of many postcolonial multiethnic states around the world. The era of European colonialism strongly influenced the long-term development of ethnic politics in a number of countries. The British experience in India, however, was unique due to a key fact: only three-fourths of India's population were ruled by British administrators. They lived in territories known as *provinces*. A massive rebellion in 1857, however, prevented the rest of the country from coming under direct colonial rule. The remainder of the population—according to the 1901 census, more than sixty million people—lived under the control of largely autonomous native kings in territories known as *princely states*.[8] This dichotomy in colonial rule resulted in the creation of two very different political cultures on the subcontinent, and ultimately forms the basis of patterns of ethnic violence today.

Explaining the Argument

This book advances a theory of ethnic conflict centered on history, culture, and institutions. It argues that historical legacies create cultures of conflict or cooperation that, reinforced over time through institutions, drive patterns of ethnic violence in multiethnic states. In India, the era of British colonialism structured long-term ethnic conflict outcomes. There are three components to this argument. First, the British and princely rulers had markedly different understandings of ethnicity. After the Rebellion of 1857, which many colonial administrators interpreted as a religious uprising, British administrators came to believe that *caste* should be promoted as the central organizing principle of a new Indian society. Princely rulers, on the other hand, had always emphasized *religion,* and they were encouraged to continue to do so by the British when they took a laissez-faire approach to princely areas after the Rebellion. Two different political cultures subsequently emerged across the provinces and princely states (Putnam 1993).

Second, given these differential understandings of ethnicity, colonial rulers created disparate policies of ethnic stratification (Hechter 1975; Horowitz 1985). Certain ethnic groups were privileged whereas others were subjugated, often for the most capricious of reasons. In the provinces, British administrators implemented policies that benefited high castes, discriminated against low castes and tribals, and protected religious minorities. In the princely states, native kings did the opposite: their policies benefited their coreligionists, discriminated against non-coreligionists, and protected low castes and tribals. Bifurcated colonial rule[9] led to the creation of different fault lines of ethnic conflict across the provinces and princely states.

Third, these differential political cultures and social fissures were reinforced through institutions. After independence arrived in 1947 the princely states were unified with the provinces, and although on paper most political organizations became identical, they operated in different environments; institutions thus reproduced cultural divides across the provinces and princely states. In addition, India's independence did not disrupt existing patterns of violence because the new government did not reform most of the vestiges of its colonial past. In the former provinces, on the one hand, low-caste and tribal groups continue to suffer under the weight of historic discrimination, and reform efforts have failed to minimize the violence. In the former princely states, on the other hand, it is mainly minority religious groups that suffer from discriminatory legacies. Once patterns of ethnic violence were created, both formal and informal institutions embedded them in society.

This book shows that the former British provinces in India experience higher levels of caste and tribal violence whereas the former princely states experience more religious violence. The reason religion forms the basis of ethnic conflict in Jaipur is that the state was controlled by a Hindu dynasty during colonialism; the reason Ajmer experiences caste and tribal violence is that it was governed instead by British administrators.

This argument relies on certain key terms that should be clarified at the outset. I follow Donald Horowitz (1985: 53) in describing the term *ethnic* as encompassing "groups differentiated by color, language, and religion; it covers 'tribes,' 'races,' 'nationalities,' and castes." The three kinds of ethnic identities examined in this book are those based on caste, tribe, and religion.[10] Relatedly, individuals have multiple ethnic identities. Kanchan Chandra (2012) carefully distinguishes between "nominal" and "activated" categories. The former is the set of ethnic identities to which a person may belong; the latter is the set of identities to which an individual professes membership or is assigned by others. These ethnic identities may also be crosscutting: members of a tribal group may be Hindu, and Muslims may have caste identities. The rich ethnic diversity of India means that in every region there are several potential fault lines of conflict, but violence tends to revolve around one dominant axis.

The term *ethnicity*, on the other hand, is about uncertainty reduction. Ethnic markers are merely one way of reducing the complexity of the social world, but they are uniquely powerful because ethnic groups share myths of a common origin, a sense of a common fate, a common culture and symbols, and physical similarities, and they face reduced barriers to communication (Brubaker, Loveman, and Stamatov 2004; Hale 2004, 2008).[11] Ethnicity is not simply instrumental; it also connotes a way of interpreting and making sense of the social world.

Ethnic violence is violence that occurs largely along ethnic lines.[12] Rogers Brubaker and David Laitin (1998: 428) emphasize two further components of this definition: at least one party must not be the state,[13] and ethnic identity must be "integral rather than incidental" to the conflict. In regard to this last point, many scholars have argued that what seem like ethnicity-based conflicts are often not explicitly ethnic but rather interpreted or officially stylized that way after the fact (Brass 1997; Mueller 2000; Kalyvas 2003). While remaining sensitive to this argument, this book shows that the historic construction and stratification of ethnic groups created distinct patterns of violence in contemporary India.

Finally, I use a broad definition of *institutions*: "not just formal rules, procedures or norms, but the symbol systems, cognitive scripts, and moral templates that provide the 'frames of meaning' guiding human action" (Hall and Taylor 1996: 947). Specifically, a number of insights are drawn from the literature on sociological institutionalism (Fligstein 1990; Dobbin 1994). Most important, according to this school, institutions are a means by which culture is transmitted over time. In India, both formal institutions like political parties and informal institutions like the collective memories of ethnic groups reinforced long-term cultural divides between the provinces and princely states. The argument here can be placed alongside a number of impressive recent works that are beginning to assess the institutional bases of ethnic conflict around the world (Cederman, Wimmer, and Min 2010; Lieberman and Singh 2012; Jha 2013).

Many of the puzzles examined in this book have been the focus of scholars across the social sciences working on the politics of a variety of regions and countries. Potential answers to several important research questions—about the causes of Hindu-Muslim riots in India, the nature of ethnic salience, and the relationship between colonial rule and contemporary ethnic violence—are offered through this study.

A number of scholars have made major advancements in the study of ethnic violence in India, specifically Hindu-Muslim riots. This literature has rightly been called "one of the most striking examples in recent years of the development of a cumulative research program in political science" (Chandra 2006b: 207). Recently, three scholars have put forward theories to explain these riots.[14] Paul Brass (1997, 2003) has argued that communal[15] riots in India are not random acts of violence but rather are driven by "riot specialists," many of whom belong to militant Hindu nationalist organizations such as the Vishva Hindu Parishad (World Hindu Council), the Rashtriya Swayamsevak Sangh (National Volunteer Association), and the Bharatiya

Janata Party (Indian People's Party). Ashutosh Varshney (2002) argues that violence occurs when intercommunal links—those that cross religious divides—do not exist in society. These links may be formal (business organizations, neighborhood peace committees) or informal (Hindu and Muslim families eating together), although formal links are stronger. Steven Wilkinson (2004) advances an electoral theory of Hindu-Muslim violence, arguing that politicians have the ability to prevent riots through their control of the police force. Local politicians will do this when Muslims form an important voting bloc, or when the party system is so competitive that the governing parties will need future coalition partners.

These works have illuminated fascinating and undoubtedly important aspects of Hindu-Muslim violence in India, but this book aims to correct two underlying problems from this literature. The first is a historical problem: all three theories focus largely on the twentieth century, especially the post-independence period. But communalism represents a significantly deeper dilemma for India. Marc Gaborieau (1985: 12) notes that Hindu-Muslim riots occurred routinely in the past, even long before the British arrived on the subcontinent. He recounts:

> The oldest evidence I came across is from Ibn Battuta, the 14th century Moroccan traveller. He speaks of the South Indian town of Mangalore which was still under Hindu rule. There was there a community of 4,000 Muslim merchants who lived in a suburb near the Hindu town (note the spatial segregation). Then, Ibn Battuta continues, "war frequently breaks out between them (the Muslims) and the (Hindu) inhabitants of the town; but the Sultan (the Hindu King) keeps them at peace because he needs the merchants."

This fact creates complications for existing arguments. For example, why did Hindu-Muslim riots occur for hundreds of years prior to the introduction of an electoral system? Though elites undoubtedly manipulated ethnic identities in the past, large-scale violence occurred despite the lack of formal electoral competition. Similarly, as responsible as Hindu nationalists may be for contemporary riots, they are not the explanation for medieval conflict. This book advances the existing literature by considering the *underlying* causes of ethnic violence in India. It analyzes conflict within a longer historical time frame, one spanning the precolonial, colonial, and postcolonial periods.

A second problem of existing research is its narrow focus on religion. The brutality of Hindu-Muslim riots is evident in India, but many kinds of ethnic conflict are plaguing the country. Violence involving secessionist linguistic groups in the northeast, rural low-caste uprisings in the so-called Hindi belt (a large region in north India where Hindi is the primary language), and tribal rebellions in the jungles of eastern India have been comparatively understudied in recent political science research.[16] Consider the impact of caste violence: in 2010 a total of 32,712 crimes were committed against members of the Scheduled Castes.[17] This book advances the existing literature by looking at religious violence in tandem with caste and tribal violence, thereby providing a more comprehensive portrait of ethnic conflict in contemporary India. Naturally one risk with such a broad scope is that different types of ethnic violence may have different causes. This is probably true—for instance, caste and tribal violence are largely driven by land issues. However, all of these conflicts may be called ethnic conflicts,[18] and patterns of violence are largely driven by legacies inherited from the past.

Another area of social science research has tried to unravel the puzzle of ethnic salience: explaining why some kinds of identities become heightened or prioritized over others. There are several studies of ethnic salience,[19] but two major arguments can perhaps simplify the debate. An historical account comes from David Laitin's (1986) work on ethnic cleavages and conflict in Nigeria. Laitin set out to explain why politics in Yorubaland revolved around ancestral city membership rather than religion, even though there was a clear Muslim-Christian divide in the region. He found that British colonial administrators had "expunged" (154) religion as a legitimate form of ethnic classification, thereby creating a hegemony of ancestral city membership, which then became the main axis of conflict. A competing rationalist account of ethnic salience comes from the work of Daniel Posner (2005), who studied why ethnic competition in Zambia focused on either tribal or linguistic identities. He posits that individuals consider the sizes of ethnic groups in a region, then form "minimum winning coalitions"—that is, they pick which identities most benefit them given specific institutional rules. In this account, ethnic identities have no major purpose other than their instrumental value. According to Posner, the salience of a particular identity can be inferred from the ethnic demography of a region.

These explanations of ethnic salience are focused on African politics, but this book advances research on this question by examining the comparative implications of these theories. In India, an historical account of ethnic salience has more explanatory value than a rationalist account in that patterns of ethnic conflict are based on colonial history, not instrumental motivations. However, building on Laitin's work, this book places special focus on the role of institutions in explaining how historical legacies are then transmitted into contemporary politics. This approach also has an important social policy corollary: in the realm of violence, ethnic identities do not change as quickly or easily as some scholars are inclined to believe.

Finally, this project contributes to the broad literature linking colonialism and ethnic conflict.[20] Scholars across the social sciences argue that colonial officials increased conflict between ethnic groups in a wide variety of ways. In some cases, new communities were formed, such as the Manyika tribe of Zimbabwe, which was a product of the British colonial imagination (Ranger 1988). Colonial censuses hardened what were often fluid identities, such as when Americans drew a distinction between "civilized" and "wild" tribes in the Philippines (Vergara 1995). New arbitrary political borders divided ethnic communities, which is why the Maasai people suddenly found themselves strewn across the unfamiliar states of Kenya and Tanzania. Favoritism toward certain ethnic groups promoted resentment among others, as in the Belgian preference for Tutsis in Rwanda, which infuriated the Hutu majority, with ultimately tragic consequences (Hintjens 1999; Mamdani 2002).

But the problem with assessing the impact of colonialism in producing ethnic violence is two alternative arguments that scholars often fail to address: that violence predated colonial rule or that it would have developed despite colonial rule. For example, tribal violence throughout the continent may have occurred long before the Scramble for Africa (Kasozi, Musisi, and Sejjengo 1994; Reid 2007). Similarly, British rule in India may have simply covaried with the explosion that appears to have occurred in the number of riots in the nineteenth century. Violence between Hindus and Muslims during this period may have been caused instead by revivalist religious movements (Hardy 1972) or by new "public arenas" for religious festivals and processions that became sites of fierce political contestation (Freitag 1989).

India is an invaluable country in considering these problems because it allows researchers the opportunity to compare colonial rule (British India) with its relative absence (princely India). Princely India was in many ways a continuation of precolonial political traditions. Furthermore, the rulers of the princely states were often remarkably free of colonial interference. Sir William Lee-Warner of the Indian Civil Service once noted that it was the Resident—an officer assigned to the princely court as the colonial government's representative—who alone made up the "slender thread that ties the State to the . . . British power".[21] In short, by comparing provinces and princely states it is possible to isolate the effects of colonialism on ethnic violence.[22] Doing so helps to avoid a recurring problem in this general area of research, which is the assumption among scholars that colonialism increased all forms of ethnic violence. This book comes to a more nuanced conclusion: although British rule is responsible for the promotion of caste and tribal violence in modern India, it likely reduced religious violence over the long term. Large-scale violence among India's religious communities long predates the arrival of the British.

British administrators considered the "Indian model" of colonialism—combining direct and indirect rule—to be a major success after 1857 because it prevented further rebellions, and this led to its adoption (with regional variations) in several other colonies located on the periphery of the Indian Ocean. The Indian model was exported to parts of eastern and southern Africa, as well as to states in Southeast Asia (Fisher 1991; Metcalf 2007). Understanding the history of India can therefore help to explain patterns of ethnic conflict in a wide array of former British colonial states—cases as diverse as Myanmar, Malaysia, and Nigeria.

Methods and Organization

This book examines patterns of ethnic violence in contemporary India by utilizing a multimethod research design,[23] drawing on a variety of qualitative methods as well as a quantitative analysis.[24] The qualitative research strategy involved spending fifteen months in the field collecting archival material and conducting dozens of elite interviews in five carefully chosen case studies. An extensive array of primary source material was collected from six repositories, both national and regional: the National Archives of India, the Jaipur City Palace Archives, the Andhra Pradesh State Archives, the Deshbandhu Press Library, the Kerala State Archives, and the British Library in London. The archival material mainly covers the late nineteenth and early twentieth centuries, which is when princely rulers had their highest level of freedom vis–à–vis the British, after the Rebellion of 1857. Both British and princely sources are included, and though the majority of the documents were written in English, I translated some of them from Hindi.

In addition to primary sources, these archives also had significant collections of secondary source material, much of it written by Indian experts whose work is little known by Western scholars. This historical material illustrates the stark differences between how ethnic politics and violence developed in the British provinces and how they developed in the princely states.

The other qualitative portion of the project involved interviewing dozens of elites, mostly in Hindi, in five case studies across India. Respondents came from a wide variety of backgrounds so that the results could be triangulated. Typical respondents included government officials (from various agencies and departments), NGO workers, police officers, journalists, and academics, among others. The purpose of these interviews was to obtain information about the contemporary state of the ethnic groups included in the case studies (because systematic data were often lacking on this question), as well as insight into the tensions and conflicts among them.

Because of India's enormous diversity, no single district or state is representative of the country, so it was extremely important to select areas to study from different regions (Snyder 2001). The cases examined therefore span northern, southern, and eastern India. The first two pairs of case studies are controlled historical comparisons. This terminology is adapted from Alexander George and Andrew Bennett's (2005: 151) idea of a controlled comparison, defined as "the study of two or more instances of a well-specified phenomenon that resemble each other in every respect but one." In other words, the two cases are similar in most regards—ethnic demography, geography, level of economic development, and so on—but different in regard to colonial history.[25] Using paired comparisons can also help to minimize the vexing problem of endogeneity—that is, determining why the British conquered certain territories and not others. The fifth and final case is the largest outlier for the theory of ethnic conflict proposed in this book. Map I.1 and Table I.2 detail the location of and basic information about these five cases.

The first controlled historical comparison is between Jaipur and Ajmer districts in Rajasthan. These two cases are remarkably similar except that during the colonial period Jaipur was a princely state and Ajmer was a British province. This difference created a key historical divergence between these two territories, one that has had major implications for patterns of ethnic violence across both areas today. In Jaipur, on the one hand, Hindu kings implemented policies that were discriminatory toward the Muslim minority,

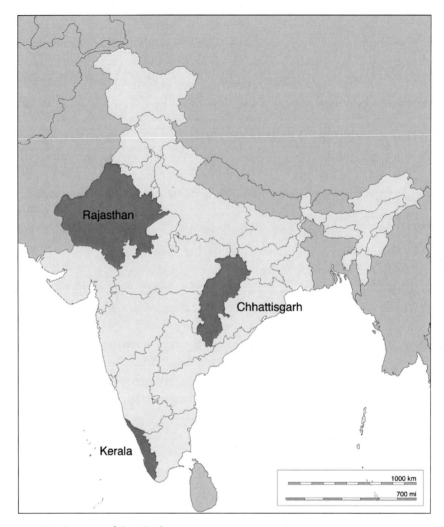

MAP I.I. Location of Case Studies.

SOURCE: Produced by Colm Fox. Original source: http://d-maps.com/carte.php?num_car=4182&lang=en.

TABLE I.2
Book Case Studies

Location	Cases	Type
Rajasthan	Jaipur	Princely
	Ajmer	Province
Kerala	Travancore	Princely
	Malabar	Province
Chhattisgarh	Bastar	Princely

thereby creating a long legacy of religious violence. In Ajmer, on the other hand, new British policies engendered violence between high and low castes.

The second controlled historical comparison comes from the south Indian state of Kerala. A southern state was chosen foremost to account for the vast historical and cultural differences between north and south India. The northern Malabar region of Kerala is compared with the southern Travancore region; the former came under the control of the British whereas the latter remained independent. Whereas the Jaipur-Ajmer study is a district-level comparison, the Malabar-Travancore study is a broader state-level comparison.

The Kerala comparison is unique for two reasons. British administrators in the early twentieth century believed that the state's divided political administration was merely a historical "accident," as they described it. Archival evidence confirms that the British were interested in conquering Travancore, but for various contingent reasons they were unable to do so. This situation creates a striking opportunity to assess directly the impact of colonial rule on ethnic violence: all of Kerala should have come under British rule, but instead the south remained independent. A second point about Kerala is that it is not a violent state and is actually considered one of India's greatest developmental success stories. Despite this fact, ethnic tension—and occasionally violence—does occur in the region, and the historical accident of divided rule has led to a discernible pattern across the north and south. British rule in Malabar led to the growth of caste politics and conflict whereas princely rule in the south created a legacy of religiosity and communal violence involving Hindus, Muslims, and Christians.

The final case—the tiny princely state of Bastar in eastern India, located in the state of Chhattisgarh—is the key deviant case for the theory of ethnic conflict proposed here. Despite the fact that Bastar is a former Hindu kingdom, this remote territory of more than two million people accounts for *one-third* of all tribal violence in contemporary India. Detailed archival evidence shows that although Bastar was nominally a princely state, it experienced an unrivaled amount of colonial interference, which constitutes the original cause of tribal violence in the kingdom.

The qualitative evidence collected from fieldwork is complemented by a large-*n* statistical analysis of ethnic conflict patterns across the entire country. The results of this quantitative study are based in part on a new dataset that offers detailed information about caste and tribal violence in India from 2005 to 2009. These conflict data were compiled from the Worldwide Incidents Tracking System (WITS), a repository created by the US government's National Counterterrorism Center using national and international press reports of violence (Wigle 2010).[26] The Varshney-Wilkinson (2006) database of Hindu-Muslim riots (1950–95) was utilized to study contemporary communal violence.

The statistical analysis also draws on control variables aggregated from a wide array of sources—colonial gazetteers, Indian census reports, and private statistical firms—in order to test competing explanations. The results of the quantitative study show that British rule is positively correlated with contemporary caste and tribal violence, but negatively correlated with contemporary religious violence. The results are also sensitive to a number of robustness checks. Both the qualitative and quantitative analyses, in other words, provide strong evidence of the impact of colonial history in explaining contemporary conflict in India.

This book proceeds as follows: Chapter 1 uses a new interpretation of British colonial history to detail a theory about the origins of ethnic conflict in India. The controlled comparisons from Rajasthan and Kerala provide qualitative evidence for this theory and are presented in Chapters 2 and 3. Chapter 4 examines and explains the deviant case of Bastar. Chapter 5 details the quantitative analysis, showcasing that ethnic conflict patterns across the entire country mirror the case studies. Chapter 6 examines the broader impact of what became known as the Indian model of colonialism. In the late nineteenth century, this model was exported to a number of other British colonies bordering the Indian Ocean. Chapter 6 argues that understanding the nature of ethnic conflict in India helps to explain variations in conflict in three other postcolonial British states: Myanmar, Malaysia, and Nigeria. The concluding chapter then summarizes the project, outlines the ways in which it has contributed to existing social science literatures, and ends by considering the social policy implications of this research. Despite an emphasis on the historical nature of contemporary violence in India, a sense of determinism is misplaced. There are lessons to be learned from the past and important ways for India to overcome that past and achieve more ethnic peace in the future.

CHAPTER I

Colonialism, Institutions, and Ethnic Violence in India

> Aspects of the British-princely distinction persisted in the political
> behavior of a generation of postindependence Indian politicians and
> their constituents. In certain contemporary Indian states, however, the
> significance of the British/princely distinction has been even greater:
> historical-political heterogeneity—briefly, the fact and the consequences
> of British versus princely rule in historically separate territorial units—
> has fundamentally influenced the formation of the contemporary state
> and its evolution as a political community.
>
> —*John Wood*[1]

Contemporary patterns of ethnic conflict in India were constructed during the period of British colonialism on the subcontinent.[2] In the mid-nineteenth century, a massive rebellion against the British East India Company ended imperial expansion and fixed the boundaries between British and princely India. Princely rulers were not simply controlled by the British; rather, they were largely autonomous within their kingdoms, especially during the run-up to independence. Colonial officials and the princes had strikingly different conceptions about ethnicity and how to organize and stratify ethnic groups, and their disparate policies created different fault lines of conflict. After independence in 1947, the institutions of the provinces and princely states transmitted the legacies of the past into modern Indian politics.

A Glimpse of Medieval India

Prior to the establishment of British rule, the most important political events on the subcontinent were a series of invasions by Islamic warlords from Central Asia. The earliest of these invasions reached the borders of modern India by the eleventh century,[3] and the last, the Mughal conquest,[4]

began in the sixteenth century. The Mughals hailed from modern Uzbeki-
stan, and the founding of their empire is dated to the victory of Zahiruddin
Muhammad Babur (who reigned from 1526 to 1530),[5] the first Mughal emperor, over the Afghan Lodi dynasty in the Battle of Panipat in 1526. Over
the next two centuries, the Mughals consolidated their rule over most of
India with the exclusion of its southern tip. Because this book's central focus
is on the influence of the British period on contemporary patterns of ethnic
violence in India, it is important to consider what is known about ethnic
politics and conflict prior to the onset of colonialism, primarily during the
period of Mughal rule.

The literature on religion during the precolonial period is fraught with
disagreement and controversy. One school of scholars tends to highlight
Hindu-Muslim synthesis and the creation of a composite or "syncretic" culture during the Mughal era, especially during the reign of tolerant emperors such as Akbar (1556–1605).[6] They argue that describing the Mughals as
Islamic is "communalizing history" because it glosses over the fact that this
category included groups as varied as Turks, Afghans, and Persians (Mukhia
1972; Jha 1998). Similarly, the term *Hindu* referred not to a consolidated
bloc but to individual sects that worshipped different gods such as Shiva
or Vishnu (Bhagat 2001: 4353). These scholars emphasize peaceful everyday interaction between the two religious communities. As Mushirul Hasan
summarizes it, "The dominant picture of the seventeenth and eighteenth
centuries is not of the Hindus and Muslims forming exclusive and antago-
nistic categories, but of their cooperating in cultural and social affairs."[7]

There is considerable evidence, however, that despite this rosy picture the
precolonial period was actually marked by significant religious discrimination and strife.[8] First, like most precolonial rulers of India, the Mughals
used religion as the main source of legitimation for their rule (Buultjens
1986; Richards 1993). And although the modern Hindu and Muslim categories may not yet have existed, there were still stark differences between these
communities (van der Veer 1994: 29–31). Francis Robinson (1974: 13) notes
that "the Hindus worshipped idols, the Muslims abhorred them. The Hindus had many gods, the Muslims had one. The Hindus revered the cow, the
Muslims ate it." Stanley Wolpert (2009: 108) concludes that it is "difficult to
imagine two religious ways of life more different than Islam and Hinduism."
Islamic rule in India also accelerated the process of consolidating the Hindu
community. Poets like Tukaram and Ramdas began to promote a more

unified version of Hinduism as early as the seventeenth century (Michaels 2004: 44; see also Nicholson 2014). Similarly, from the fourteenth to the seventeenth century, the Vijayanagara Empire politically united Hindus throughout south India to oppose Islamic invasions from the north.

Some quantitative data are available on the integration of Hindus into the Mughal imperial system. Figure 1.1 details the percentage of Mughal *mansabdars* (rank-holders) who were Hindus and Muslims during the reign of three emperors: Akbar, Jahangir, and Shah Jahan. Mansabdars were non-hereditary leaders of the empire who commanded armies and governed territory. They were granted different rankings (the term *mansab* means rank) by the Mughal emperor. Despite constituting an overwhelming percentage of the population, Hindus were generally relegated to a subordinate position within the system.[9]

In terms of communal violence, John F. Richards (1993: 2) finds that the earliest Islamic forces in India "appealed regularly to Muslim militancy in the *jihad* or holy war against the idolatrous Hindus of the subcontinent." Muslim scholar al-Biruni, writing in the eleventh century, remarked about the "wonderful exploits [of Muslim conqueror Mahmud of Ghazni], by which the Hindus became like atoms of dust scattered in all directions."[10]

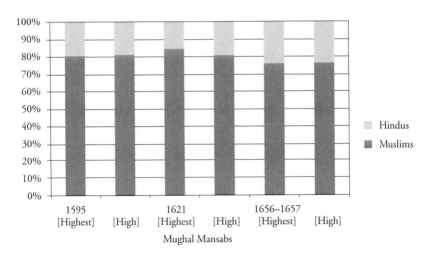

FIGURE 1.1. Communal Composition of Mughal Mansabdars. Percentage of Hindus and Muslims holding Mughal highest and high mansabs during the reign of three emperors: Akbar (1595), Jahangir (1621), and Shah Jahan (1656–57).
SOURCE: Char 1991: 159.

Before the Turko-Mongol ruler Timur sacked Delhi in 1398 and slaughtered countless Hindus, he recounted, "My officers told me that the inhabitants of Hindustan were infidels and unbelievers. In obedience to Almighty God, I determined to make an expedition against them."[11]

Regardless of the significant historical divide on the question of religion in precolonial India, there is some agreement that during the period of Mughal decline (in the late seventeenth and early eighteenth centuries), and especially during the reign of Aurangzeb (1658–1707), communal violence intensified (Sarkar 1932; Chand 1962; Richards 1976). This period saw an increase in the influence of Islamic officials at the Mughal court, as well as forced conversions and the widespread destruction of Hindu temples.[12] Aurangzeb was also responsible in 1679 for reinstating the *jizyah* (tax on non-Muslims), which had been abolished during the reign of Akbar. Saqi Mustad Khan, employed in Aurangzeb's court and author of an authoritative account of the emperor's life, *Maasir-i-Alamgiri,* wrote about the decision:

> As all the aims of the religious Emperor were directed to the spreading of the law of Islam and the overthrow of the practice of the infidels, he issued orders to the . . . officers that from Wednesday, the 2nd April, 1679 . . . in obedience to the Qur'anic injunction "till they pay commutation money (*jizyah*) with the hand in humility" and in agreement with the canonical traditions, *jizyah* should be collected from the infidels . . . of the capital and the provinces.[13]

The reign of Aurangzeb saw the rise of numerous religious revolts, such as those initiated by the Hindu Marathas from Maharashtra,[14] the Sikhs from Punjab, and even the once loyal Hindu Rajputs from Rajasthan. And when Delhi's Hindu population massed outside the Red Fort to protest the emperor's discrimination, Mughal elephants were dispatched to stampede them (Wolpert 2009: 162–72). The only area that was spared the endless communal violence of this period was the peninsular south; states such as Kerala never came under Mughal hegemony and, therefore, in those regions the salience of the religious divide did not resonate as strongly.

In comparison, there are fewer examples of caste and tribal conflicts during the Mughal period, although the imperial religious policies of this era have certainly aroused the lion's share of scholarly interest. The caste system in the precolonial period was not fixed, and there was mobility outside the top of the hierarchy (Cohn 2008; Mayaram 2008). More important is that caste divisions were not as rigid as divisions based on religion, especially because Islam arrived in north India through centuries of invasion. So although precolonial identities may have been "fuzzy," they were not all equally fuzzy. Nirad Chaudhuri explains: "In its emotional aspect the new [religious] division was infinitely more embittered than the old opposition between the primitives and the civilized Hindus . . . it did not generate a fraction of the venom which the Hindu-Muslim enmity engendered."[15]

Al-Biruni's detailed account of medieval India further illustrates this point. On the difference between Hindus and Muslims he famously wrote:

> They (the Hindus) totally differ from us in religion, as we believe in nothing in which they believe and vice versa. . . . Their fanaticism is directed against those who do not belong to them—against all foreigners. They call them *mleccha,* i.e. impure, and forbid having any connection with them, be it by marriage or any other kind of relationship, or by sitting, eating, drinking with them, because thereby they think they would be polluted. The Hindus claim to differ from us, and to be something better than we, as we on our side, of course, do vice versa.[16]

But about differences within the caste system he noted a quite different situation: "Between the latter two classes [castes] there is no very great distance. Much, however, as these classes differ from each other, they live together in the same towns and villages, mixed together in the same houses and lodgings."[17] And whereas those outside the caste system were considered untouchable by high-caste Hindus, Muslims were depicted in temple inscriptions from the medieval period as something markedly worse—demonic hordes, an allusion to the Ramayana, in which Ram battles the demon army of Ravana (Pollock 1993; Talbot 1995).

In terms of caste conflict, it is not clear that Muslim rule in India led to increasing stratification or violence between different Hindu castes, and the Mughals "generally refrained from intrusive meddling" in the caste system (Richards 2003: 32). Moreover, the rise of widespread caste politics dates instead to the immediate post-Mughal period (Bayly 1999: 369). And though it is true that there were peasant uprisings against the Mughals that presumably involved Hindu cultivators, Kathleen Gough (1974: 1392) notes that it was "British rule [that] brought a degree of disruption and suffering among the peasantry which was, it seems likely, more prolonged and widespread than had occurred in Mogul times."

Conflict involving India's *adivasis* was also relatively limited during Mughal rule. Christoph von Fürer-Haimendorf (1982: 34), noted tribal anthropologist of India, writes about the relationship between tribals and the

Mughal administration that "for long periods the hillmen and forest dwellers were left undisturbed [by the Mughals]. Under British rule, however, a new situation arose. The extension of a centralized administration . . . deprived many of the aboriginal tribes of their autonomy." The Mughal policy of not disturbing tribal society generally promoted peace, but it was subsequently upended during colonialism.[18]

In sum, scholars have located extensive religious conflict during the Mughal period, but there is less evidence for widespread caste or tribal conflict. This was the legacy of ethnic violence that the British inherited when they reached the subcontinent in the early seventeenth century.

The British Provinces and the Princely States

In 1608, William Hawkins, a representative of the court of King James I of England, arrived in the port city of Surat in modern-day Gujarat as part of a mission to request trading rights from the Mughal emperor Jahangir (1605–27). This expedition marked the humble start of the British Raj. The British East India Company (BEIC) would eventually come to control a vast portion of the subcontinent, and the empire that succeeded it at its peak governed around four hundred million people. India was the most important of the British colonies—the so-called jewel in the crown of the empire. Lord Curzon, Viceroy of India from 1899 to 1905, once stated: "We could lose all our [white settlement] dominions and still survive, but if we lost India, our sun would sink to its setting."[19]

When the British first arrived on the subcontinent, the Mughal Empire was firmly consolidated. After the death of Aurangzeb in 1707, however, the empire quickly fractured. A number of new powers, especially the Marathas, began to challenge Mughal supremacy, and although regional leaders remained officially tied to the Mughal emperor, in Bengal, Hyderabad, and other areas they carved out independent kingdoms.

The period of British rule on the subcontinent constituted a singular era in Indian history, marking the greatest extent to which any state had, until that point, come to exercise centralized control over the country. That this state was a European, technologically advanced power only amplified the effect. One beachhead of British rule was Bengal, an area in which the BEIC had significantly expanded its commercial ventures. After trading rights were granted to the British in 1615, they gradually began to expand their clout in the region. In 1698 they began purchasing *zamindari* (landlord system) rights—the ability to collect taxes—from villages in territory around Calcutta. The Company at this time officially operated as a client of the Mughal emperor. This relationship continued until the aggressiveness of the British in their commercial expansion resulted in a backlash from the local *nawab* (Mughal regional governor) of Bengal, who managed to briefly expel the Company from Calcutta. The British responded by defeating the nawab's armies at the historic Battle of Plassey in 1757.

The Battle of Buxar in 1764 marked another major turning point because it allowed the British to expand into the Gangetic plains, and it prompted the first dispatching of Residents to the courts of princely rulers (Fisher 1991: 49–50). The BEIC then, in 1765, obtained *diwani*—chief land revenue collector—rights in Bengal. Philip Mason (1985: 36) recounts that this "was the biggest single step in the transformation of traders into rulers." Among the significant changes in this "post-Plassey" period was the introduction by Governor-General Lord Cornwallis (1786–93) in 1793 of the Permanent Settlement, a new system of revenue collection and land ownership that attempted to create a class of landlord rulers (zamindars) in India similar to the large-scale landowners of England (Guha 1981).

The period from 1765 to 1813 was marked by a policy of creating a "ring fence," or buffer, between the Company's territories and their external threats. During this period, the British were one of many powers in India, and they were largely concerned with consolidating territory. From 1813 to 1857, however, the Company became more aggressive, implementing a policy of "subordinate isolation" that was intended to establish British supremacy in India by annexing native states and increasing the power of Residents. The years 1848 to 1856 were especially important; it was during this period that Governor-General Lord Dalhousie established the Doctrine of Lapse. Prior to this policy, the British had allowed princes to adopt heirs when they did not have a son in line for the throne. Once the Doctrine of Lapse was instituted in 1848, the British disallowed this practice and annexed territories where princes did not have natural male heirs (Chopra et al. 2003: 137–40).

The expansion of British power throughout India during this time was, on the whole, haphazard, with "no conscious plan or coherent organization" (Fisher 1991: 123). Most likely the entire subcontinent would have come under British control if not for rebellion (Copland 2002: 15). But colonial administrators were strategic in how they annexed territory; they conquered areas that were agriculturally productive (that is, had fertile land) or near one of the coasts, and by the mid-nineteenth century the remaining princely states "were located mainly in less economically productive areas" (Ramusack 2004: 186).

Company political rule continued to strengthen in India during the nineteenth century, until the Rebellion of 1857. This conflict began when *sepoys*—native Indian soldiers serving in the Company army—refused to use new rifle cartridges allegedly coated with either beef fat (offensive to Hindus) or pork fat (offensive to Muslims). Several insubordinate sepoys were imprisoned, which resulted in army mutiny throughout the whole of north India. A few princely rulers joined the revolt, but the vast majority did not. The rebels eventually marched to Delhi to restore the Mughal Empire under the aging emperor Bahadur Shah II.

It took a full year for the British to suppress the Rebellion, and colonial power in India was fundamentally altered in the wake of the revolt. The Government of India Act 1858 was subsequently passed in British Parliament. It contained a number of far-reaching reforms. Most important, it transferred rule of India from the BEIC to the crown, and Queen Victoria was eventually styled as the Empress of India. It also led to the creation of a Secretary of State for India (in London), a Viceroy of India (the crown's representative in India), and a new bureaucracy named the Indian Civil Service. The Mughal Empire was dissolved, and Bahadur Shah II was exiled to Burma.

The Rebellion of 1857 was a critical juncture in Indian history, locking in place the boundaries between the provinces and the princely states. As Queen Victoria stated in a declaration to the princes after the conflict, "all treaties and engagements made with [India's princes] by or under the authority of the Honourable East India Company are by us accepted, and will be scrupulously maintained."[20] She further assured the princes that the British sought "no extension of [their] present territorial possessions," and no further states were annexed after the Rebellion. Map 1.1 showcases the divisions between British India (shaded) and the princely states. The provinces constituted roughly three-fifths of the area of the country and three-fourths of its population.

After the Rebellion, the boundaries between British and princely India became permanent. There were at one point more than six hundred native

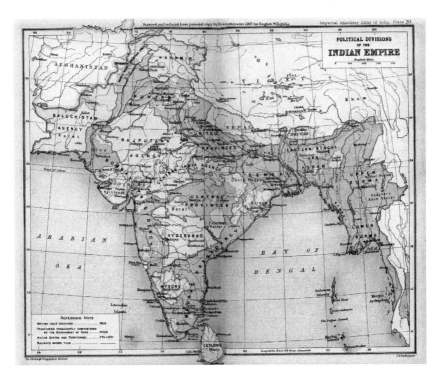

MAP 1.1. British Provinces and the Princely States, 1909.
SOURCE: Imperial Gazetteer of India, 1909, inside front cover, created by J. G. Bartholomew.

states in princely India, consisting of both gargantuan kingdoms like Hyderabad (with a 1901 population of more than 11 million) and tiny states like Faridkot (roughly 125,000). The vast majority of these states, however, were small. Dick Kooiman (2002: 18) notes that the twenty-four states that received a gun salute of seventeen or higher at ceremonial events accounted for roughly 70 percent of the entire princely state population.[21] Because of the immense variation among the states it is hard to generalize about them. Table 1.1 displays the twenty-four major kingdoms in 1931.

Whereas the provinces were governed directly by British administrators, the princely states were placed under a system of indirect rule,[22] alternatively referred to by colonial officials as *paramountcy* or *suzerainty*. The way this system operated was not altogether clear; in 1928, in response to princely inquiries, the British defined the relationship between themselves and the princes rather obliquely: "Paramountcy must remain paramount" (Rudolph and Rudolph 1966: 139). However, the British were unquestionably the dominant power in India. Responding to complaints from the *nizam* (ruler) of Hyderabad, Lord Reading, Viceroy of India from 1921 to 1926, noted in 1926, "The Sovereignty of the British Crown is supreme in India, and therefore no Ruler of an Indian state can justifiably claim to negotiate with the British Government on an equal footing."[23]

TABLE I.I.

Major Princely States in India, 1931. Ranked by gun salute, then population. States in bold are case studies examined in this book. Location refers to the modern location; some princely states overlap several modern states, so the largest one is cited. AP: Andhra Pradesh; GJ: Gujarat; JK: Jammu and Kashmir; KA: Karnataka; KL: Kerala; MP: Madhya Pradesh; MH: Maharashtra; PB: Punjab; and RJ: Rajasthan. Size is area in square miles.

Princely State	Location	Size	Population	Gun Salute	Ruler
Hyderabad	AP	82,698	14,436,148	21	Muslim
Mysore	KA	29,475	6,557,303	21	Hindu
Jammu and Kashmir	JK	85,885	3,646,243	21	Hindu
Gwalior	MP	26,383	3,523,070	21	Hindu
Baroda	GJ	8,135	2,443,007	21	Hindu
Travancore	KL	7,625	5,095,973	19	Hindu
Udaipur	RJ	12,915	1,566,910	19	Hindu
Indore	MP	9,570	1,318,217	19	Hindu
Kolhapur	MH	3,217	957,137	19	Hindu
Bhopal	MP	6,902	729,955	19	Muslim
Kalat	Pakistan	73,278	342,101	19	Muslim
Jaipur	RJ	16,682	2,631,775	17	Hindu
Jodhpur	RJ	35,066	2,125,982	17	Hindu
Patiala	PB	5,932	1,625,520	17	Hindu
Rewa	MP	13,000	1,587,445	17	Hindu
Cochin	KL	1,418	1,205,016	17	Hindu
Bahawalpur	Pakistan	15,000	984,612	17	Muslim
Bikaner	RJ	23,315	936,218	17	Hindu
Kotah	RJ	5,684	685,804	17	Hindu
Cutch	GJ	7,616	514,307	17	Hindu
Bharatput	RJ	1,993	486,565	17	Hindu
Tonk	RJ	2,553	317,360	17	Muslim
Bundi	RJ	2,220	216,722	17	Hindu
Karauli	RJ	1,242	140,525	17	Hindu

Throughout this book, the provinces and princely states are treated as distinct political realms; the reality, of course, is more complex. First, there was migration between the two areas, so political developments in one region could naturally spill over into the other region.[24] Second, as noted earlier, there were major variations among the princely states, and this was also true for the British provinces. For instance, the Bengal Presidency enforced the zamindari system, a disruptive and detrimental land policy that relied on landlords more than did the Madras Presidency, which utilized instead a *ryotwari* system, in which revenues were collected directly from *ryots* (peasants). The cases examined in this book span north, south, and east India in order to capture some of this variation in governance across the country.

This model of colonialism in India after 1857 was unique compared to other British colonies. Lange, Mahoney, and vom Hau (2006) identify four broad types of British colonial rule: (1) settler territories like the United States, (2) indirectly ruled states like Ghana and Malawi, (3) directly ruled states like Hong Kong, and (4) the "hybrid model" (1429–30) represented by India, which combined direct and indirect forms of colonial rule. British India experienced *direct rule,* meaning that British officials governed these territories, although Indians were involved in the lower rungs of the bureaucracy. The princely states experienced *indirect rule,* meaning that native kings had autonomy within their territories.[25] Prior to the colonization of the subcontinent, most British areas had been brought fully under direct rule (Lange 2009: 31).

A central question is whether the British, even after 1857, continued to exert extensive control over the native states. For example, colonial administrators instituted the aforementioned Residency system in which advisors (Residents) were sent to princely courts to offer "advice" to princes. During the early history of British power in India, no less a figure than Governor-General Warren Hastings (1773–85) admitted that "in our treaties with [princes], we recognize them as independent sovereigns. Then we send a Resident to their courts. Instead of acting in the character of ambassador, he assumes the functions of a dictator."[26] The British policy toward princes from 1813 to 1857 was likewise focused on limiting them from exercising control over foreign affairs and external communications. Many princes were forced to provide a large subsidy to the British in return for military protection. They were also threatened with removal in the case of "misrule."[27]

Although there is no agreement among historians of India on the question of princely sovereignty, this book argues that princely rulers after

1857—and especially in the early twentieth century, during the run-up to independence—largely had autonomy within their territories. This argument is, at least in part, a reflection of changing historical scholarship on the princely states. It was once the case that most historians did not treat princes as serious rulers, instead viewing their kingdoms as "hollow crowns" (Dirks 1987). At worst, *rajas* (rulers of the princely states) were portrayed as collaborating with British rule. Waltraud Ernst and Biswamoy Pati (2007: 3) document "earlier, hegemonic [historical] accounts that depicted princes as at best mere decorative stooges of British imperial power." Edward S. Haynes (1990: 492) best summarizes this position: "rajas [during British rule] became princes fit only for the garden party."[28]

On the whole, however, newer scholarship on the native states has cast significant skepticism on the claim that princes were controlled by the British. A number of scholars argue that the princes were semiautonomous rulers.[29] Barbara Ramusack (2004) elaborates this position, writing that although they did not control their defense or external affairs, princes did control tax collection, the allocation of state revenues, criminal and judicial power, internal law and order, and cultural activities and institutions. Even some earlier historical accounts had stressed this position. John Hurd II (1975: 171) argued, "Nevertheless, in spite of British influence and control, whether potential or actual, the Government of India rarely tried to force princes to alter their political systems to any significant degree." John Wood (1984: 71) wrote about the Residency system specifically: "Ordinarily, however, the prince possessed preeminent substantive and personal power. It often appeared, in fact, that the Resident was more zealous of the prerogatives of 'his' princes than they themselves were."

This argument is not solely the view of modern historians interpreting Indian history; there is evidence that even contemporary audiences understood princes in this way. In 1911 the *Times* collected a series of articles for Empire Day. Their reporting on the princely states noted that "[princes] are not independent sovereigns, for they cannot wage war, or form alliances, or maintain foreign relations, but they direct the internal government of their States, and some have the power of life and death over their own subjects" (*Times* 1911: 21).

Princes retained autonomy within their territories for four key reasons. Most important was that after 1857 the British needed them. As Lord Canning, Governor-General of India (1856–62), famously put it, during the Rebellion princely states were "breakwaters in the storm which would have swept over us in one great wave."[30] The vast majority of princely states had supported the British during the Rebellion, and in the postconflict period they expected to be repaid for their loyalty. The uprising had shocked colonial officials, especially some of its more brutal episodes, such as the infamous massacre of British civilians at Cawnpore. Fears of another large-scale revolt were never far from the minds of British administrators in post-1857 India (Metcalf 1965).

For instance, Hyderabad State did not join the uprising, and administrator John Bruce Norton of the Madras Presidency noted that "if Hyderabad had risen we could not escape insurrection practically over the whole of [the] Deccan [plateau] and Southern India."[31] Prior to the Rebellion, the state's Resident, General Fraser, had written to Lord Dalhousie suggesting that he intervene more actively in the internal affairs of the kingdom, which Fraser believed to be hopelessly corrupt. Once the Rebellion was put down, however, the British tone changed considerably in light of Hyderabad's loyalty. They signed a fresh treaty with the nizam, gave him more than £13,000 worth of presents, canceled 50 lakhs of his debt,[32] and in 1861 presented him with the Order of the Star of India, the highest chivalric honor for princes (Regani 1963: 322–23). It is also important to note that during the early twentieth century, the British engaged in two world wars, and they needed to maintain princely support during both of them. This was one reason that, at the conclusion of World War I in 1918, the British bestowed upon the nizam the unique title "His Exalted Highness" and declared him a "Faithful Ally of the British Government."[33]

A second reason for princely autonomy is that the British began to realize that princes could be effective allies not only in preventing rebellion but also in perpetuating colonial rule—provided that they were kept happy. As Sir John Malcolm, Governor of Bombay (1827–30), put it in 1825, "the . . . security of our vast oriental possessions is involved in the preservation of native principalities which are dependent on us for protection. . . . their co-existence with our rule is of itself a source of political strength."[34] This understanding necessitated nonintervention in the princely states. By 1867 this policy had proceeded far enough that Secretary of State for India Stafford Northcote (1867–68) suggested to a British administrator that he should avoid lecturing a prince "as if he were a minor of whom we are the guardians."[35]

The model of indirectly ruling certain parts of India was also recognized as being less expensive for the British—certainly in a monetary sense, but also in terms of sheer manpower. India was one of the largest and most populous colonies in the imperial system, and it presented rough terrain for British officials. An inhospitable climate and a host of native diseases led to high settler mortality rates (Acemoglu, Johnson, and Robinson 2001). Furthermore, India's enormous cultural diversity made it a difficult nation to govern. Due to these challenges, at no point did British administration account for more than .05 percent of the country's total population (Maddison 2006: 111), and as few officials as there were in the British provinces, there were fewer still in the princely states.

Finally, during the early twentieth century, the British began the process of devolving authority to Indians in preparation for self-rule. As a result, princely rulers were also given more autonomy within their territories. In 1909, Lord Minto, Viceroy of India from 1905 to 1910, presented the Udaipur Declaration, which instituted an official laissez-faire policy toward the states. This policy became further entrenched in the 1920s and 1930s. Akbar Hydari, prime minister of Hyderabad State, summarized the situation in 1930:

> Luckily, for the States, the present situation is favourable. On the one hand, the pressure exerted by British India for devolution of power, all along the line, has awakened the British Government to their obligations to the States; on the other, the abandonment of the policy of isolating the States has enabled them to discover that their grievances are common and, on that common ground, to unite in pressing their demand for the removal of those grievances.[36]

In fact, whereas princes had previously been forbidden to form alliances, by 1920 the British formed the Chamber of Princes in order to allow them to communicate on issues of mutual interest. British administrators recognized that they could not devolve power in the provinces without also doing so in the states. Newspaper editor Lovat Fraser wrote in 1911, "We cannot . . . on the one hand announce our intention of giving greater liberty to the people of British India, and on the other, turn the screw upon the Indian princes."[37] By the twentieth century, India as a whole had "witnessed a marked and notable revival in the authority, prestige and efficiency of [princely] State administrations" (Majumdar 1988: 967).

All four of these factors—that the British required princely support, recognized princes as potential allies, lacked financial resources, and had to devolve power in preparation for independence—created a situation in which princely rulers had considerable autonomy within their territories after 1857. This is not to say that the British were powerless over these areas. Rather, every native kingdom featured some level of British intervention, and some more than others. But princely territories were not puppet states in which the British had a free hand to interfere as they pleased. Chapters 2 and 3 illustrate that British officials were often surprisingly limited in what they could achieve in these kingdoms. As one Resident of Hyderabad State, Sir Arthur Lothian, detailed, no matter what the British tried "there has been no real change of heart on the part of the Nizam," who maintained a "proclivity for short-circuiting the Resident. . . . H.E.H. [His Exalted Highness] is still at his old tricks. . . ."[38]

The British, the Princes, and Ethnic Identity

After the Rebellion of 1857, there were two distinct Indias: British India and princely India. This was a critical historical era, a period when the main ethnic cleavage structures that still dominate Indian politics were constructed. Colonial administrators and princely rulers had markedly different conceptions about ethnicity: the British in the provinces emphasized the centrality of caste whereas princes in their states emphasized religion.[39]

The British were confronted after the Rebellion with the sobering realization that their knowledge about India was severely lacking. After the conflict ended in 1858, colonial administrators undertook a sustained program to gain information about the country, mainly through massive data-gathering projects (Cohn 1996). Through their quest to understand better their prized colony, British officials reached several important conclusions. Foremost among them was that they began to view and promote caste as the central organizing principle of Indian society. As Nicholas Dirks (2001: 5) summarizes it, "under the British . . . 'caste' became a single term capable of expressing, organizing, and above all 'systematizing' India's diverse forms of social identity, community, and organization."

The concept of caste refers to two specific structures: *varna* and *jati*. The varna system contains four broad categories: Brahmins are priests, Kshatriyas are kings or warriors, Vaishyas are agriculturalists or merchants, and Shudras are laborers. Untouchables are below these groups and technically outside the boundaries of the system; they do work that is considered ritually unclean, such as removing animal carcasses. The jati system classifies according to endogamous birth groups, and throughout contemporary India this system is utilized much more than varna categories. Unlike the broad typology associated with varna, there are thousands of jati groups all over the country, and each region features a different mix of castes.

The British did not conjure caste out of thin air. Varna is an ancient system of classification derived from Vedic and Hindu religious texts, although these same texts have also been used to justify opposition to the centrality of caste.[40] The word *caste* is Portuguese in origin—*casta,* which refers to animal husbandry. Many scholars accept that the British at the very least placed a new and distinct emphasis on caste,[41] which was partly a function of the fact that they centralized power through more technologically advanced means than had previous rulers of India.

The British focused on caste for a variety of reasons. Most important was that many colonial officials (in both India and London) believed the Rebellion of 1857 was an Islamic uprising, which has come to be known as the "Muslim conspiracy" interpretation.[42] They were certainly aided in this perception by the rebels' decision to march to Delhi, the last capital of Mughal India, and reinstate the old Mughal emperor. The Collector of Agra, Charles Raikes, summarized this widespread view by describing the violence of the rebellion in these terms: "The green flag of Mahomed too had been unfurled, the mass of the followers of the false prophet rejoicing to believe that under the auspices of the Great Mogal of Delhi their lost ascendancy was to be recovered, their deep hatred to the Christian got vent, and they rushed forth to kill and destroy."[43] Although the Muslim conspiracy angle was quite widespread, other officials placed a more general emphasis on the religious nature of the uprising. For example, administrators noted that Hindu sepoys also revolted in 1857 because their religious sensibilities had been offended.

Consequently, administrators embraced an overarching policy of depoliticizing the religious cleavage in the provinces. Caste was promoted because it was regarded as a modern form of social organization, unlike identification by religion, which was considered traditional and backward. This attempt to minimize religion was a British policy that took root in, but was not specific to, India. David Laitin (1986: 150–58) shows that in Yorubaland British administrators sought to expunge religion as a legitimate mode of ethnic classification in order to avoid the fanaticism that they believed was associated with religious mobilization, especially Islamic mobilization.

Contemporaneous conflicts between the British and Muslims in Sudan and Somaliland only heightened this fear in India (Robinson 1998: 276). According to many colonial administrators, the British were petrified of Muslim militancy. As British writer W. S. Blunt admitted, "In England we were perpetually scared at the idea of a Mohammedan rising in India."[44]

Though British administrators had originally regarded caste as a fundamentally religious category—as a core component of Hinduism—this understanding began to change in the mid-nineteenth century. A new imperial sociology of India morphed caste from a religious to a largely social system (Dirks 1992: 66–72). Several examples illustrate this transformation. Some colonial administrators began to think of caste as comparable to race, and "racial scientists" subsequently embarked on projects classifying supposed physical differences between high and low castes, and identifying the so-called "martial races," or those best suited for military service. Other administrators believed that caste shared similarities with the hierarchical class structure of Victorian society, with which they were familiar (Metcalf and Metcalf 2001: 112). Many administrators who came to India were inclined to believe that caste was not only the proper mode of social organization but also a method of social control. Unlike religion, caste was a ranked system; low castes could therefore be expected to provide a massive supply of labor as the servants of colonial officials. Some figures, such as Indologist Max Müller, began to argue that caste was more fundamental than religion, noting that "modern Hinduism rests on the system of caste as on a rock which no arguments can shake."[45] By the early twentieth century, as Herbert Risley, director of the census, summarized it, "caste [was] regarded as the natural law governing human society."[46]

The British also considered tribal identities to be intertwined with the caste system. This idea touches on the broader debate about whether adivasis are outside the caste system. In his study of the adivasis of Bastar, Alfred Gell (1997: 433) argues that "India's 'tribals' (or Adivasis) are not really tribes . . . at all, but are numerically dominant agricultural castes which hold, or used to hold, land in clan-based village communities in the more remote, forested and hilly parts of the subcontinent." Other scholars maintain that tribes are functionally distinct from castes. V. C. Simhadra (1979: 2) notes that tribes, unlike castes, do not have links to specific occupations. Whatever the case, the British believed there was a clear connection between the two categories. British government handbooks known as District Gazetteers, for instance, recorded "Castes and Tribes" together. Other important government reports and periodicals did the same—for example, Edgar Thurston's seven-volume *Castes and Tribes of Southern India* and Herbert Hope Risley's *Tribes and Castes of Bengal.*

Beginning with the assumption that caste should define British India, colonial administrators then increased the salience of the caste system through a variety of new social policies. The central mechanism was the census, first implemented in 1871. In explaining their focus on caste in the census, the colonial state noted:

> It is unnecessary to dwell at length upon the obvious advantages to many branches of the administration in this country of an accurate and well-arranged record of the customs and the domestic and social relations of the various castes and tribes. The entire framework of native life in India is made up of groups of this kind. . . . For the purposes of legislation, of judicial procedure, of famine relief, of sanitation and dealings with epidemic disease, and of almost every form of executive action, an ethnographic survey of India, and a record of the customs of the people, is as necessary an incident of good administration as a cadastral survey of the land and a record of the rights of its tenants.[47]

The process of officially classifying and enumerating caste groups had a significant effect on, as sociologist G. S. Ghurye put it, "a livening up of the caste-spirit."[48] The census was seen as an important tool in laying the foundations for a new social order—one that was, as Dirks (2001: 51) notes, removed from the religious and supernatural. By the late nineteenth century, caste had become the dominant ethnic category in provincial India.

This argument about the centrality of caste runs counter to an alternative view that the British understood India primarily in religious terms. Many influential colonial policymakers believed, for example, that India was above all the land of Hindus and Muslims. Paul Brass (1974) notes that the colonial state hardened a divide between religious groups that was previously fluid. Gyanendra Pandey (1990) argues that the British constructed a history of India that emphasized religious divisions. Ayesha Jalal (1994: 11) writes that the colonial state viewed the nationalist movement "erroneously . . . in terms of the great religious divide between Hindus and Muslims." Most important, several major historical decisions—the partition of Bengal in 1905, the introduction of separate electorates in 1909, and especially the partition of the colony into India and Pakistan in 1947—are taken as overwhelming evidence that the British emphasized religious divisions in India.

Colonial administrators certainly did not ignore religion, but after the Rebellion they began to prioritize caste. Although they placed importance on Indian religious traditions, they ultimately subverted their significance to the broader project of creating a secular government in the provinces. Mridu Rai (2004: 93) notes that "in British India religion was, even if only theoretically, relegated to a space subordinate to the 'secular' and the 'public.'" This was especially the case post-1857, when colonial officials initiated a policy of de-emphasizing religion in the political sphere. Pandey (1990: 67) notes that during this period caste rose in administrative importance: "In the early nineteenth century the 'village community' had been the prime candidate for the role of *basic unit* of Indian society—that which symbolized its essence. By the latter half of the century 'caste' had taken over that position. It was largely after the 1840s that 'caste' emerged as the central organizing principle in the colonial records, from village level upwards."

The British also perceived religious divisions in India at the level of the nation—that is, they came to believe (not without considerable assistance from religious organizations themselves) that Hindus and Muslims constituted two separate nations. However, the case-study chapters of this book show that this emphasis on religion did not filter down to the level of provinces, where instead the focus was on castes and tribes.[49]

The rulers of the princely states, however, had an altogether different view on the social organization of their territories. While caste defined the provinces, religion was the foundation of princely society. This was in keeping with the precolonial tradition of Indian rulers, who had also asserted their sovereignty in religious terms. The native states were essentially theocracies[50]—often explicitly Hindu or Muslim kingdoms—and princely rulers promoted the salience of their religion above all other categories.

The culture of the princely *darbar* (court) revolved around elaborate religious displays and functions. In Hindu kingdoms, Brahmins were at the right hand of the raja throughout his reign—first educating him, then serving as court chaplain, and always acting as his primary advisor. In Muslim kingdoms, the *ulama* (Islamic religious scholars) were likewise central to the process of governing. Princely rulers made large donations to religious institutions, abolished their taxes, and granted religious groups large tracts of land for temples, mosques, and shrines. Many princely territories were governed by religious law, and many states also enacted anticonversion laws in order to maintain the strength of the dominant religious group in the society. Raigarh created such a law in 1936, followed by Patna (1942), Surguja (1945), and Udaipur (1946). Many other states that continued to allow conversion still stripped converts of basic rights. In the provinces, however, there were no restrictions on conversion (Lee-Warner 1910: 19).

Native kings created theocracies, but in the nineteenth century the British also assisted in reifying the princely states in this way. As Pamela Price (1993: 495) argues, "imperial administrators and Western-educated elites came to assume that authoritarianism in government and community identification by religion were indigenous to India."[51] Accordingly, Rai (2004: 89) notes that in preparation for Queen Victoria's Imperial Assemblage (a ceremonial event in India that celebrated the coronation of a new monarch) in 1877, the British created an official chronicle of India prior to colonialism in which they constructed historical ages derived from the religions of rulers. This view was widely held—for instance, administrator James Grant described to Warren Hastings in 1786 that the Muslim invasion of India "effected the total subversion of the ancient inferior empire of the Hindoos" (5th Report, 1786: 107). And James Mill's famous *History of British India* (1817) periodized the history of the country into Hindu, Muslim, and British eras. Princely rulers were encouraged to rule their territories as religious polities because this is how the British perceived India's indigenous political systems.

After the Rebellion, many British administrators came to believe that one cause for the uprising was that they had interfered too much in the religious customs of India. In her 1858 proclamation, Queen Victoria therefore carefully noted, "We disclaim alike the right and the desire to impose our convictions on our subjects. We declare it to be our royal will and pleasure that none be in anywise favored, none molested or disquieted, by reason of their religious faith or worship of all of our subjects, on pain of our highest displeasure."[52] Consequently, after the Rebellion the British were invested in taking a laissez-faire approach to the states and allowing them to maintain their existing political cultures. Kooiman (2002: 19) explains that "British colonial officers, who were largely responsible for the creation of the two Indias, tended to see them as almost different worlds. William Barton, who after a distinguished career in the political service became Resident in Hyderabad, wrote in 1934 that the achievements of the Indian political genius were to be found at their best in the states."

Princely rulers did not ignore their caste or tribal ties but they did prioritize their religious identities. As Ian Copland (1998: 211) notes, "princes, by definition, were practising Hindus or Muslims. Their rule had religious sanction." All of the princely states examined in this book illustrate this fact; the rulers of Jaipur, Travancore, and Bastar all emphasized their religious identities more than other kinds of identities. Like precolonial rulers, they relied on religion as the basis of their political power (Ramusack 2004: 207). Whereas castes and tribes were the dominant ethnic categories in British India, religion was the main form of ethnic identification in the native states.

Ethnic Stratification in the British Provinces

Given the differential understandings of ethnicity in the provinces and princely states, the rulers of these territories ordered ethnic politics in fundamentally contrasting ways. Certain ethnic groups came to enjoy most-favored status whereas others saw their positions deteriorate. In the provinces, British administrators created ethnic policies that benefited high castes, discriminated against low castes and tribals, and protected religious minorities. Native kings did the opposite: they pursued policies that benefited their coreligionists, discriminated against non-coreligionists, and protected low castes and tribals. Figure 1.2 diagrams these different sets of policies. These disparate forms of ethnic stratification ultimately created different fault lines of ethnic conflict during the colonial era.

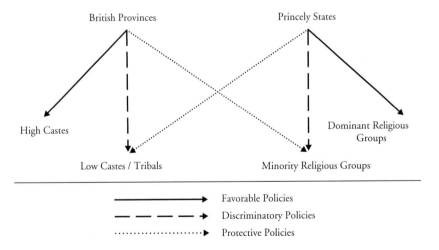

FIGURE 1.2. Ethnic Stratification in Colonial India.

As caste came to be the dominant ethnic category of the provinces, the British implemented policies that increased caste stratification. As British power grew and consolidated in India, colonial officials began to form relationships with the dominant castes throughout the country. Governor-General Charles Canning supported this view to his colleague Charles Wood in 1860 after the Rebellion: "If we are wise, we shall lose no time in binding to ourselves the Chiefs, the Landholders, great and small, and the wealthy classes. . . . We must impress them all with this plain conviction that, come what may, the fall of our power will be no gain to them."[53] This policy was also implemented because the British faced a credible commitment problem: as foreigners—and Christians specifically—they could not rule via religious legitimation like native princes. They therefore emphasized the caste system, and high castes were viewed as a kind of natural aristocracy with which the Company could engage.

For their part, the dominant castes also wanted to create formal linkages with the BEIC, and they bought titles and ranks in order to cement their position within a changing country (Cohn 1960). As the power of dominant castes grew, the position of low castes deteriorated. Not only was this a function of increasing political, economic, and social disparities between castes, but also the colonial state actively enforced policies that discriminated against those at the bottom of the caste hierarchy. A variety of mechanisms led to their declining power, especially census enumeration, new landholding policies, and a new judicial system.

Census enumeration hardened caste identity, leading to increased antagonism as certain groups fought to achieve higher status, or as some castes tried to designate rivals as untouchables. For example, Census Commissioner William Plowden remarked that low castes would be easy to categorize as those groups "which the popular voice designates as inferior."[54] The 1901 census was a pivotal iteration because it ranked caste groups, a practice that was later disavowed, although its effects were felt long afterward. Because of the political nature of rankings, the mid-nineteenth century saw an explosion in the number of caste organizations and associations in British India (Rudolph and Rudolph 1960).

Some administrators were cognizant of the negative effects that the census had on the caste system, and on low castes in particular. L. Middleton, a census commissioner in Punjab, wrote in 1921 that

> our land records and official documents have added iron bonds to the old rigidity of caste. Caste in itself was rigid among the higher castes, but malleable

amongst the lower. We pigeon-holed every one by caste, and if we could not find a true caste for them, labelled them with the name of an hereditary occupation. *We deplore the caste system and its effects on social and economic problems, but we are largely responsible for the system we deplore.* Left to themselves such castes as Sunar and Lohar would rapidly disappear and no one would suffer. . . . Government's passion for labels and pigeon-holes has led to a crystallization of the caste system.[55]

A second major detrimental change for low castes had to do with land-holding. The Mughal agricultural system was an Asian form of royal absolutism, to use the terminology of Barrington Moore Jr. (1966: Chapter 6). But a number of new British policies worsened an already oppressive system. The biggest change was that colonial administrators transformed zamindars into private proprietors. In addition, the British also levied an onslaught of new taxes and revenue burdens on rural India, increasing inequality and promoting violence.

The zamindars of India were originally intermediaries between Mughal rulers and the peasantry (Habib 1963).[56] They collected taxes and supervised the cultivation of agricultural lands. With the rise of the British, however, throughout north India zamindars were transformed into a powerful new class of landlords. The introduction of the Permanent Settlement in Bengal in 1793 formed the foundation of this experiment. The thinking behind this policy lay in English liberal ideas about the importance of property rights, as well as about the need to establish a landed aristocracy in the country (Metcalf 1965; Guha 1981). Administrators were interested in improving the land; they reasoned that if they granted proprietary rights to zamindars, the zamindars would in turn reinvest in the land and develop it. Eric Stokes (1978: 2) writes, "The British believed they were innovating. . . . [They] proclaimed their purpose as being not to overturn existing rights but to give amplification and legal certainty to rights that had hitherto remained vague and inchoate."[57] But it was not clear that colonial officials generally understood existing rights; Chapter 3, for example, details how British administrators completely misunderstood and then reformulated the nature of agrarian relations in Malabar, with devastating results. The granting of a proprietary right in north India led to extreme land concentration: by 1963, for example, some two million individuals out of a total population of 63 million controlled every acre of land across the massive United Provinces (Stokes 1978: 205). Peasants consequently became tenants-at-will, and evictions increased throughout India during colonialism (Gough 1974).

The zamindari model was not implemented everywhere. Throughout parts of south India, under Governor of Madras Thomas Munro (1820–27), the British implemented the ryotwari system. In other areas they gave control of the land to village communities (*mahalwari*). Across India there was a high degree of experimentation with land policy. Karl Marx remarked on this in *Das Kapital:*

> The history of the English in India is a string of futile and really absurd (in practice infamous) economic experiments. In Bengal they created a caricature of large-scale English landed estates; in south-eastern India a caricature of small parcelled properties; in the north-west they did all they could to transform the Indian economic community with common ownership of the soil into a caricature of itself.[58]

Although the introduction of the zamindari system was more detrimental for peasants than the ryotwari or mahalwari systems, the rapid implementation of different tenurial models also provoked conflict. Chapter 2 details how the British changed the tenurial system in Ajmer several times during the nineteenth century, which bred deep resentment among the agricultural population.

Increased British revenue demands were also tied to these changes in landholding. Colonial administrators placed enormous new tax burdens on rural economies. This was a sharp change from the Mughal period; for example, even during the reign of the ruthless emperor Aurangzeb, crop failures often led to remissions and extra produce being left with cultivators (Majumdar 1991: 533). British administrators in many areas, however, established fixed land tributes. One result of this policy was that famines, such as the massive Bengal Famine of 1943, became routine on the subcontinent. And while Indians perished from starvation, the British government continued massive crop exports from the country (Lange 2009: 1–2). Colonial administrators also stipulated that provinces begin producing cash crops such as indigo, sugar, and rice, as well as open their domestic markets for British goods (without import taxes), which subsequently crippled a number of native industries.

The last major change was a new judicial system implemented by the British, which in turn was captured by high castes to provide legal justification for their rule. Courts became a central tool of landlords—for instance, to displace peasants from their land. In many areas, British land reforms empowered zamindars not only as landlords but also as the final judicial authority in their territories. Chapter 3 showcases how the new judicial system in Malabar was used to steadily increase the number of peasant evictions during the nineteenth century.

The position of tribals in India also deteriorated considerably during colonialism. Adivasis, most of whom were concentrated in forests and jungles, attracted the ire of a colonial government intent on expanding control over land and extracting natural resource wealth. British officials approached the jungles with an overarching goal of bringing "primitive" tribes under the control of a modern bureaucracy (Sivaramakrishnan 1999; Skaria 1999). Three key policies harmed India's tribal population: the British taking direct control over forests, heavy immigration into adivasi lands, and "Criminal Tribes" legislation.

The British colonial government became the conservator of India's vast forests in 1878 through the Indian Forest Act. This was a singular event in the history of the country; never before had any native power claimed ownership of forests. Adivasis were therefore transformed into tenants-at-will on land they had occupied for centuries. Ramachandra Guha and Madhav Gadgil (1989: 145) note that "by one stroke of the executive pen [this bill] attempted to obliterate centuries of customary use of the forest by rural populations all over India." The bill allowed the government to designate certain areas as reserved forests, and these lands were then cut off from local populations and opened to a variety of commercial interests. Later reforms to the system of forestry rights were ineffectual; for example, the revised Indian Forest Act, 1927, "contained all the major provisions of the earlier Act" (Kulkarni 1983: 192).

Tribal land displacement also skyrocketed under colonial rule. An influx of new groups such as immigrants, moneylenders, and Forest Department officials all contributed to a steady encroachment on tribal land. K. S. Singh notes that as a result "the self-contained subsistence economy based on agriculture and forest produce was weakened and destroyed."[59] Illiterate adivasis were also routinely cheated out of their property, with colonial administrators often complicit in the process (Culshaw 1945).

The British concurrently implemented "Criminal Tribes" legislation— laws that governed the actions of tribes with a history of criminal behavior (Simhadra 1979; Radhakrishna 2001; Hasnain 2007). But this legislation did little to blunt the problem of criminality among tribes. For example, it criminalized all members of a Criminal Tribe, including those who had never actually committed a crime. These tribes were heavily stigmatized, prevented from moving about freely, and jailed for not reporting their travel to colonial authorities. In 1949, A. V. Thakkar, a member of the Bombay Depressed Classes and Aboriginal Tribes Committee, noted that "a much larger percentage of these tribes were led into criminality by giving them the stigma of criminal tribes."[60] Aside from the three central mechanisms highlighted here, there were also a number of other significant changes to the lives of adivasis under British rule: the colonial state replaced the customary tribal barter system with a monetary economy, tribal law with state decrees, and local *panchayats* (village councils) with foreign bureaucracy.

All of these new discriminatory policies against low castes and adivasis led to a sharp increase in the number of peasant revolts in colonial India.[61] As discussed previously, there is a paucity of data on precolonial violence, but peasant revolts became a routine occurrence during the British period. In 1855 the Santhals rebelled; in 1868, the Naikdas; and in 1873, the Kolis. In 1875 the massive Deccan Riots occurred, and in 1895 the Birsas revolted. This is only a fraction of the total number of conflicts. Ranajit Guha (1999) has documented more than 110 colonial-era peasant revolts, and Gough (1974) records 77 since the beginning of British rule.

The British were not unaware of the deleterious effects of their rule on low castes and tribals, and in response they did initiate certain reforms. The Chotanagpur Tenancy Act of 1869 (amended several times thereafter), for instance, was implemented to protect adivasis in northeast India by prohibiting the transfer of tribal land. In the early twentieth century, throughout the south the British government implemented reservations for depressed castes. In fact, the term *Scheduled Caste* was first used by the Government of India in 1935. But these reform efforts came only at the end of a long history of discrimination, and their effects are unclear. For instance, despite reforms in Chotanagpur, after the 1970s the illegal timber trade was booming in the area, generating 10 crore per year (Prasad 1998: 27).[62] Similarly, the impact of low-caste reservations in the south may have reduced Hindu-Muslim conflict (Wilkinson 2004: Chapter 6), but caste conflict remains a major problem throughout the region, as Chapter 3 details. In short, colonial policies on low castes and tribals were not uniformly detrimental, but they tilted overwhelmingly in that direction (see also Srinivas 1957: 531–32).

As colonial policies in the provinces created increasing levels of conflict among caste and tribal groups, a very different set of policies was simultaneously being implemented with respect to religion. The overarching and long-term goal in British India was to depoliticize the religious cleavage and create a new secular form of governance. To achieve this outcome, especially after the 1857 Rebellion, British administrators advanced a policy of religious neutrality.[63]

To the colonial officials of nineteenth-century India, secularism had two key components. First, in the most basic sense, in a secular state all religions were considered equal under the law, irrespective of the size of any particular group. Religious neutrality aimed to create a government that would, in Viceroy Lord Curzon's famous turn of phrase, hold even the scales between Hindus and Muslims. The colonial state actively worked to limit the political domination of any religious group, including Christians. Despite the fact that most British administrators were Christian and that many Evangelicals at home pushed for explicitly Christian policies, after 1857 European missionaries were always kept at arm's length by the colonial government (Sarkar 2007).

A second component of British secularism was a distinction between church and state (van der Veer 2001: 16–24). The policy of religious neutrality was meant to achieve this outcome in a number of ways. One example was the establishment of a system of secular education in the provinces beginning in the mid-nineteenth century. In the aftermath of the "Islamic" rebellion, for example, *madrassas* (Islamic religious schools) in many parts of India were shuttered by colonial officials (Zaman 1999: 296–97). Secular schools that were run by Muslims, however, attracted significant British support (Metcalf 1982: 328). A second initiative that aimed to produce this church/state separation in the provinces pertained to the law. For the first time in Indian history the British implemented a uniform criminal code instead of one derived from religious precepts (Smith 1963: 69–70).

Some scholars contend that, instead of secularizing the population, this attempt to implement religious neutrality had the opposite effect of increasing religious fervor (van der Veer 2001: 24; Adcock 2013). They suggest, for example, that the imposition of secularism, an ostensibly Western concept, was doomed to fail in a state like India where religion was so central to the lives of the people (Madan 1987; Nandy 1988). At the outset, this argument about provoking religiosity assumes that religious politics did not exist prior to British rule, which is not the case. In the short run, it seems persuasive, but as the case studies of Ajmer and Malabar show, the populations of these territories became quite secularized over the long run. This is especially surprising in the case of Malabar, because scholars argue that in the early twentieth century the region experienced a number of religious revolts (detailed in Chapter 3). Religious neutrality in Ajmer and Malabar did not divide Hindus and Muslims; rather, it created cultures of cooperation that persisted long after the end of colonial rule. Moreover, the privileging of caste in these areas diminished the importance of religion and ultimately reoriented the local ethnic cleavage structure.

Kooiman and colleagues (2002: 56) elaborate on the overall effect of religious neutrality by looking at the specific workings of the Madras Presidency:

> The British Government in Madras had arrived at a reasonably firm policy of not involving itself in matters of religion and of upholding a stance of imperial arbiter in secular matters. The state was firmly in British hands and there was little ground for any community to see the ruler-subject relationship in a proprietorial manner, even though some groups were strategically better placed than others. The British were convinced that this neutral bureaucracy was a major factor in the discouragement of communal strife.

Because, compared to Hindus, Muslims were such a small minority in India, this policy of religious neutrality had the result of being quite protective of them. After the Rebellion, the British initially distanced themselves from the Muslim community because colonial officials perceived the uprising as Islamic. In response, Muslim leader Sir Syed Ahmad Khan formed the Aligarh movement to bring Muslims and the British government closer together and repair their relationship. As independence loomed, Muslims began to fear that they would be left, in the words of such leaders as Maulana Muhammad Ali, "at the mercy of an angelic majority."[64] Due in part to the Aligarh movement, in the twentieth century British administrators and Muslim leaders resolved their differences. Many of the circumstances that revived the position of princes in the early twentieth century also applied to Muslims, and they came, once again, to be viewed as strong pillars of support for colonial rule (Metcalf and Metcalf 2001: 106). By 1905, the *Islam Prachak* newspaper summarized this outcome by writing, "under British rule we are undeniably dwelling in great peace and happiness."[65]

Many scholars maintain that the British did not pursue religious neutrality in India but instead implemented a policy of divide-and-rule.[66] According to this argument, the British promoted antagonism between Hindus and Muslims for their own political benefit, and the rise of communalism throughout India is a direct legacy of colonial rule.

It is undeniable that the British made communal decisions at certain times. But the divide-and-rule hypothesis makes two faulty assumptions. First, it assumes that Hindus and Muslims were not significantly divided prior to the arrival of the British. This unlikely argument was discussed at the beginning of this chapter. As Cynthia Keppley Mahmood (1993: 373) elaborates, it rests on a shaky foundation:

> The political myth of communal conflict today is that it is a modern phenom-
> enon out of sync with the rest of Indian history. The cultural reality is that,
> insofar as its roots are in fact historically deep, communalism unfortunately rep-
> resents a far more intractable problem than most current dialogue admits. An
> image of India based on the notion of consensus, deviations from which require
> explanation, must be replaced by a paradigm according full weight to the long-
> term dialectic of communalism that is, unhappily, showing no signs of abating.

The second assumption is that communal conflict was not a major feature of Indian politics prior to British arrival. This is also doubtful, because religious violence not only occurred throughout the pre-British period (Bayly 1985; Gaborieau 1985; Subrahmanyam 1996, 2001) but was also more extensive than other forms of ethnic violence.

British policies that took on the complexion of being based on communal thinking were in part perceived this way because colonial officials had to contend with a Hinduism and Islam that were going through revivalist periods.[67] Hindu revivalism attempted to create an explicitly Hindu state in India whereas Islamic revivalism led to increased calls for Muslim separatism. During this time, Hindus and Muslims created a number of new associations and began to focus more on religious conversion. These political organizations played a large part in dividing the two communities irrespective of British policy. For example, from its earliest days the Indian National Congress (INC) used explicit Hindu imagery and mythology to gain adherents (Wolpert 2009: 268–70). The INC also contained a contingent of Hindu nationalists who actively worked to alienate Muslims from the movement (Gould 2004). The song Vande Mataram, for instance, was often played at INC gatherings even though Muslims despised it. On the other side, the Aligarh movement led by Sir Syed—who, as Rafiq Zakaria (1970: xxii) notes, is more the real father of Muslim nationhood than Muhammad Ali Jinnah—did much to increase Muslim separatism. He pushed for Muslims to embrace Western education and argued that only through closer ties to the British would they be able to survive in the modern era.

During colonialism, Hindus and Muslims in India were already sufficiently divided and needed no assistance from the British to exacerbate tensions between them. Copland (2005: 11) writes that newer historical scholarship has "effectively demolished the romantic notion that, prior to the coming of the British, the prevalence of tolerant attitudes towards variant beliefs ensured complete harmony between Hindus and Muslims." Ultimately Robinson (1974: 348–49) draws the following conclusion about the divide-and-rule thesis: "Does this mean that the British divided and ruled? In the crude sense, no. There was no deliberate attempt to foster communal hostility; indeed the aim was to avoid it." Or as an Indian delegate to the 1931 Round Table Conference concisely put it to a British administrator, "We divide and you rule."[68]

As a corollary to the divide-and-rule argument, most scholars believe that during colonialism the provinces experienced significantly more religious violence than the princely states. This position has rarely been challenged and is usually offered with little in the way of evidence. For example, Asghar Ali Engineer (1989b: 2467) writes that generally "the princely states were less prone to communal conflict." Even those who question the divide-and-rule thesis are convinced that British areas experienced more communal conflict than princely India (Kooiman et al. 2002: 49). At the same time, the Indian Statutory (Simon) Commission, sent to India in 1927 to oversee a variety of government reforms, commented that the princely states seemed relatively free of violence. On the face of it, it seems like most of the major communal centers in India are former British cities, such as Bombay, Ahmedabad, and Aligarh.

There are several problems, however, with this conventional wisdom. First, it is not surprising that the vast majority of communal violence occurred in British India, because three-fourths of the population lived there. Second, many of these British cities had a precolonial legacy of violence that was difficult to erase immediately. This fact is often overlooked; as Christopher Bayly (1985: 178) notes, for most historians of India "the existence of religious riots before the late nineteenth century has hardly been considered." Studies of communalism in Bombay, for example, usually begin in the mid-nineteenth century and focus especially on the 1893 riot over cow protection (Menon 2011). But communal conflict has been prevalent in Maharashtra at least since the Hindu Marathas challenged Mughal supremacy in the seventeenth century. Scholars may argue that Shivaji Bhonsle, founder of the Maratha Empire, was not a "Hindu king," but he drew explicitly on ancient notions of Hindu kingship and crowned himself Chatrapati (Lord of the Universe) in a ceremony in which eleven thousand Brahmin priests recited Vedic texts (Wolpert 2009: 169). Finally, most studies of communalism during the British period look only at the national picture or at British cities but rarely include comparisons across provinces and princely states.[69]

One exception is the work of Ian Copland (1998), who in a comparison of data on communal violence collected from the Simon Commission, press reports, and various other sources offers at least one systematic analysis. He finds that during the period from 1920 to 1940 the provinces "suffered between fifteen and eighteen times more" religious violence than the princely states (213). But there are several weaknesses with this study. It is not clear, for instance, that reports of religious violence in the princely states were well-covered by the press. Princes were known, for instance, to ban newspapers that recorded unflattering portraits of life in their territories. Chapter 2 details this tendency by the rulers of Jaipur.

Most important, only one control variable—population—is used in Copland's analysis. Yet there are many other factors that presumably matter: for instance, the relative size of the Muslim population, the level of economic and social development, and the strength of the police in a particular area. Chapters 2 and 3 show that in carefully selected paired comparisons from Rajasthan and Kerala, British areas experienced less religious violence than princely states during and after colonialism. Furthermore, a host of control variables are considered in a statistical analysis of modern violence in Chapter 5; and, when included, the results of the study confirm that across India princely states experience more violence than provinces. Even if Copland's analysis is correct, he notes that by the 1930s the princely states became as violent as the provinces (1998: 214). During Partition, for instance, several princely states accounted for an immense amount of violence; kingdoms in the Punjab, as well as Alwar and Bharatpur in Rajasthan, saw wholesale ethnic cleansing (Mayaram 1997).

British policies of ethnic stratification in the provinces favored high castes, discriminated against low castes and tribals, and protected religious minorities. These policies in turn led to increased caste and tribal violence, but the policy of neutrality minimized religious discord over the long term.

By the late nineteenth century, the main fault line of ethnic conflict in the British provinces had been formed.

Ethnic Stratification in the Princely States

Traditional India—the India of the princely states—was defined by religion. This definition was largely due to the way native kings had always identified themselves, a custom that dates back to precolonial times. But it was also reinforced by the British, who after 1857 attempted to reify princely states as religious polities. Princely power and legitimacy derived from the dominant religious group in the state: Hindu kings favored the Hindu community, Muslim rulers favored Muslims, and Sikh rulers did likewise. Chapters 2 and 3 demonstrate how the rajas who governed Jaipur and Travancore time and again favored the Hindu communities in these states.

One of the arguments discussed at the beginning of this chapter contends that prior to the arrival of the British, India was marked by a religiously tolerant or syncretic culture. To scholars who accept this argument, once the British took control of India, syncretism continued on as the major practice of princely rulers in their states. The main evidence offered for the perpetuation of this syncretic culture is the way in which native kings patronized rival religious traditions. Copland (1998: 212) offers several examples:

> Every year in Gwalior the Hindu maharaja rode at the head of the tazia [a replica of the tomb of Husain, the martyred son of Muhammad] procession which marked the end of the Muslim festival of Mohurrum. The Jaipur government patronized Mohurrum as well as the tomb of the Sufi saint Mu'in al-din Chishti at Ajmer. In 1930, the Sikh maharaja of Kapurthala spent £30,000 on the construction of a mosque in his capital. In 1939, the nizam of Hyderabad endowed a chair at the Benares Hindu University.

Most important, princely rulers are said to have guaranteed freedom of worship to religious minorities, unrestricted access to mosques and temples, and the ability to carry out religious festivals without interference.

Like the argument about religious tolerance in the precolonial period, this argument about syncretism in the princely states is greatly overstated—or as Kooiman (in Kooiman et al. 2002: 49) puts it, "This picture of social harmony in the states is too good to be true." The main problem is the often glaring disparity between official pronouncements and the actual religious policies of princely governments. Most native rulers adopted the language of tolerance and acceptance (often for the explicit purpose of warding off British intervention in their territories), but in practice they were not syncretic. The last nizam of Hyderabad, Osman Ali Khan (1911–48)—whose government was dominated by Muslims—liked to lovingly proclaim that Hindus and Muslims were the "two eyes of the [kingdom]."[70] Even the communal record of states like Jaipur and Travancore, widely considered among the most progressive kingdoms on issues of religious freedom, differed considerably from traditional narratives.

Contrary to their tolerant reputations, princely rulers throughout India tended to be discriminatory toward non-coreligionists. The Hindu rulers of Kashmir were brutally repressive toward the overwhelmingly majority Muslim population. A contemporary account from 1941 notes, "The poverty of the Muslim masses is appalling. Dressed in rags and barefoot, a Muslim peasant presents the appearance of a starving beggar. . . . Most are landless laborers, working as serfs for absentee [Hindu] landlords."[71] James Tod (1829: 420), a famed British expert on Rajputana, noted that Zalim Sing, the raja of Kotah, was a "zealot in all the observances of religion." Jai Singh, the ruler of Alwar, instituted Ram as the state deity in the 1930s, banned Urdu and Persian from all state schools, and even prohibited men from growing beards. Alwar and Bharatpur became sites of massive communal violence during Partition (Mayaram 1997). The Muslim nizams of Hyderabad discriminated against the overwhelmingly Hindu population enough that the Lahore newspaper *Milap* editorialized in November of 1931, "How regrettable is the matter that the Hindus [of Hyderabad] . . . are compelled to spend their life [sic] like slaves."[72] Donald Smith (1963: 98) summarizes as follows: "The religious policies of the Indian states were a part of the heritage which India received with her independence in 1947. With few exceptions these policies were not nearly as conducive to the realization of a secular democracy as those [that] evolved in British India."

Forms of discrimination varied in the states; non-coreligionists could be prevented from freely practicing their religion, from constructing houses of worship, or from forming religious organizations and holding public meetings. Minority religious groups were more generally blocked from access to educational spots and government jobs, and they were on the whole much poorer and less educated than dominant religious groups. For example, literacy rates for non-coreligionists were lower than for majority groups across princely India (Chaudhary and Rubin 2013). In the powerful princely kingdom of Hyderabad, religious minorities received a paltry level of political representation. The periodical *The Leader* detailed the institutionalized discrimination against Hindus during the reign of Osman Ali Khan:

> The Executive Council is composed of eight members; of this, one is a Hindu and one an Englishman—the rest are Muslims. Every official in the executive council drawing a salary above Rs. [rupees] 225 is a Muslim. Not a single Hindu is admitted anywhere near the precincts of the highest office under Government or his Exalted Highness's household. The High Court consists of 10 judges; eight are Muslims and only two are Hindus. A vast Hindu population is deliberately treated as hewers of wood and drawers of water.[73]

While non-coreligionists suffered at the hands of princely rulers, state policies toward low castes and adivasis were entirely different, because these groups were protected during colonialism. There are a number of reasons for this, but the most important is that the peasants in the princely states had closer links to their princes than to the zamindars or British administrators because the princes were the native rulers of India. Viceroy Lord Lytton (1876–80) remarked along these lines that "the Indian peasantry is an inert mass. If it ever moves at all it will move in obedience, not to its British benefactors, but to its native chiefs and princes."[74]

The treatment of low castes in the princely states was superior to their treatment in British India. Although late in the colonial period there were a number of British policies that ostensibly attempted to help depressed castes, princely rulers pursued the process of low-caste uplift long before the British. Several princes were noteworthy for taking hard stands against caste discrimination. The ruler of Baroda personally paid for the education of *dalit* reformer B. R. Ambedkar. The rulers of Kolhapur responded to low-caste agitation by stipulating that 50 percent of all government jobs were to be reserved for non-Brahmin castes (Mendelsohn and Vicziany 1998: 129). In Mysore, all non-Brahmins were designated as backward and were also entitled to ameliorative government policies (Bayly 1999: 279). In Travancore, Maharaja Shri Chithira Thirunal Balarama Varma (1924–47) took the most liberal measure by allowing untouchables to enter Hindu temples. The subsequent case-study chapters highlight various other examples.

The new policies implemented in British India that caused the position of low castes to deteriorate were muted or simply nonexistent in princely India. For example, the census was also conducted in princely India but did not have the equivalent effect on politics. Chapter 3 on Travancore details that the Hindu rulers of the state used the census to attack the position of non-coreligionists such as Christians rather than as a means of increasing caste stratification. In the realm of landholding, the princely states employed a variety of tenurial models, but princes generally treated cultivators on their lands as hereditary and did not displace them arbitrarily if they paid the revenue (Singh 2003).

In the twentieth century, many princes also established ryotwari settlements in which land tributes were collected directly from cultivators, thus curtailing the intermediary groups that were a source of endless strife in British India. In many princely states there were hereditary nobles who controlled large portions of the land, and princes often had little control over these areas. The position of cultivators was generally worse in noble-controlled lands, but princes also mounted efforts to reform these territories. For example, in the 1930s Jaipur's raja initiated a strict set of reforms for the nobles of Sikar, a large principality within his kingdom where peasants were constantly in rebellion (Rubin 1983). Baroda was another state that was progressive on rural issues; it implemented several reforms geared toward the peasantry, lowering agricultural taxes and incorporating cultivators into a more direct relationship with the government (Hardiman 1978). During the same time, Mysore, Bikaner, and Cochin all began to spend more state revenues on agricultural improvements such as irrigation networks (Ramusack 2004: 191).

Though the princely states faced new revenue burdens placed on them by British administrators, their own taxes on the land were often lower than those of the British provinces. The British-controlled areas in Rajputana and Kerala had higher levels of taxation and, subsequently, more peasant unrest than neighboring princely areas, as illustrated in Chapters 2 and 3. Similarly, princes also maintained control over their judicial systems, and the courts did not become a mechanism for expropriating peasants.

Princes all over India were similarly protective toward adivasi groups. In Rajputana, both the Bhils and the Meenas were incorporated into the structure of the princely government. These tribes were charged with ceremonially placing the *rajatilaka* on the brow of the newly crowned king.[75] In Jaipur, the Meenas were the guardians of the royal treasury (Ramusack 2004: 210). In Travancore and Cochin, tribes were given ownership of their land, government subsidies to improve it, and special policies that limited the imposition of the outsiders (immigrants, moneylenders, Forest Department officials) who were a major problem for tribes throughout British India (Mo-hanty 2006: 178). In Jammu and Kashmir, many members of the Bakkarwal tribe were employed as tax collectors (*zaildaars*) and became an important part of the government (Tandor 2005: 24). In 1942, most of the rulers of the Eastern Feudatory States approved a draft policy (although it was not implemented) declaring that tribal groups ought to be the first claimants to forest lands and should also have the right to be governed by independent panchayats (Edmunds and Wollenberg 2003: 184). Princes displayed greater tolerance for tribal groups, and adivasis fared better under their rule than under the British administrators in the provinces. For Verrier Elwin, noted anthropologist of adivasis, it was "most refreshing to go to Bastar from the reform-stricken and barren districts of the Central Provinces."[76]

In the native states, princes implemented policies of ethnic stratification that benefited coreligionists, discriminated against non-coreligionists, and protected low castes and tribal groups. These policies—the mirror image of how ethnic politics was organized in British India—intensified religious violence but minimized caste and tribal conflict.

Institutions and the Persistence of the Old Regime

It has become commonplace to suggest that around the world colonialism shaped contemporary ethnic conflict, but one aspect often missing from these studies is a clear explanation of why it should still matter. Scholars studying this question often resort to some form of a path-dependent argument in which the mechanisms of transmission are rarely detailed.[77] The colonial period is still relevant to contemporary Indian politics primarily because the differential cultures and social fissures of the provinces and princely states were reinforced through institutions.

At the dawn of Indian independence in 1947, one of the fundamental problems facing the new republic was the integration of several hundred princely states (Furber 1951; Menon 1956; Wood 1984). Most states were eventually incorporated into the union through what was called a "merger agreement," which allowed princes to retain their wealth and titles in return for giving up jurisdiction over their territories. Other states that refused accession, such as Hyderabad, were annexed. Despite these significant changes, in the broadest sense India did not experience what Barrington Moore Jr. terms a "revolutionary break from the past" (1966). There was a large sense of continuity between the colonial and postcolonial periods (Chatterjee 1986; Brass 1994). For instance, the primary organization spearheading independence, the INC, transitioned from a broad-based mass movement into a broad-based political party, one that dominated elections for decades after independence. India was not unique in this sense: postcolonial continuity was also the norm throughout Africa (Mamdani 1996; Young 1994).

Postcolonial India maintains key continuities with the past. There are two components to this explanation. Foremost, the salience of ethnic categories and patterns of violence that were constructed across provinces and princely states during colonialism became embedded in a variety of formal and informal institutions. Second, largely because institutions continued to reflect colonial-era power disparities, new postcolonial governments were unable to implement (or in some cases undermined) effective reforms of the past, especially with respect to policies governing ethnic minorities.

Once the provinces and princely states were integrated into the new Republic of India, political organizations from the former were transported to the latter. The British-era civil service bureaucracy, police, courts, and so on that had existed solely in the provinces began to operate in the princely states as well. Despite this convergence, these organizations continued to operate in quite different political cultures (Putnam 1993), and they continued to reflect different preexisting social fissures. Pamela Price (1993: 495) describes this effect: "particularistic values and segmented political thinking have continued to affect political behavior in a number of, perhaps all regions of India."

At one level, patterns of violence were reinforced by formal institutions, such as party systems. Parties have been a focus of emphasis for constructivist scholars of ethnicity as an engine of identity change (Chandra 2004, 2012; Posner 2005; Wilkinson 2012). However, there is a critical problem of causal directionality in this argument. Party systems do not appear spontaneously; in India these systems are based on ethnicity and not the other way around. As detailed in Chapter 3, for instance, it is not that caste matters in Malabar because of the Communist Party but rather that the Communist Party matters in Malabar because of caste. This argument is important because of the way parties operate in India. Congress has defined itself as a "catchall" party—that is, representative of all castes, religions, and classes. However, as Pradeep Chhibber and John R. Petrocik (1989: 196–97) note, "A more accurate description comes from [Richard] Sisson, who finds that the national Congress is 'organized into mutually exclusive factional coalitions which tend to nucleate around a dominant leader or faction which has its own regional base of political support.'"[78]

Even during the early days of dominance by Congress, state-level parties were built on local ethnic cleavage structures, which were different across provinces and princely states. For instance, when Hyderabad was integrated into the Indian Union in 1948, Congress was, according to officials at the time, "prepared to recognize the historical position of the Muslim community by agreeing to special weightage for it."[79] In this way, local politics in Hyderabad, which had been dominated by religious identification, did not change after colonialism (Varshney 2002: 180–81). The creation of durable ethnic cleavage structures during the colonial period therefore affected the creation of parties more than parties themselves created ethnic cleavages.

Similarly, in the native states, princes continued to play a large role in the early postcolonial period when they served as *rajpramukhs* (governors) of their former states and maintained control over the selection of civil servants. Many princes ran for elected office in the early postindependence period, and they had an overwhelming success rate (Richter 1971). Princely families continue to exercise influence through political dynasties; for instance, Jitendra Singh, recently Minister of State for Home Affairs and a former Member of Parliament representing the erstwhile princely state of Alwar, is the grandson of the last maharaja of the kingdom.

The functioning of other formal colonial-era institutions further illustrates the continuing divide across provinces and princely states. Consider the Indian Civil Service, which became the Indian Administrative Service (IAS) after independence and was extended into former princely kingdoms. In former native states such as Indore and Gwalior, however, most of the postcolonial IAS contingent came from the former princely bureaucracy, even though the majority were legally required to come from outside the state. These officers even entered the IAS without taking the standard entrance exam, which emphasized the strength of princely rulers to coopt organizations imported from the provinces (Jones 1974: 100).

Patterns of violence also became embedded in informal institutions. For instance, violence during the colonial period created narratives that came to define specific regions, or as Roger Petersen (2012: 409) succinctly notes, "Violence becomes memory." Members of ethnic groups recognize these histories of conflict, conveyed through either written or oral accounts. The long legacy of communal violence in Hyderabad led to the city becoming known throughout India as a communally sensitive place. Since communal riots became a feature of the city's politics in the 1920s, Hyderabad has remained a major site of Hindu-Muslim violence. Despite a world of economic and demographic changes since independence, it is still known throughout India as one of the country's most riot-prone cities. In former provinces like Ajmer or Malabar, however, memories fixate on previous episodes of violence centering on local castes and tribes.

Along these lines, several scholars have noted that acts of violence themselves harden ethnic identities (Van Evera 2001; Kaufmann 1996; Bates, De Figueiredo, and Weingast 1998; Byman 2000). Ornit Shani (2007: 158), for example, has noted the following in her work on Hindu-Muslim riots in Gujarat: "An act of large-scale violence that is widely labelled or perceived to be taking place along a Hindu–Muslim divide clearly defines the boundaries between two such groups. . . . the general representation of violence as communal, in official and popular discourses, simplified this complexity and hardened its communal characterization." Violence serves a dual purpose—it both rigidifies ethnic divides and maintains the salience of ethnic categories. This effect can be incredibly long-lasting; recent research has shown, for example, that as far back as the medieval period political violence in Africa is correlated with stronger violence even after colonialism (Besley and Reynal-Querol 2014).

A question here is why, after the end of colonialism, disadvantaged groups—especially ethnic majorities—did not seek out revenge for colonial-era policies. For example, Hindus in British areas may have wanted to instigate violence against Muslims precisely because they had been a protected minority during the British period. Certain ethnic groups may have felt resentment about their past treatment (Petersen 2002). On the contrary, the colonial period in India created different political cultures and commonsensical notions of how conflict should and should not be organized. As Laitin vividly demonstrates about Yorubaland, the way individuals are conditioned to think about ethnicity and ethnic relations matters greatly in the production of violence. The situation is similar in India; for example, a common refrain from interview respondents in Ajmer, a former British province, was, "But everybody knows that Hindus and Muslims do not fight here"[80]—despite the fact that, as Chapter 2 details, the large Hindu majority of the province was forced to share power with a small Muslim minority during the colonial period. The Hindu-Muslim divide in Ajmer nevertheless receded during colonialism, and a new narrative of ethnic conflict based on caste began to emerge.

Because new institutions continued to reflect colonial-era ethnic divides, attempts at reforming the position of ethnic groups in contemporary India have met with limited success. The failure of reform is the second major reason that the colonial past still casts a shadow over contemporary India. For example, consider policies on landholding. On the surface, the early postindependence period featured an impressive array of reforms aimed at British landholding policies, the most important being the abolition of zamindari tenure. However, as Barbara and Thomas Metcalf (2001: 244) note, "the extent of the transformation can easily be exaggerated. . . . landlords were guaranteed compensation for all property taken. . . . Landless peasants gained little from zamindari abolition." After peasant uprisings in Hyderabad State in the late 1940s, Swami Ramanand Tirtha of the Hyderabad State Congress toured local villages and noted about the landlords who had been under siege that "the feudal elements are taking shelter and surreptitiously managing their affairs. They are waiting for an opportunity. They feel that once the Communists are crushed, they would go back and continue as before. They have not changed a bit. They are the same hard nuts."[81] The next several chapters highlight how postcolonial land reform has stalled, especially in former British areas. Former princely states often reformed their agricultural policies decades before independence. Chapter 3 illustrates this fact from Kerala: the princely region of Travancore initiated widespread land reforms prior to the end of colonialism whereas the former British region of Malabar lagged decades behind.

Along these lines, consider one of the other major reforms intended to push for caste and tribal uplift: the Mandal system of reservations.[82] Despite these national-level reservations, Chapter 2 shows that identical reservation policies across Jaipur and Ajmer are perceived quite differently by the low-caste students whom the reforms are meant to assist. In places like Ajmer, with its long legacy of caste violence, polling indicates that Scheduled Castes have generally found the reservation system of little benefit.

Another example is the way the postindependence government has approached colonial forest policies, one of the main drivers of tribal conflict. The post-British governments of India have not significantly altered colonial policies; the state still controls forest lands, implements reservations, and has done little to prevent adivasi land displacement (Guha 1983; Haeuber 1993). In some cases, the postcolonial government exacerbated existing policies; Richard Haeuber (1993: 49–50) notes that "despite the transition from colonial to independent status, forest resource management changed little: exclusionary processes *accelerated . . .* to consolidate state authority over forest resources" (emphasis added). This inherited legacy was fatal in places like Bengal, where the Naxalite movement, a Maoist uprising against the Indian state led by poor adivasis, began.[83] But because princes in such places as Jaipur and Travancore had been pursuing protective policies for adivasis, new forest policies in these regions did not have the same negative effect.

Despite a wide variety of reform efforts, the hierarchy of ethnic groups in different parts of India today exists largely as it did during the colonial period. Key distinctions between ethnic groups in British India and those in princely India have persisted over time. The state of low castes and tribals is still poorer in former British areas; the position of Muslims and other religious minorities remains poorer in former princely states. One important caveat here is that this failure of reform is not uniform throughout India; it would be too simplistic to suggest that reforms failed everywhere they were instituted. There were exceptions to the rule. The case-study chapters of this book highlight this variability. Jaipur and Ajmer in Rajasthan, as well as Bastar in Chhattisgarh, have failed to displace their colonial legacies. But the case studies from Kerala illustrate that effective reform is possible, and even if this reform does not ultimately alter patterns of violence inherited from the past, it can significantly reduce the overall amount of bloodshed.

Summary

In the mid-nineteenth century a massive rebellion among the native population led to the creation of two Indias: one was governed directly by British administrators whereas the other remained under the control of native princes. These native rulers maintained autonomy within their territories, especially in the run-up to independence. British administrators and princes had markedly different ways of thinking about ethnicity and ordering ethnic politics. In the provinces, British administrators placed a new focus on caste identity and pursued policies that benefited high castes and discriminated against low castes and tribals. In the princely states, as in precolonial India, native rulers emphasized religion and pursued policies that benefited coreligionists and discriminated against non-coreligionists. Furthermore, the British goal of religious neutrality created protective policies for religious minorities (mainly Muslims), whereas princely rulers enforced protective policies for low castes and tribals. These disparate sets of ethnic policies led to more caste violence in the provinces but more religious violence in the princely states.

Ethnic identities and patterns of violence initially constructed during colonial rule remain salient in the postindependence period. Patterns of violence were first reinforced through institutions. Formal institutions such as political parties were built on the ethnic cleavage structures of colonial India, and informal institutions such as the narratives and memories of past conflict became embedded in specific regions, thereby creating commonsensical notions of how conflict should be organized. Also, the postcolonial government in India failed to reform the socioeconomic conditions of minority ethnic groups. Despite a number of reforms geared toward Scheduled Castes and Scheduled Tribes or Muslims, the positions of these groups have not altered considerably in the decades since 1947. In both of these cases—institutional persistence and the failure of reform—a divide was maintained between provinces and princely states after independence. The colonial past continues to play the paramount role in producing patterns of ethnic violence across the contemporary Indian state.

CHAPTER 2

Violence in North India: Jaipur and Ajmer

Muslims have a good situation here. Go into their neighborhoods.
They eat chicken biryani all the time.

—*Police inspector, Ajmer district*[1]

During the colonial period, the north Indian state of Rajasthan was known as Rajputana (the land of the Rajput clan) and was a conglomerate of primarily Hindu kingdoms. The sole territory in the region that came under the control of British administrators was the small province of Ajmer, or Ajmer-Merwara,[2] as it came to be known during the colonial period. When Ajmer became a British territory, the nature of ethnic politics in the area was fundamentally altered, especially in comparison to the neighboring princely state of Jaipur. Caste and tribal identities became hegemonic in Ajmer, but religion remained the bedrock of Jaipuri society. Political leaders in both areas implemented different policies of ethnic stratification, policies that were reinforced by institutions even after independence. This historical divergence from the early nineteenth century explains the pattern of ethnic violence visible across Jaipur and Ajmer today.

The Case Studies

Jaipur and Ajmer are neighboring districts located in the heart of Rajasthan. Both territories are located along the eastern divide of the state, slightly north of the Aravalli mountain range. Maps 2.1 and 2.2 indicate the location of both areas during the colonial and postcolonial periods, and Table 2.1 shows basic comparative figures for both regions over time. Though Jaipur has always been a more populous territory than Ajmer, both areas are otherwise comparable: they have similar geographies, economies, languages, and cultures, and they have roughly the same ethnic demography.

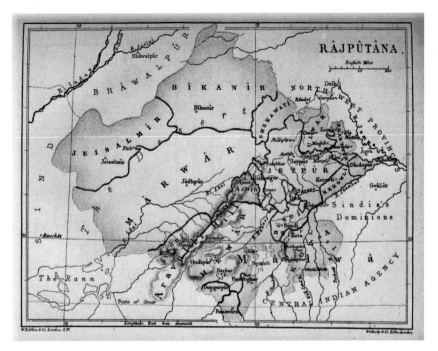

MAP 2.1. Colonial Rajputana.

SOURCE: Pope 1880.

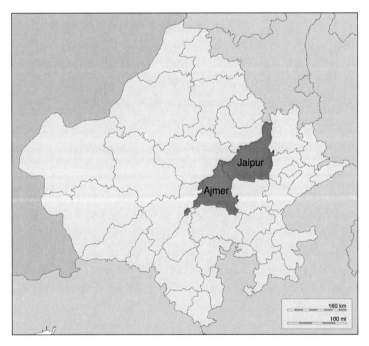

MAP 2.2. Postcolonial Rajasthan.

SOURCE: Produced by Colm Fox. Original source: http://d-maps.com/carte.php?num_car=9036&lang=en.

TABLE 2.I.
Jaipur and Ajmer Historical Comparison

	1901		2001	
	Jaipur State	Ajmer Province	Jaipur District	Ajmer District
Population	2,658,666	476,912	5,251,071	2,181,670
Hindus	90%	80%	88%	86%
Muslims	7%	15%	10%	11%
SCSTs	–	–	23%	20%

SOURCE: Data from 1901 and 2001 Censuses.

During the colonial period, Rajputana was a massive landlocked territory extending over 330,000 square kilometers, and it was made up almost entirely of Hindu princely states. These various kingdoms were considered patrimonial and backward (Rudolph and Rudolph 1984). British administrators liked to compare them to the dominions of feudal Europe. They were called "antique states" (Ramusack 2004: 43) in which tradition and lineage were paramount. Most of the Rajput territories were formed by clans who used Hindu mythology to trace and legitimize their kingdoms. In the medieval period, one clan—the Kachhawa, who were from the Kshatriya caste and claimed to be descended from Ram—established a kingdom in Rajputana called Amber, which later became Jaipur State.

Amber was incorporated into the Mughal political constellation as an imperial client state during the medieval period. Due to their military prowess, the Rajputs had close relations with the Mughals during the reign of Akbar. One of Amber's earliest rulers, Bahar Mal, was given a nobility mansab, and the house of Amber intermarried with the Islamic rulers of India. Later kings of Amber, such as Jai Singh I and Sawai Jai Singh II, were called on to serve Aurangzeb during his Deccan military campaigns in the late seventeenth century.[3] It was during the reign of Aurangzeb, however, that relations between the Mughals and the Rajputs—whom the emperor described in a letter as "those Satans in a human shape"[4]—deteriorated into open rebellion.

Mughal power in India precipitously declined after Aurangzeb's death in 1707, and Amber eventually emerged as an autonomous state. In 1727, Jai Singh II (1699–1743) began to construct the city of Jaipur as the new capital of his expanded kingdom, which he renamed Jaipur State. Its relationship with the British began at the start of the nineteenth century. By this time, Rajputana, trapped in a power vacuum in north India after Mughal decline, had become a war-torn region. Emergent powers such as the Marathas and Pindaris led vicious raids against the Rajput states that decimated the area. In the midst of this mayhem, in 1803 the British, under Lord Gerard Lake, signed a treaty with Jaipur's ruler Jagat Singh (1803–18). Jaipur State had initiated contact with the British in the hopes of securing military aid. The treaty stipulated that Jaipur would pay an annual tribute and provide troops to the British in return for military protection. Within only three years, however, the British abruptly terminated the agreement because officials in London had become skittish about imperial overextension in India (Stern 1988: 13). For the next decade Jaipur was left isolated and the outside raids resumed in force.

In another about-face, in 1818 the British (now with recently renewed ambitions in India) demanded that Jaipur sign a new treaty. Jaipur eventually relented and became a protected state once more.[5] In 1820 the British then sent a Resident to the Jaipur court. Over the ensuing decades colonial officials interfered repeatedly in the kingdom's internal administration, especially after an 1835 agitation in the capital city. After the Rebellion, however, the British began, as they did throughout India, to take a hands-off approach to governance and devolved more internal authority to Jaipur's rulers (Sarkar 1984: 360–62). For example, because Maharaja Ram Singh (1835–80) had supported the British during the uprising, he became a recipient of the Order of the Star of India. Jaipur State was given a seventeen-gun salute. Robert W. Stern (1988: 18–19) writes that the kingdom eventually became, in relation to the British, "a client tail wagging a patron dog," and that Sawai Madho Singh II (1880–1922), the second-to-last ruler of Jaipur, was essentially an "absolutist monarch."

The neighboring territory of Ajmer was also once a regional kingdom whose precolonial history was not unlike that of Jaipur. Ajmer became an imperial client state once the Mughals conquered India. It was designated a *subah* (province) of the empire and was even briefly the headquarters of Aurangzeb. There is evidence, however, that Ajmer, more so than Jaipur, experienced serious precolonial communal conflict. In 1192 it was the site of the defeat of the last Hindu king, Prithvi Raj Chauhan, in battle against Muhammad Ghori, who laid the foundations of the Delhi Sultanate, one of the earliest Islamic empires in India.[6] It was also the first recorded city in

India to have had a Hindu temple destroyed, in 1193 by Ghori. And during the Mughal period the emperor Jahangir destroyed another temple there in 1613 (Eaton 2000: 73).[7]

Once the Mughal Empire began to decay, regional warlords attempted to establish their own autonomous kingdoms in Ajmer. The state came under Maratha domination in the mid-eighteenth century and was later placed under the control of a Maratha regional governor. By 1816 the British had determined to crush Maratha power once and for all in north India, and they enlisted the support of Daulat Rao Sindhia, the maharaja of the nearby Gwalior State. After the Marathas were defeated, in 1818 Ajmer was ceded to the British for more than 500,000 rupees by Sindhia (Baden-Powell 1892: 321). Over the next several decades, British administrators in the state negotiated and signed treaties with the surrounding princely kingdoms in order to pacify the borders of their new outpost.

Ajmer-Merwara would become the only British province in the whole of Rajputana, and colonial administrators intended it to be "a model to the surrounding States."[8] Despite its remote location, it was not an inconsequential area. Ajmer became a British province before such well-known cities as Delhi, Agra, Lahore, Lucknow, and Allahabad.[9] It was governed by a Chief Commissioner who was directly responsible to the Foreign Department of the Government of India. One of those Chief Commissioners, Robert Holland (1919–25), noted the following about the state: "The province resembled in some way a spoilt child because it is equipped with loving grandparents, namely the Government of India, devoted and fussy parents, in the Chief Commissioner and the Commissioner, and a host of other fond relations in the shape of officials who would not be found in an area corresponding in size in British India."[10]

After Indian independence in 1947, Rajputana was designated a "Part B" state—that is, a former princely state or conglomerate of princely states. In the next year it was incorporated into the Indian Union. The maharaja of Jaipur was named the rajpramukh, and Jaipur city became the capital of the new state. Under the States Reorganisation Act of 1956, Ajmer-Merwara province (considered a "Part C" state because it was formerly a Chief Commissioner's Province) was integrated into the state. The boundaries of present-day Rajasthan have remained largely the same as those of the colonial period.

The central concern underlying the choice of these two districts for comparison is to explain why Ajmer came under the control of the British but

Jaipur did not. From their earliest days on the subcontinent, the British had selected for annexation areas of India where there was fertile land. In this sense, Rajputana on the whole was not appealing because the massive Thar Desert stretched across most of the region. Ajmer in particular was not a productive area; records from the time noted that "agricultural conditions in Ajmer-Merwara are precarious. . . . The soil is generally shallow, and the rocky strata are near the surface. . . . rainfall . . . is uncertain, and its frequent failure makes the Province peculiarly liable to scarcity and famine."[11] The British also wrote that adjoining Merwara was "a wild and hilly tract, giving little opportunity for productive agriculture."[12] Ajmer-Merwara did, however, have one clear benefit for the British: it was well-placed in the center of Rajputana. Chief Commissioner Holland noted that "Akbar realised the great importance of Ajmer as a 'point d'appui' in the midst of Rajputana, commanding the route to Gujarat on the one side and to Malwa on the other."[13] He added that "every power who became paramount in Upper India has striven to possess Ajmer as one of the symbols of sovereignty."[14] In 1818 the British took control of Ajmer for precisely this reason, using it as their lone station within Rajputana.

In the same year, the British also concluded a treaty of "subordinate cooperation" with the ruler of Jaipur. Why didn't they take control of this state as well? Stern (1988: 66) explains: "The British knew what they wanted in Jaipur, but not yet how exactly to go about getting it. They wanted, of Rajputana in general, a pacified border area bordering on their empire proper; and from Jaipur, in particular, they wanted money." Jaipur was a considerably more prosperous princely state than Ajmer, and the British needed to pay for their wars in Rajputana. In 1818 they therefore set the tribute for Jaipur at a staggering 8 lakhs. Even colonial officials residing in the kingdom at the time considered the amount excessive. In 1842 British authorities relented and reduced the tribute to 4 lakhs annually, and they also remitted 46 lakhs to the Jaipur government.[15] Stern (1988: 1–2) notes that the British, instead of conquering the kingdom, intended to "maintain, more-or-less, Jaipur's own political system and try to establish over it controlling British influence." They had limited success in this endeavor, but they preferred this option over fighting another costly war in the region.

The British did not select Ajmer on the basis of the dependent variable of interest in this study: patterns of ethnic violence. Furthermore, the actual selection criterion—geographic location—is not related to ethnic conflict.

Ajmer's location would have no effect on violence: being in the center of Rajputana would not have made it more or less likely to experience any particular kind of ethnic conflict. Moreover, its geographical attributes were incredibly similar to those of Jaipur. Therefore, the problem of endogeneity can be minimized with the paired selection of these two cases.

Colonial-Era Religious Policies in Jaipur and Ajmer

Throughout its history Jaipur State has often been described as a kingdom of communal peace. Shail Mayaram (1993: 2524), for example, writes that Rajasthan as a whole "has hardly had a history of communal violence," and princely states like Jaipur "by and large, maintained their record of communal harmony" (2525). Stern (1988: 276) similarly notes that Jaipur "enjoyed a well-earned reputation for . . . communal peace."

These quotes are representative of the argument that princely rule throughout India was marked by syncretism, a concept discussed in the previous chapter. In contrast to these existing accounts, this chapter argues that Jaipur was in fact a kingdom beset by communal conflict for much of its preindependence history. This religious violence began with the discriminatory policies of Jaipur State toward its minority Muslim community. Policies of ethnic stratification widened the gulf between Hindus and Muslims. In contrast, communal violence was curtailed in Ajmer, where British administrators did not stratify ethnic groups by religion. Instead, they implemented a policy of religious neutrality, which had the practical effect of protecting the small Muslim minority. This policy expunged religion as the primary mode of ethnic classification in the province and reduced violence over the long term.

The rulers of Jaipur State were orthodox Hindus and they established and ruled the kingdom as a Hindu polity. The religiosity of the state's founder, Jai Singh II, was well-known throughout India:

> [Singh] was personally very religious and well versed in theology. About the time that he began to construct Jaipur, he received from the Mughal emperor the titles of Maharaja, Mirza Raja and Sawai. . . . Mirza Raja, which denotes a kinship relation with the Mughals, was not used in his own documents since it did not fit his image as a ruler. . . . by 1727, when Jaipur was founded, a new Kachhwaha seal was adopted that proclaimed allegiance to the deity Sita Rama, not to any Mughal overlord. (Datta 2008: 236)

After the death of Aurangzeb, Singh was finally able to break free from Mughal hegemony. He began to embrace Hindu customs and traditions openly, designing the kingdom's capital city according to religious precepts and intending it for his Hindu subjects (Roy 1978). He considered himself the *dharmaraja* (righteous king) and performed in Jaipur the Vedic *asvamedha* ritual (horse sacrifice), an important symbolic gesture because at that point it had not been undertaken by any Hindu ruler in some nine centuries (Datta 2008: 232; see also Narayanan 2014: 105–7). The religiosity of Jai Singh II also extended to later kings of Jaipur. For instance, in 1911 the *Times* singled out for their readership the maharaja of Jaipur (Madho Singh II) as a "prominent . . . ardent supporter of orthodox Hinduism" (*Times* 1911: 26).

This focus on religion was rather typical of all the Rajput kingdoms. James Tod (1829: 403) noted in his detailed chronicle of Rajputana that "there is scarcely a state . . . in which one-fifth of the soil is not assigned for the support of the temples, their ministers, the secular Brahmins, bands and genealogists." He also observed the powerful role Brahmins played in the raja's life: "The [king] is often surrounded by lay-Brahmins as confidential servants, in the capacities of butler, keeper of the wardrobe, or seneschal [majordomo], besides the Guru or domestic chaplain, who to the duty of ghostly comforter sometimes joins that of astrologer and physician, in which case God help the prince!" (406–7). Like many other princely states in Rajputana, a large portion of the land in Jaipur was given to priests tax-free as *inam* (gift) and used for the construction of temples. Rajas throughout Rajputana dispensed large amounts of patronage to religious institutions. The rulers of Jaipur exemplified this practice. They primarily understood ethnicity in terms of religion, and they fashioned the kingdom as a Hindu theocracy.

In the eighteenth century, when the city of Jaipur was initially being constructed, Jai Singh II brought a large contingent of Muslim laborers to his new capital. Jaipur is well-known as one of the earliest planned cities in India, and Muslim labor played an important role in constructing it. Later, once the city had been built, Jaipur's Muslims worked in primarily two occupations: as artisans or in the large gemstone trade. In the latter, they mainly worked on the manufacture of gems—they purchased stones and polished them—whereas most of the sellers were Hindus.

It has been argued that Muslims were integral to the fabric of Jaipuri society, and that the state had a general record of tolerance and inclusion toward them. Mayaram (1993: 2525) notes that "although [Jaipur] was theocratic, its rulers were known . . . for their financial support to the Ajmer dargah[16] and to tazia processions. Persian was the language of the state administration and Muslims were an integral part of the ruling elite and revenue administration." Rajat Datta (2008: 236) notes that "Jai Singh saw himself as a *dharmic* [religious] king . . . but his state did not promote policies that discriminated against non-Hindus." Ian Copland (1998: 212) comments that the "Jaipur government patronized Mohurrum as well as the tomb of the Sufi saint Mu'in al-din Chishti at Ajmer." It is also frequently noted that the last maharaja of Jaipur, Sawai Man Singh II (1922–47), personally intervened during Partition to prevent violence against Muslims and implored them not to leave for Pakistan.

A deeper look into the record of the state, however, reveals a quite different picture. Beginning with their conceptualization of Jaipur as a religious kingdom, the rulers of the state embraced ethnic policies that stratified and divided the Hindu and Muslim communities. In contrast to numerous official pronouncements and public displays of tolerance and inclusion, the princes of Jaipur in reality enforced many discriminatory policies against the Muslim minority, policies that were consistent across several rulers of the kingdom.

First, consider Mayaram's argument about the inclusion of Muslims in the Jaipur government elite. This is an important measure for two reasons. First, most communal violence occurred in urban areas where government capitals and departments were located. Second, in India it was argued that "office is everything" (Zakaria 1970: 2), therefore communal representation was extremely important in limiting violence. Using data collected from the City Palace Archives in Jaipur, Table 2.2 displays communal representation in the state during the late 1920s. In reality Hindus dominated the upper echelons of the princely government. The Council of State, known as the *Mahakma Khas,* was the central governing institution of the kingdom and consisted almost entirely of Hindus. From 1929 to 1930, only the Public Works Ministry was headed by a Muslim.

Only one Muslim headed a ministry in 1934–35 and again in 1937–38 (which covers the main period for which data were available).[17] The posts headed by Muslims also tended to lack security. One British administrator in the region commented about this in 1940: "I spoke to Resident [sic] and also to the Prime Minister at Jaipur a few days ago about the question of a successor to Khan Bahadur Abdul Aziz as Revenue Member, Jaipur. Apparently the Maharaja has now decided that he would definitely prefer to have

TABLE 2.2.
Jaipur State Civil List, Mahakma Khas, 1929 to 1930. Muslim member in italics.

Position	Officeholder
Vice Presidency	Mr. B. J. Glancy
Foreign and Home Minister	Rai Bahadur Pandit Sri Gopi Nathji
Finance Minister	Rai Bahadur Pandit Amar Nathji Atal
Revenue Minister	C. L. Alexander
Public Works Minister	*Khan Bahadur Maulvi Mahomed Ashfaq Hasan Khanji*
Military Minister	Thakur Devi Singhji of Chomu
Education Minister	Rao Bahadur Thakur Narendra Singhji of Jobner
Chief Justice	Raj Bahadur Pandit Seetla Prasadji Bajpai
Inspector General	Mr. L.C.B. Glascock

SOURCE: Jaipur City Palace Archives, Report on the Administration of the Jaipur State, 1929–1930.

a Hindu Revenue Member and intends to appoint a Muslim to hold some other portfolio."[18]

In 1941 Jaipur's ruler Sawai Man Singh II did appoint as his *diwan* (Chief Minister) a Muslim, the acclaimed Mirza Ismail (1941–46). Prior to coming to Jaipur, Ismail had become well-known throughout India for his efforts to rapidly modernize the southern Kingdom of Mysore. Despite having one of their own in the kingdom's second-highest office, the Muslim community of Jaipur hardly benefited. For example, when Mirza Ismail instituted a constitutional reform process, Muslims were left untouched by its changes. Stern (1988: 317) writes:

> The Muslim members of the constitutional reform committee wanted for their constituency in Jaipur the same pattern of positively disproportionate representation, "weightage," and separate electorates that had been enjoyed by Muslims in British India since the Morley-Minto Reform of 1909. They didn't get it. . . . Most of Jaipur's Muslims were among the state's poorest and least educated people, and they were for the most part unenfranchised by Mirza's constitutional reform.

Muslims in the princely states often held as their standard for treatment the way their counterparts lived in British India. This was a common pattern, and Chapter 3 details that Muslims in Travancore demanded similar treatment.

In the early twentieth century, most of the princely states were devolved greater levels of autonomy in their internal affairs. During this time, Jaipur became more hardened in its religious discrimination. Because of its treatment of Muslims, during the 1930s and 1940s the princely government periodically became the target of complaints by the Muslim League. For example, the League wrote about the lack of responsiveness by the Jaipur government toward the condition of the Muslim community: we have "every sympathy with the Muslim *Muhajirin* from Jaipur who have been undergoing great hardships and suffering. . . . The Committee urges upon the Jaipur Durbar to meet the just demands of the Jaipur Muslims."[19] They commented later on the princely states more broadly, especially regarding "the various Indian States, namely Jaipur, Jodhpur, Bhavanagar, Cutch and Patiala. . . . The Committee most earnestly urges upon the rulers of the States concerned to redress the grievances and protect the lives, honour, properties and liberties of their Muslim subjects, thereby creating a sense of security amongst them and preventing the situation from taking a serious turn."[20]

British administrators in Rajputana were also concerned about Jaipur's religious discrimination. They believed that Man Singh II was biased against Muslims and had connections to the Hindu Mahasabha, a Hindu nationalist organization (Stern 1988: 304). The situation for Muslims under Man Singh II continued to deteriorate. One of the rights taken for granted by authors who have argued that the princely states were syncretic is the freedom of religious minorities to worship without interference or harassment. But even these basic rights were curtailed in Jaipur. In January 1939, the Muslims of Jama Masjid (the largest mosque in the city) submitted an application to Man Singh II to expand the entrance of their mosque because the walkway was too small for Muslims to enter and exit at the same time. This simple request was denied, but Muslim leaders ordered the construction to begin anyway. In response, the prince sent his police to halt the project. A small disturbance ensued and six Muslims were shot and killed. Syed Ghulam Bhik Nairang, a member of the Central Legislative Assembly, created a report on the incident for the Muslim League Party of the Central Legislative Assembly entitled "The Jaipur Juma Mosque Tragedy."[21] Even the Muslims of British India, including those from Ajmer, protested against the actions of the Jaipur darbar.[22]

As a result of these discriminatory policies, instances of communal violence in Jaipur State increased in the early twentieth century. One communal riot broke out in 1926 on the outskirts of Jaipur city. A larger riot occurred in

1927 and the entire city was shut down for five days.[23] In 1931, Mohammed Ishaq, editor of the newspaper *Muballigh,* wrote to the editors of the *Muslim Outlook* newspaper about another riot that year: "Hindu Muslim tension at [Jaipur] has assumed [a] dangerous aspect."[24] He continued: "Hindus have completely boycotted Muslims who, threatened with starvation, scarcity of water and intolerable aggressiveness of Hindus, have left home and migrated to neighbouring places. Cemetary [sic] fences have been burnt by Hindus and no legal steps are taken against perpetrators while Muslims are being involved in false cases. . . . Police Officers are doing their worst to oppress Muslims."[25] Muslims wrote to the British Resident at that time:

> [Hindus] have combined together to reduce us to abject misery and distress and to compel us to leave our homes. . . . They made undue claims upon our religious rights and places of worship, they stopped business and dealings with us and they have banned their schools and dispensaries upon us. We are poor and helpless and depend upon our Hindu brethren. Our plight can therefore be well imagined.[26]

Hindus blamed the 1931 conflict on Muslims, noting in their own letter to the Resident that "the direct and the immediate cause of the present disturbance is that the Mohammedans forcibly constructed a wall in night hours on Mohurram night with beat of drums and 500 armed persons outside the mosque on Khalsa . . . land and took a Pipal tree inside it."[27] A. C. Lothian, the British Resident in Jaipur, sided with the Muslim interpretation, although he could do little to stop the violence. He noted in 1933 that the Jaipur government played a key role in promoting communal conflict: "Relations between Hindus and Muslims of the Jaipur State are very strained. One of the main grievances of the Muslims is that they are being denied services in the Household and other departments under the verbal orders of the Maharaja. The posts which were formerly occupied by Muslims are now being given to Hindus in general and to Rajputs in particular."[28]

Another major incident occurred during Mohurrum in 1936. It is impossible to know with certainty on the basis of contemporaneous accounts and documents what happened. However, a press communique from the time noted the following:

> The Moharram processions on the Ashra or 10th day of Moharram were marred in Jhunjhunu town, the Head-Quarters of the Shekhawati district of the Jaipur State, by an untoward incident which occurred when the Chejaras or Mohammedan masons completely demolished a wall of a Hindu house, which they

alleged interfered with the passage of their Tazia. The demolition was carried out by a large mob of Mohammedans in defiance of the orders of the Nazim or District Magistrate, who was present on the scene. . . . Next day the Hindus observed a complete hartal [strike].[29]

In 1942–43 there were two more riots in Jaipur.[30] Then, in 1946, another incident occurred and this time the Muslims tried appealing to their new diwan, Mirza Ismail. They described the incident as follows:

> In the Jaipur State . . . the Musalmans are of late facing circumstance [sic] which are far from happy. . . . On the 18th March, 1946, certain local Hindu goondas [thugs] decided to take out their holi[31] procession with music being played before the mosque, with threats of social boycott and violence to the Musalmans in case they placed obstructions in their way. . . . When the Musalmans were engaged in their Zor (afternoon) prayers, the goondas raised a huge noise and pounced yelling upon the defence-less Namazis inside the mosque. The Police Constables were also helpless. The Mussalmans were taken unaware and received bullet wounds, lathi [truncheon] blows and beatings.[32]

This sharp increase in discrimination and episodes of communal violence prompted the *Sarosh*, an Urdu weekly in Bombay, to write tellingly on the eve of independence in 1946 that "so far as repression and excesses against the Musalmans are concerned, this state *[Jaipur] has surpassed even the states of Kashmir and Gwalior*," two states with among the worst communal reputations in India at that time.[33] The Jaipur police superintendent noted the next year that "[this all] goes to show that the feelings amongst the Hindus and Mohammedans in Jaipur are somewhat strained, and might burst forth any day."[34] The final colonial-era riots occurred in Jaipur during 1947 and 1948 as India was partitioned.

The actual state of the Muslim community in Jaipur contrasts sharply with traditional accounts that stress religious tolerance and communal harmony. Muslims were instead subjected to economic, social, and political discrimination by the Hindu-dominated princely government. Periodic explosions of violence resulted from this discrimination: Jaipur's Muslims agitated against their maltreatment while the princely government and the Hindu majority of the state responded with force to maintain their strength. Tensions between the two communities consistently ran high. The syncretism that existed on the face of Jaipur State was largely illusory; the government mistreated Muslims throughout the twentieth century. Even after Partition, several Muslim members of the Jaipur government who had emigrated to Pakistan complained that their back wages were never delivered to them.[35]

The communal situation in neighboring Ajmer during colonialism was altogether different. The British officials who governed the area were more focused on the nature of the caste system and on relations between different caste and tribal groups, because they understood ethnicity primarily in these terms (detailed later in this chapter). In the realm of religious policy, British administrators in Ajmer-Merwara sought to secularize the province, to prevent both Hindus and Muslims from dominating politics, and to expunge religion as a legitimate mode of social organization.

In Ajmer, British administrators implemented a policy of religious neutrality. Even though the province was overwhelmingly Hindu, all religions were considered equal under the law. In effect this meant that Muslims were protected because they were a small minority in the province (only 15 percent of the population). The best example of this neutrality is the fact that, in contrast to their situation in Jaipur, Muslims actually did form an integral part of the ruling elite within British-controlled Ajmer-Merwara. Table 2.3 displays the number of government posts occupied by Muslims in 1925.

Ajmer's Muslim community held almost half of all jobs in the province. These jobs were distributed across various branches of the government, unlike in Jaipur, where Muslims were generally relegated to only one department. Muslims also held several of Ajmer's top government posts—Additional Sessions Judge, Public Prosecutor, and Inspector of Police, for example. The British noted in 1925 that "out of 73 posts of a superior nature 27 are held by Mohammedans and 46 by Hindus,"[36] meaning that Muslims controlled almost 37 percent of the top posts in the province. They even comprised a majority of the Ajmer police force. This fact may have played a crucial role in limiting communal violence: a majority-Muslim police force may have worked hard to prevent spasms of violence in which Muslims suffered disproportionately. Moreover, Muslims dominated the key police

TABLE 2.3.
Communal Representation in Ajmer Government, 1925.

Total Jobs	Hindus	Muslims	Percentage Muslim
2340	1241	1051	44.91

SOURCE: National Archives of India, Foreign and Political Branch, Establishment Branch, 1925, #509–E.

posts; of eighty-seven Head Constables, fifty-nine (67.8 percent) were Muslim and twenty-eight (32.1 percent) were Hindu.[37]

This information about Muslim representation in government was released by the British in response to complaints from local newspapers that Ajmer constituted, as they put it, a "Hindu Raj."[38] Colonial administrators responded to this criticism by conducting an internal audit and publicly releasing the information. The whole process was carried out in stark contrast to the autocracy of princely India. Religious minorities there had fewer outlets through which to complain or organize to redress grievances. In 1939, for instance, Jaipur banned several major newspapers—the *Hindustan, Vir Arjun, Jaiya Praja, Sainik,* and *Qaumi Gazette*—due to "scurrilous editorials intending to excite disaffection both towards the Ruler of the State and his Government."[39] This practice was common in princely states throughout India. Critiques of the government, especially on the grounds of religious intolerance, were simply prohibited.

Regarding the number of Muslims employed in government service in Ajmer in 1925, Chief Commissioner S.B.A. Patterson (1925–27) told his superiors that the data "will show that taking into account the complete total of employees a larger number of Mohammadans is employed than their proportion to the population warrants."[40] The Commissioner likewise noted that Muslims "enjoy a position of very considerable weight."[41] Another Ajmer official, Denys Bray, responded to complaints from Muslim newspapers by noting, "In view of the fact that Mahommedans number about one third of the urban and one fifth of the rural population of Ajmer-Merwara, it would appear from these statistics that the need for special measures to safeguard their interests in this respect has not been clearly established. The local Administration are [sic] not unmindful of the matter."[42] At the same time, however, Bray also emphasized a general policy of neutrality and implored those within the Ajmer-Merwara government to understand the "undesireability [sic] of any one community [holding] an unduly disproportionate share of posts in Govt. service."[43]

The British also undertook other efforts to push for religious neutrality in Ajmer. One of these initiatives dealt with education policy, a principal way in which the province could be secularized over time. Table 2.4 details the percentage of Hindu and Muslim children enrolled in primary schools in 1933–34 in Ajmer-Merwara. Although all of the figures are extremely low, a higher percentage of Muslim boys than Hindu boys were enrolled in school,

TABLE 2.4.
Hindu and Muslim Education Statistics in Ajmer, 1933 to 1934. The denominator in the archival file was the total Hindu and Muslim population, not simply the population of children; therefore the actual figures for primary school attendance are probably much higher than these estimates.

	Hindus		Muslims	
	Male	Female	Male	Female
Primary School Enrollment	5.02%	1.10%	6.87%	1.05%

SOURCE: National Archives of India, Home Department, Public Branch, 1935, #31/38/35.

and the percentage of girls from both religions was comparable. The latter statistic is surprising because of the cultural reluctance at the time to enroll Muslim girls in school.

The British administration of Ajmer-Merwara utilized a policy of religious neutrality that created the same protective policies for Muslims as throughout the rest of provincial India. Even well into the twentieth century this minority community provided almost half the manpower of the Ajmer-Merwara administration. Government documents from the time show that British officers were concerned foremost about maintaining a sense of equality between Hindus and Muslims, making them equal under the law.

As a result of these policies, Ajmer remained largely peaceful during British rule. Only two communal riots occurred prior to Partition. The first was in 1923.[44] Authorities at the time noted that "as a result of Hindu processions playing music near mosques in Ajmer, two collisions have occurred between Muhammadans and Hindus. Bitter feeling prevails between the two communities."[45] Another contemporaneous telegram noted that "the first signs of trouble occurred on the night of the 15th . . . when a Hindu procession was set upon in the Durgah Bazar by Mohamedans. This was a small affair and was adequately dealt with by the Police in half an hour at the cost of a dozen arrests and the disappearance of a gold bangle from the idol."[46] During this riot five people died and more than one hundred were injured.

Over the entire next decade—when Jaipur began its slide into communal chaos—there was only one minor riot in Ajmer, in 1936, and no individuals were killed. The Deputy Superintendent described it as follows:

> On May 22nd, at 11.10 a.m. Constable Lahri Singh of the local C.I.D. reported to the Kotwali [police station] on telephone that a riot of communal nature was

taking place at the gate of the Carriage shops and that stones were being freely pelted. The S.O. Kotwali accompanied by some Sub-Inspectors, Head Constables and constables hastened to the scene. The rioting was then going on but it was brought under control. . . . It was ascertained that 19 workmen, including 11 Hindus and 8 Muslims, had received injuries during the course of fracas [sic].[47]

The *Fortnightly Reports* located in the British Library in London contain detailed police reports about the communal situation in Ajmer during a wide swath of the early twentieth century. The reports describe a relatively peaceful province: most communal incidents recorded were minor in nature. Most important, over time the British policy of neutrality worked to lessen the religious divide between Hindus and Muslims. For example, a dispatch from February 1931 shows how community leaders worked together to prevent violence from erupting: "In consequence of the fact that the month of Ramzan coincides this year with the Hindu marriage season, there has been some slight friction over the playing of music by Hindu processionists when passing Mosques at the time of Tarahvi prayers. The attitude of the leaders on both sides appears to be reasonable and no serious developments are apprehended."[48] Or consider this dispatch from May 1931: "The Muharram celebrations passed off peacefully, although there were one or two contretemps. In one case it was alleged that water had been thrown from a house occupied by Hindus on the party accompanying a Tazia. The police pacified the Taziaars and induced them to pass on."[49]

At other times the British noted no disturbances whatsoever. In January 1922 a dispatch stated, "There is a distinct lull in agitation in the City of Ajmer. The Commissioner states that the City is quieter than it has been for 13 months."[50] Around the time that Jaipur was experiencing serious rioting in 1943, a dispatch for Ajmer-Merwara noted plainly under the heading of communal conflicts, "Nothing of interest."[51] The reports also detail that most of the demonstrations and rallies in Ajmer were not ethnic in character but related to the independence movement, probably because the INC was able to organize within the district. The last major incident of communal violence in Ajmer was during Partition, although almost the whole of north India experienced some violence during that time.

There are a few alternative ways to account for the lack of communal violence in Ajmer during the colonial period rather than the British policy of neutrality. First, Jaipur may have been less able to prevent violence than Ajmer-Merwara. To consider this explanation, figures were collected on the size of the military and police force in both areas during colonialism. In Ajmer in 1903 there were a total of 2,515 men in the Imperial and Native Armies and 704 policemen in the regular police force.[52] Jaipur, however, had a much larger military and police presence. The state had 11,660 men in the army, 5,782 cavalry were under the control of nobles who served the darbar, and the combined city and district police employed 12,666 men.[53] Using population figures from the 1901 census, this means that Ajmer had one officer for every 148 persons while Jaipur had one for every 88 persons. Jaipur was therefore well-equipped to handle communal violence.

A second explanation for the lack of violence in Ajmer comes from the unique nature of Islam in the district. Mu'in al-din Chishti, founder of the *dargah* (shrine) in Ajmer, was a prominent Sufi saint, and Sufism—a mystical Islamic tradition—was central to the history of the city. Yet the existence of a strong Sufi identity in Ajmer is a poor explanation for the lack of violence. It is not clear, for example, that militant Hindu groups make any distinction between the different sects of Islam. Also, other cities with a strong lineage of Sufism, such as Aurangabad in Maharashtra or Gwalior in Madhya Pradesh, have not been spared communal violence like Ajmer. A better explanation may be that the dargah in Ajmer brings together the Hindu and Muslim communities, thus creating social and economic ties that can prevent violence (Mayaram 2005). But Saumitra Jha (2007: 20) has found some statistical evidence that Muslim pilgrimage sites actually have increased chances of experiencing religious violence because rival religious communities frequently practice their rituals in close proximity to one another. After all, the Babri Masjid in Ayodhya was a contested site for both Hindus and Muslims, and this is precisely why it experienced significant communal violence. Moreover, the economic interaction within the dargah is not the kind that promotes peace: it is not complementary, nonreplicable, and does not involve trade (Jha 2013).

Finally, perhaps it is the case that violence in Jaipur was contagion from Ajmer. This seems unlikely, however, for several reasons. Most important, it was the rulers of Jaipur who decided to discriminate against Muslims, which formed the original cause of communal violence in the kingdom. They did so despite—not because of—the British. British officials did not want to interfere in princely India, but they were nevertheless concerned about religious discrimination in those kingdoms. In fact, in their treaties with princely states, British officers insisted that laws for religious toleration be "written in large characters on the Statutes of the realm" (Lee-Warner 1910: 199). Moreover, in the 1930s Ajmer was one of the only places in Rajputana where the Hindu nationalist Rashtriya Swayamsevak Sangh (RSS) was active (Mayaram 1993: 2538). They did not have a presence in Jaipur.

Overall, Ajmer-Merwara experienced significantly less communal conflict during the colonial period than the neighboring Jaipur State. On the one hand, before Partition there were only two small riots and much less total bloodshed in Ajmer-Merwara, even taking into account the population disparity between the two territories. On the other hand, Jaipur State was plagued with communal discord.

This fact must also be considered in context. In many ways, Ajmer is a likely case for Hindu-Muslim conflict. As mentioned at the beginning of this chapter, Ajmer had a precolonial legacy of religious violence. During colonialism, it was also home to several powerful Hindu organizations. The RSS had a strong presence there, but Ajmer was also the headquarters of the Hindu reform movement Arya Samaj (Noble Society). In 1925 a massive gathering of Hindu Jats (a peasant caste) occurred right outside Ajmer. It was overseen by the ruler of the princely state of Bharatpur, and during the event the crowd passed a resolution demanding the forced conversion of Muslim Jats (Sikand and Katju 1994). Also, David Ludden (1999: 112) notes that the local fort of Prithvi Raj Chauhan became "an icon of militant Hindu nationalism." Yet despite all these factors that might have produced high levels of communal conflict, Ajmer was a relatively peaceful province and experienced less violence than neighboring Jaipur. Considering the precolonial legacy of violence in Ajmer, the absence of conflict by the end of the colonial period suggests that British rule played an important role in reducing it over the long term. A firm policy of religious neutrality secularized the province, kept the peace, and created a sense of equality between the two communities that persisted even after independence.

Postcolonial Religious Violence in Jaipur and Ajmer

The pattern of religious violence in Jaipur and Ajmer inherited from the colonial period became embedded and reinforced through local institutions after independence; the postcolonial period has therefore not seen major changes in how ethnic conflict unfolds. Formal institutions in both areas have continued to reflect divisions from the colonial past: the leaders of Jaipur and Ajmer immediately after independence came largely from the cadres of, respectively, the former princely state and province. Likewise, educational and employment opportunities have continued to differ widely for Muslims in both cities. Informal institutions, such as commonsensical perceptions of ethnic organization, as well as memories of previous conflicts have resonated differently in both areas. In conjunction, reform efforts (in this case, those geared toward Muslims in Jaipur) have largely failed to alter the past.

There is a considerable lack of credible information on the state of religious groups in both districts today, especially on the Muslim community. To overcome data insufficiencies, qualitative interviews were conducted with a wide array of respondents in both Jaipur and Ajmer to piece together as much information as possible on Hindu-Muslim relations. Respondents included government officials, members of the police administration, NGO workers, religious leaders, academics, and journalists.[54]

Policies of ethnic stratification in Jaipur from the colonial period severely stunted the development of the Muslim community. In almost three hundred years their position has not improved. Remarkably, Muslims have not moved even from the neighborhoods they inhabited earliest—the ghettos of the Old City—nor have they changed their major professions or sources of income. For Jaipuri Muslims, time has stood still: they were born a marginalized group and have remained one. Muslim religious leaders in the city are best-informed about the community's overall situation. One religious leader noted the following about its long history: "Sawai Jai Singh brought labor class Muslims here when Jaipur was constructed. Because most of them were poor, they were never integrated into society and did not achieve quality education. They live in the same areas even today—mainly in the eastern part of the Old City."[55]

Though it is hard to come by systematic figures on the state of these Old City Muslim neighborhoods, Shail Mayaram (1993: 2525) uncovered a Jaipur Development Authority report that included some basic information. About public goods she recounts the following:

> It is significant to note that all those four wards, namely chowkri [ward] Gangapol, chowkri Topkhana Huzuri, chowkri Topkhana Desh and chowkri Ramchanderji, where proportion of households per public tap is considerably high, have quite a high percentage of Muslim population residing there. And these are mostly the poor Muslim households, living under slum-like conditions, who

depend on public taps for their water requirements. . . . The story of draining, sanitation and public utility services, such as police chowkis [stations], post offices, medical facilities, reading rooms, is very much the same.

In addition to residing in decrepit neighborhoods, most Muslims also work in the same kinds of occupations as they did during the princely period (but now without opportunities for princely patronage). A Muslim NGO activist put it like this: "Muslims here today work as artisans, in handicrafts, polishing gemstones, textiles, printing, handmade paperwork. They've done the same thing for a long time."[56] Work in the gemstone trade has remained perhaps the most important source of economic stability for Muslims. But just as they did during the colonial period, Hindus form the majority of the sellers of gemstones. Exact figures are unavailable, but it is estimated that around 25 percent of the Muslim workforce in Jaipur are children involved in the gemstone trade. Hindu children, in contrast, constitute only about 7 percent of their respective workforce (Wal 2006: Chapter 19).

The state of Muslims in neighboring Ajmer is quite different. Although their position is not great in absolute terms, interviews conducted in the district revealed that it is better than that of Muslims across the border. One religious leader in the city summarized the difference between Ajmer and Jaipur: "Things for Muslims are not so bad here. In Ajmer the Hindu-Muslim situation is roughly equal. There is not a lot of enmity between the two groups due to one being ahead of the other."[57] When asked about the historical situation, the respondent stated, "During British rule the situation was good. In the princely states everything was done according to religion. But British India was different. There was not this kind of favoritism for the dominant group. Muslims received government jobs. And most important they were protected from Hindus. The British and the Muslims both feared Hindu India." Another religious leader echoed these sentiments: "I wouldn't say that the situation of Muslims is great here. But there is a sense that there is some equality between Hindus and Muslims; that there is not a huge gap here. There is some discrimination against Muslims, but no real hatred between the two groups."[58] The equality that was created between the two communities in Ajmer during the colonial period has been reinforced and persists even decades after independence.

Many respondents associated with Muslim NGOs also spoke about the economic situation of the community. Most pointed out that Muslims worked in a variety of industries, unlike in Jaipur where they were concentrated as artisans or workers in the gemstone trade. One respondent stated that "In the rural areas Muslims work in agriculture, but in the urban areas Muslims work in lots of different jobs: they own their own businesses, work in construction, work for the government. Of course, a lot of them work for the dargah."[59] About the dargah the respondent continued: "Go to the dargah area. You'll see it's not like the situation of most Muslims. They [those that run the dargah] are powerful people. They are well-off." A member of the dargah's Anjuman Committee confirmed this: "The situation of Muslims is good here. We are at the top. Hindus and Muslims are united in this area, around the dargah."[60]

The position of Muslims in contemporary Jaipur and their position in Ajmer are mirror images of each other, and religious interaction in each district differs greatly from interaction in the other. Muslims in Ajmer, although still constituting a backward group, work in a variety of industries, and interview respondents were more apt to display optimism about their community. Furthermore, Hindu-Muslim relations are not a major source of tension in the district. That peace seems to emanate from a sense of equality between the two communities that was fostered over time.

A second factor that has resulted in the persistence of colonial patterns of religious violence in Rajasthan is the failure of reform efforts. A variety of government organizations in the state did attempt to reform the position of Muslims after independence. At the national level, these policies have largely been a failure.[61] The contemporary Jaipur-Ajmer comparison provides additional evidence. The main administrative organizations responsible for improving the situation of Muslims in Jaipur are poorly staffed, poorly funded, and largely ineffective. One interview respondent at the Rajasthan State Minorities Commission (RSMC) noted that the administrative board had no chairman and no members because they were still waiting for stalled political appointments.[62] And consider the Rajasthan Minority Affairs Department, which oversees the distribution of scholarships to members of minority religious groups: from 2009 to 2010 more than ten thousand scholarships were stripped from their fixed allotment.[63]

Muslims in Jaipur have not seen much change in their fortunes since the princely period; they work the same jobs and live in the same neighborhoods. Muslims in Ajmer, however, have remained in a better position than their Jaipuri counterparts despite the exodus of a large number of wealthy Muslims to Pakistan after Partition.

Just as the religious communities in Jaipur and Ajmer seem no different today than during the past, so do their patterns of conflict remain unchanged. Systematic data on modern religious violence in both districts were compiled from a number of sources. The first two were the *Varshney-Wilkinson Dataset on Hindu-Muslim Violence in India* (Varshney and Wilkinson 2006) and the Worldwide Incidents Tracking System (WITS) database (Wigle 2010). The former database was compiled by Ashutosh Varshney and Steven Wilkinson from *Times of India* (Bombay) newspaper reports and covers the years 1950–95. The latter was compiled by the US government's National Counterterrorism Center from national and international press reports and covers the years 2005–2009. A third source was additional riot data from the Ministry of Home Affairs (MHA) published by Gopal Krishna in 1985. These data are unique because MHA figures are rarely disaggregated to the district and town level, but Krishna was given special access to this information. The main drawback is that the data cover only a truncated period (1961–70). Nonetheless, they offer a rare highly detailed glimpse into riot metrics for the entire country. The results of the contemporary Jaipur-Ajmer comparison are laid out in Table 2.5.

Since independence, Jaipur has continued to experience more communal violence than neighboring Ajmer. According to the Varshney-Wilkinson dataset, Jaipur is listed as one of India's "riot-prone" cities.[64] There have been thirty-two riot-related deaths and 123 injuries since 1950, although because the data are recorded from only one source it is likely that the overall toll is much higher. The number of events is also noteworthy: Jaipur experienced riots in 1952, 1969, 1989, 1992, 1993, and 1995.[65] In contrast, Ajmer did not have a single riot between independence and 1995.

The WITS data, on the one hand, record one major instance of violence in Jaipur: the June 2008 bombing that killed sixty-four people and injured two hundred. The terrorist group Indian Mujahideen took responsibility

TABLE 2.5.
Contemporary Religious Violence in Rajasthan (per 100,000). These figures are calculated per capita; the denominator is the combined Hindu and Muslim population (2001) of each district. *Casualties* means combined deaths and injuries.

	Hindu-Muslim Riot Casualties	WITS Casualties
Jaipur	3.01	5.13
Ajmer	0	1.04

for the attack. In Ajmer, on the other hand, there were only three deaths and nineteen injuries in a 2007 bomb attack by Muslim assailants from the group Harakat ul-Jihad-I-Islami (Islamic Jihad Movement).

Krishna's dataset unfortunately does not present figures on the total number of casualties from Hindu-Muslim violence; however, it does note that Jaipur was the most violent city in Rajasthan during the 1960s. Jaipur experienced enough violence during four of the ten years of that decade to be labeled an "urban centre . . . prone to periodic rioting" (1985: 69). Ajmer does not appear on Krishna's list. When all three sources are taken together, they show that Jaipur is a district of communal strife and Ajmer is a district of communal peace.

This view was reinforced by a number of interviews conducted with members of the police administration in both districts, from high-level inspectors to street-level constables. One police officer in Jaipur noted that "there are periodic Hindu-Muslim riots here in Jaipur. There is not a lot of understanding between the two communities. They are segregated. And all it takes is one miscreant to start a large conflict."[66] Another police officer stated, "The violence erupts from time to time, but it's especially bad during 'tense' moments. Think of Ayodhya or other problems like that. Whenever things like that happen, Jaipur will become violent."[67]

Riots are only one form of religious violence. Many other types of smaller, everyday conflict typically go unnoticed. A member of the RSMC noted that during 2010, for example, there were more than five hundred statewide complaints by Muslims in Rajasthan, and Jaipur was a central problem area. Of these complaints, approximately 50 percent dealt with some form of violence being committed, and its main cause was the demand by Hindus for Muslims to leave their neighborhoods.[68]

Police officers from Ajmer offered a contrasting view of communal relations in their district. An overwhelming number of them indicated that riots were not a major problem. One inspector noted generally that "the communal condition here in Ajmer is cool. There is not a lot of Hindu-Muslim violence at all—at least not a lot of riots. There are small things here and there, like one Hindu shopkeeper fighting with a Muslim shopkeeper. Or maybe a Muslim hits a Hindu with his scooter. But not riots."[69] One constable noted about "tense" moments that "when Babri Masjid happened I was in the police. I remember it. A lot of people were very worried, but there weren't any major riots. Definitely we have to be much more vigilant at those times."[70]

Existing political science explanations for communal conflict in India struggle to interpret this pattern of religious violence across both districts. All three of the most well-known political scientists working on Hindu-Muslim riots have pointed to Hindu nationalist organizations as the central promoters of violence (Brass 1997, 2003; Varshney 2002; Wilkinson 2004). All of their analyses highlight important features driving contemporary ethnic violence, but none of their arguments can explain the particulars of the Rajasthan comparison.

Brass (2003: 6) summarizes his primary argument as follows: "Hindu-Muslim opposition, tensions, and violence have provided the principal justification and the primary source of strength for the political existence of some local political organizations in many cities and towns in north India linked to a family of militant Hindu nationalist organizations whose core is an organization founded in 1925, known as the Rashtriya Swayamsevak Sangh." It is certainly true that Hindu nationalist organizations have played a major role in promoting religious violence. But riots in Rajasthan predate the rise of these organizations. Even if we take into account that the Bharatiya Janata Party (BJP) traces its roots to colonial organizations such as the Hindu Mahasabha, riots still predate these organizations. Second, if these organizations are the main promoters of violence, then we would expect Ajmer to have more Hindu-Muslim conflict than Jaipur. As noted previously, in the 1930s the RSS was active in Ajmer but not in other areas. Only in the final years of colonial rule were Hindu nationalist organizations able to begin organizing in Jaipur. And in modern times, the BJP has been successful in both districts as a local party—the party that dominated Lok Sabha (lower house of the Indian parliament) elections in both constituencies from 1989 to 2009—so its strength cannot be the source of the variation that exists in religious violence outcomes.

Next, recall Wilkinson's (2004: 1) argument, which he summarizes as follows: "My argument . . . is that ethnic riots, far from being relatively spontaneous eruptions of anger, are often planned by politicians for a clear electoral purpose. They are best thought of as a solution to the problem of how to change the salience of ethnic issues and identities among the electorate in order to build a winning political coalition." The main problem with this hypothesis is that political parties and competitive elections did not exist during most of the colonial period, yet riots still occurred. There can be little doubt that contemporary politicians manipulate ethnic issues and offer protection to minority ethnic groups who are politically valuable to a coalition. However, riots in Rajasthan occurred well before the introduction of any kind of electoral system. Furthermore, the particular constellation of ethnic groups is similar in both Jaipur and Ajmer: Muslims form roughly the same percentage of the population in both areas, so they are not more valuable as political actors in one district.

Finally, Varshney (2002) argues that civil society plays the key role in determining where outbreaks of communal violence occur. Specifically, he claims that networks (whether associational or quotidian) that link Hindus and Muslims can prevent violence. Varshney finds survey evidence that where intercommunal networks exist, violence is minimized. Therefore, perhaps Ajmer has more intercommunal organizations than Jaipur and this has led to the minimization of conflict. This is unfortunately a difficult argument to test because local-level data on associational life are hard to come by.[71] As a basic test, however, all interviewees in Jaipur and Ajmer were asked about local Hindu-Muslim organizations, but no one was able to name any (at least formal) associations.[72] This makes some analytical sense considering that across India formal associational life is among the weakest in the world (Chhibber 1999).

The religious politics of modern Jaipur and Ajmer do not differ considerably from their religious politics in the colonial period. Colonial policies and patterns of religious violence became embedded in both formal and informal institutions. It is this factor, combined with the failure of governmental reform efforts in the postindependence period, that has led to Jaipur remaining a district of Hindu-Muslim discord while Ajmer remains a district of Hindu-Muslim peace.

Colonial-Era Caste and Tribal Policies in Jaipur and Ajmer

During the colonial period, the Hindu rulers of Jaipur State emphasized the centrality of religion and discriminated against Muslims whereas British administrators in Ajmer emphasized religious neutrality and tried to promote secularism and equality between rival religious communities. In the realm of caste politics, however, the opposite happened. The British discriminated against low-caste and tribal groups in Ajmer whereas these same groups were protected by the rulers of Jaipur. Although detailed data on caste and tribal conflicts (like those pertaining to communal rioting) for Rajputana during the colonial period do not exist, archival evidence indicates that ethnic policies governing these communities differed considerably between Jaipur and Ajmer, ultimately creating different fault lines of conflict.

The basic comparative caste compositions of Jaipur and Ajmer in the early twentieth century are displayed in Table 2.6. Brahmins were the numerically superior caste in Jaipur, and more than 53 percent of the population made their living from the land. In Ajmer-Merwara, however, the Mahajans (a mercantile caste) were the largest group, and approximately 55 percent of the people made their living from the land. The dominant castes—Brahmins and Rajputs—were not involved in agriculture (considered a degrading occupation). Low castes and, to a lesser extent, tribal groups populated the countryside.

The main adivasi groups in each district were the Bhils and the Meenas, but there were numerous smaller tribes as well. Neither Jaipur nor Ajmer was a heavily forested area: according to the 2001 census, only 4.53 percent and 4.19 percent of the respective land was covered by forest. Most of the tribes lived in these small forested tracts or in rural hill regions.

When the British arrived in Ajmer, they came with the assumption that caste should be the central organizing principle of Indian society. While the rulers of Jaipur created a Hindu state, in Ajmer-Merwara province colonial officials ordered society around caste and tribal identities. For example, R. C. Bramley, a British Superintendent, was sent to the district in preparation for the 1901 census. This was the first census in British India that attempted to rank caste groups. Bramley and Captain A. D. Bannerman may have been

TABLE 2.6.
Composition of Castes in Jaipur and Ajmer, 1901.

Jaipur State	Ajmer Province
Brahmins – 349,000	Mahajans – 37,027
Jats – 265,000	Gujars – 36,278
Chamars – 218,000	Rawats – 32,362
Mahajans – 212,000	Shaiks – 31,972
Gujars – 184,000	Jats – 27,952
Rajputs – 124,000	Brahmins – 25,896
Malis – 116,000	Rajputs – 15,430

SOURCE: *Imperial Gazetteer of India* Vol. 5: 145–146 (Ajmer-Merwara) and Vol. 13: 389 (Jaipur).

the first Englishmen to officially employ the term *untouchable* in a government document (Charsley 1996: 2). In his reports Bramley painstakingly noted all the castes in the district that (according to his estimation) constituted the untouchables, such as the Balais, Chamars, and Regars, among others. The very process of determining untouchability promoted long-term caste antagonisms, and the stigma associated with this new designation was difficult to erase. Census operators were also sent into kingdoms like Jaipur, but the rulers of the native states emphasized religious identities and subverted caste to a secondary position of importance in their territories.

Believing that caste should be the basis of social organization in Ajmer-Merwara, the British then implemented ethnic policies that widened the gulf between high castes, low castes, and adivasi groups. Furthermore, as the British linked with high castes throughout India, policies toward low castes and adivasis took on a discriminatory character. The main policies in Ajmer that harmed the peasantry revolved around land; it is therefore imperative at the outset to understand the nature of landholding in Rajputana.

There were two main types of land in Jaipur and Ajmer: *khalsa* land and *jagirdari* land. Khalsa land (also known as crown land) was directly controlled by the government. In princely states, for example, the maharaja often owned these lands and received revenue directly from the cultivators who worked on it. On khalsa land, cultivators had no proprietary rights, but they were still "as a rule, treated as hereditary, being seldom interfered with so long as they [paid] the revenue."[73]

Jagirdari land, on the other hand, was controlled by a hereditary noble, and the darbar did not exercise strict rights over these areas, although they did collect revenue from them. *Jagirs* (land grants) in Rajputana had historically been granted by the raja for some kind of service (often military), and the rights to the land typically expired upon the death of the grantee. However, over time jagirs evolved into hereditary grants as new claimants (such as the son or nephew of a nobleman) simply paid a *nazarana* (fee) to the darbar and thereby retained control of the territory. In their estates the *jagirdars* (Rajput noblemen) were "assignees of the rights of the State, [but they had] the same rights as the State itself."[74] Jagirdari lands could be small parcels or massive estates; the larger ones were often known as *thikanas* and could have their own courts, tax collectors, and police forces. Powerful jagirdars could assign smaller jagirs within their kingdoms. These jagirdars were known by a wide variety of names: *sardar, thakur, thikanedar,* and *rao raja.*

There were also small allotments of land in Rajputana known as *bhums,* which were free land parcels. They did not require any kind of tax payment and were granted for life. They were given both by the darbar and by jagirdars. This outline summarizes the general contours of the Rajput landholding model, but in reality every kingdom in Rajputana was different.

It is difficult to know with certainty what exactly the system of landholding was in Ajmer-Merwara prior to British arrival. The British administrators who governed the region and surveyed existing land records believed that khalsa lands were governed under the ryotwari system, in which the tribute was collected directly from the cultivators. Once Ajmer came under the direct control of British administrators in 1818, however, colonial officials began to disrupt the existing landholding system in a number of ways (Gold and Gujar 1997). The results were disastrous to low-caste groups and produced a high level of rural unrest.

Ann Grodzins Gold and Bhoju Ram Gujar (2002: 67) note that during the early days of colonial rule in Ajmer, the British were focused "above all [on] tax assessment and revenue collection." In 1818, one of the most important tasks of the first Superintendent of Ajmer, Francis Wilder (1818–24) was calculating and instituting a new land-revenue policy. Wilder determined the land revenue as one-half of the value of all crops produced in the district. This amount was calculated even after the Superintendent commented that the Ajmer population before British rule had been "sadly thinned by oppression."[75] This new figure mirrored the crushing revenue demands made in direct-rule districts throughout British India. Later British administrators noted the following about Wilder's policy: he "had made the mistake of over-estimating the resources of the District, and the baneful effects of this error extended many years. This, added to several years of distress . . . reduced the District to a state of abject poverty."[76] The last tribute collected by the Marathas in 1818 totaled 128,978 rupees. Wilder increased it within two years to 179,457 rupees, although it was subsequently lowered after widespread protest.[77] Later administrators wrote that high taxation left "cultivators and landless labourers . . . generally in debt, and the latter live hand to mouth."[78]

Aside from increased revenue demands, the British did not otherwise alter the system of khalsa lands until 1849, when a *mouzawar* system was established in which proprietary rights were given over to village bodies. In essence this new policy "effected a radical change in the [khalsa] tenure. It transformed the cultivating communities of the *khalsa*—each member of which possessed certain rights in improved land, but who as a community possessed no rights at all—into . . . proprietary bodies."[79] Yet this new system was, as administrators complained, "hardly understood, and . . . not appreciated by the people."[80] This kind of land policy experimentation was common among the British in Ajmer. If a certain policy did not work, it was abandoned and replaced. For example, Ajmer-Merwara was originally opened up to the cultivation and sale of opium, but once the district became rife with smuggling, this policy was reversed (Indian Department of Statistics 1908: 41).

Another important change with the onset of colonialism in Ajmer was an increase in the number of khalsa villages. They almost doubled during the early years of British rule in the district, increasing the number of revenue-bearing villages under the control of the government. Although many of the early caste conflicts over land originated in the Bengal Presidency (home of the Permanent Settlement), British officials in Ajmer-Merwara noted that they actually had comparatively stronger proprietary rights over the land in their district.[81]

The main change on non-khalsa land in Ajmer-Merwara was the increasing power of zamindars. By 1901, for example, 1,693,728 acres of land were cultivated under the zamindari system whereas no areas were under ryotwari tenure (Keltie 1903: 152). In Ajmer the chiefs of non-khalsa land became independent property holders and were called *istimradars*. They claimed that they had always been private property holders—a dubious assertion but one accepted by the British. Colonial administrators in the district generally practiced nonintervention in zamindari areas. Cultivators in these regions were therefore subjected to the caprices of the istimradars; peasants became tenants-at-will and could be thrown off their land for any reason.[82]

The cumulative effect of these new British agricultural policies was the economic deterioration of the peasantry. In 1926, Commissioner of Ajmer-Merwara Lieutenant Colonel R.J.W. Heale traveled to an "average village" in the district to conduct an inquiry on the state of cultivators. He concluded that "the village is typical to the extent that it suffers from the difficulties and presents the problems that are common to the whole District, but it is more backward than very many villages. . . . The difficulties may be summed up in three words; ignorance, poverty and lack of water."[83] Mukat Behari Lal Bhargava, member of the INC and future Lok Sabha member from the Ajmer constituency, summarized the state of peasants in Ajmer in 1938:

> The condition of the peasantry in the province in general and in the Istamrari area in particular is indeed miserable. In the latter the system of Begar[84] is in vogue and the tenants have to pay a number of "lags" [taxes] besides the usual share of the produce, and are liable to be ejected at the whim and caprice of the Istamradar though they may have been cultivating the same plots of land for generations. . . . The lot of the five and [a] half lacs of people of this important but unfortunate province is no better than the hewers of wood and drawers of water and they drag on their miserable existence as mere dumb driven cattle.[85]

These various changes in agricultural policy in Ajmer-Merwara also made the province suddenly prone to famine. In the nineteenth century there were episodes of food scarcity of varying degrees in 1819, 1824, 1832–33, 1848, 1868–69, 1891–92, and 1899.[86] Part of the problem was that the British failed to make long-term investments in the land—irrigation, for example—and famines therefore hit the district especially hard.

British policies on adivasis in the province were also heavily discriminatory. The tribes of Ajmer-Merwara resided primarily in hilly regions or in small forested tracts in the district. The British, as they did throughout provincial India, commandeered these areas as property of the state when they came into power in 1818, arguing that they had the right of "management of any tract of waste or hilly land, the proprietary right . . . being invested absolutely in Government as long as the land is required for forest purposes."[87] The result was the alienation of lands that tribal groups had used without interference for centuries. Colonial administrators were led by their belief that without conservation policies the forests would be destroyed by villagers, who, British administrators contended, "wanted the free run of the forests to help themselves as they pleased with no thought to the future."[88] There is little evidence, however, that prior to British arrival Ajmer suffered from excessive deforestation.

The British also established Criminal Tribes legislation in Ajmer, and members of the large Meena tribe were criminalized. British administrators noted that there were actually two "classes" of Meenas: "the zamindari or agriculturalists, and the chaukidari or watchmen; the former are industrious and well-behaved, while the latter were, and to some extent still are, famous as marauders. As noticed later on, it is not always easy to distinguish one class from the other."[89] Members of the Meena tribe who were not actually criminals were stigmatized and suffered discrimination. In 1933, for example, hundreds of Meenas, as well as Sansies, Baories, and Chakras were convicted under Criminal Tribes legislation in the province.[90] Policies against the Mers tribe were especially brutal. They were designated a "predatory tribe" and in 1824 the British conducted military operations against them[91]—or as official B. H. Baden-Powell (1892: 319) described this process, the Mers were "rude tribesmen . . . reclaimed under British rule."

Across the border in Jaipur, social organization was completely different. Jaipur State was an explicitly Hindu kingdom; caste and tribal identities were therefore relegated to a position of secondary importance. In Jaipur it could hardly be argued that the situation of low-caste groups was good. Yet compared with British-controlled Ajmer-Merwara, Jaipur—far from its reputation as a "feudal" state—pursued a variety of protective policies for low-caste groups. These policies in turn reduced the likelihood of caste violence in the state.

First, the state of landholding in Jaipur differed considerably from that of Ajmer. The darbar probably controlled only about two-fifths of the land while the rest was "alienated in grants to nobles, ministers, priests or courtiers."[92] This percentage was extremely low in comparison to most of the other princely states.

The Jaipur government had a markedly different set of policies in its khalsa areas than in those instituted by the British in Ajmer's crown lands. Beginning in the early twentieth century, Jaipur State "followed a strategy similar to that in Baroda to achieve peasant support and political stability. [In the 1920s and 1930s] . . . a *ryotwari* settlement began to bring peasants into direct relations with the central administration."[93] Jaipur's ryotwari system cut out middlemen, an endless source of corruption in British India, and produced more security in land tenure. In 1939 Jaipur State went further and abolished a large number of land taxes that had previously been levied only on low castes.[94] In contrast to the excessive land tributes demanded by the British in Ajmer, less was requested by the darbar in Jaipur, where tributes could be as low as one-sixth of the crop, although the autumn demand could be much higher.[95]

The protective nature of the darbar was also reflected in the difference between tenure rights in khalsa lands and those in the jagirdari areas. On khalsa land the economic condition of the peasantry was superior. Richard Sisson (1971: 27) notes about Jaipur that "primarily in *khalsa* areas, the position of tenants was neither so tenuous nor their economic obligations so severe. Frequently tenants enjoyed *katedari* and *pattedari* rights which provided permanent rights of occupancy and inheritance if certain rules of tenure were met and in some cases provided for the right of transfer and the assumption of mortgage." Susanne and Lloyd Rudolph (1984: 29) add that "in the judgment of an inquiry committee of high civil servants from British India that reported on tenant rights at the time of independence, 'the tenant [of khalsa] has rights defined and secured, and there is, on the whole, little cause for him to complain.'"

In jagirdari areas over which the darbar had limited control, however, the position of tenants was much less secure and more prone to strife. The Rudolphs note that even by 1947 only 32 percent of all (16,780) jagir villages in Rajasthan had settled revenue obligations, meaning the rules that governed taxes and revenue were not codified and therefore tended in practice to be capricious. Jaipur State pushed for settlement in jagir lands in the late 1930s and 1940s, although with mixed success. The main point of contention was that some nobles in Jaipur did not believe themselves to be subservient to the darbar, but rather considered themselves independent rulers of hereditary estates. This enabled them to govern their territories in any fashion they chose, which usually resulted in feudal tenures. In fact, most associations or organizations that emerged to fight for peasant rights in the princely states targeted not princes but jagirdars. Barbara Ramusack (2004: 228) writes, "Although these princes were hardly utopian reformers and peasants on khalsa lands still had significant grievances, the conditions of peasants in jagirdari areas could be much worse."

The differences between peasants on khalsa land and those on non-khalsa land are well illustrated by the political history of Sikar, the largest thikana in Jaipur State. In 1935 Sikar was the site of Jat uprisings in which hundreds of cultivators refused to pay excessive revenue demands and protested their feudal conditions, which resulted in a violent backlash by Sikar officials (Rudolph and Rudolph 1966: 158). Thousands of Jats then traveled from Sikar to Jaipur city to speak to the maharaja, and Stern (1988: 282) notes that "one of the *sabha's* [group's] leaders, Harlal Singh, remembers a courteous reception at the palace and a sympathetic hearing of the Jat's [sic] complaints." Yet the raja of Jaipur had limited ability to interfere in the Sikar thikana. In fact, in response to Jaipur's attempts to meddle in state affairs, the rao raja of Sikar launched an armed rebellion against the maharaja in 1938 (Rubin 1983).

During this struggle the Jats sided with the maharaja against the rao raja. The Jats understood that their situation in Sikar—uncertain land tenures, excessive revenue demands, harassment by petty officials—was appreciably worse than that of the peasants of the khalsa lands of Jaipur. Sisson (1969: 947) notes that, on the whole, Jat movements in the princely states were "most intense in areas ruled by jagirdars . . . rather than in those under the direct rule of the royal house." The Sikar rebellion was eventually put down by the Jaipur raja with the assistance of the British, and the thikana was finally subjected to a set of serious land reforms.

The peasants of Jaipur fortuitously benefited from this endless infighting between the raja and his nobles. It was partly because of an attempt to weaken the nobles that the rajas of Jaipur in the twentieth century sought improvements in the lives of the peasantry. For example, when Mirza Ismail initiated constitutional reforms in the 1940s, "the Praja Mandalists on the constitutional reform committee were so successful in reducing the general franchise qualifications of wealth and/or education for Jaipur's untouchable castes as to enfranchise a positively disproportionate number of untouchables" (Stern 1988: 317). These specific reforms were ultimately blocked by high castes, but the darbar succeeded in passing legislation that tried to eliminate the more feudal aspects of jagirdari tenure (Kumar 2001: 265). By aligning themselves with the peasantry, the rulers of Jaipur were thus able to stunt the autonomy of the large landholding jagirdars in the state.

In contrast to the British in Ajmer, Jaipur State was also proactive in response to famines.[96] During the 1868–69 famine, for instance, the darbar distributed large amounts of cooked food from the capital and started a massive relief works program. Low-caste groups were specifically targeted and were allowed to graze freely in the forests to acquire enough produce to prevent starvation.

In total, the position of low castes in Jaipur was superior to that of the low castes in Ajmer-Merwara. The darbar, even if it was slow to act and limited in its reforms, pursued policies that were more protective than those in British-controlled Ajmer. There was more security in land tenure, better government response to famines, and over time the darbar connected more closely with the peasantry in land settlements. Furthermore, the darbar did its best to curb the most feudal aspects of jagirdari rule, eventually pushing for peasant land rights in those areas as well.

Jaipur State, like a number of other princely territories, also implemented protective policies toward tribal groups. The main reason was that princely rulers considered the tribes of the area to have been among the earliest inhabitants of Rajputana. Several other states in the region, such as Dungarpur, Banswara, and Pratapgarh, considered the Bhil tribe the earliest occupant of the land (Varma 1978). The rulers of Jaipur were no different. One account of the history of the state argues that "Meenas . . . held a good deal of this part of the country in the twelfth century"[97] before the Rajputs came to control it. Due to this belief, many tribes were treated with a large amount of respect. When a new raja was placed on the throne in Jaipur State, it was a member of the Meena tribe who placed the ceremonial rajatilaka on the king's forehead. Also, an official allotment of government jobs was reserved for the Meenas: specifically, they guarded the royal treasury and were hunters employed by the state (Ramusack 2004: 210). In 1939, Jaipur also created a new job-training program for members of the Dais tribe.[98]

The British, for their part, were not happy about Jaipur's protective treatment of its tribal population. They tried to enforce in Jaipur the same Criminal Tribes legislation that prevailed in Ajmer-Merwara, though they met with little success. For instance, when the British discussed Criminal Tribes legislation at a conference in Ajmer in 1923, Jaipur simply did not send a delegate. Inspector of Police D. R. Wright complained, "I see no officer from Jaipur was present at this conference but the Darbar had been informed of it and had intimated that one would attend."[99] In 1930, the British Resident wrote to the Jaipur government to complain that "if there are really members of Criminal Tribes—Minas and Baories—[there,] they should be dealt with according to the Criminal Tribes Rules." The Jaipur government responded: "we have the honor to state that these Minas & Baories are living here since the [state] was founded & are only cultivators. There is also no complaint against them. We, therefore, recommend that these Minas & Baories . . . may not be declared as Criminal Tribes."[100] Attempts by the British to limit the movement of the Meenas in Jaipur also failed: Jaipur State refused to implement these policies, much to the chagrin of British administrators.[101]

Overall, there were stark differences between Jaipur and Ajmer in their treatment of low-caste and tribal groups. In Ajmer, on the one hand, new census operations produced antagonism between castes as they were officially ordered and ranked for the first time. Low castes were subjected to crushing new revenue demands, were alienated from their land, and suffered an increase in the power of local landlords. For their part, tribal groups were cut off from their forests, and many were criminalized. In Jaipur, on the other hand, the darbar pushed for several protective policies for low-caste groups, even trying to improve their condition in jagirdari areas. Adivasis were also protected; they formed an important part of the princely administration, were allowed to remain in their forests, and were shielded from British attempts to criminalize them.

Postcolonial Caste and Tribal Violence in Jaipur and Ajmer

In the postindependence period, patterns of caste and tribal violence in both districts have not changed. On the one hand, caste issues still dominate the politics of Ajmer, and the caste system remains extremely rigid. In Jaipur, however, contemporary politics revolves around religion. Formal and informal institutions reflect this: political leaders in Ajmer utilize the language of caste, but in Jaipur they use the language of religion. Commonsensical understandings of how ethnic conflict is organized also differ: whereas in Jaipur caste and tribal violence is considered illegitimate, in Ajmer it is the norm.

A variety of respondents were interviewed in Jaipur and Ajmer to gain understanding of the contemporary socioeconomic position of SCSTs, as well as of relations between different caste and tribal groups. One Jaipuri journalist summed up the comparative state of caste and tribal violence in these areas as follows:

> Ajmer struggles with caste and tribal issues in a way that Jaipur does not. You can read the papers and you'll see the violence that happens there on a daily basis. The dalits are usually the victims, but STs suffer too. The high castes will do anything to ensure that the position of dalits does not change. They will prevent them from getting an education, from getting political representation—anything.[102]

The inherent caste divisions in Ajmer were reinforced via formal institutions such as political parties. In fact, a *Times of India* article from 2009 sums up the political history of Ajmer by noting that the district "has been dominated by caste politics."[103] This has been the case since the earliest days after independence. In the 1950s, India's first prime minister, Jawaharlal Nehru, wrote that the local Congress Party was badly split into caste factions, and that consequently development efforts there were among the least successful in Rajasthan (Naipaul 1971).

After independence, Rajasthan, like most states, tried different reforms to improve the condition of marginalized castes and tribes. The caste system was technically abolished. The state also embarked on an ambitious set of land reforms. In 1949 the central government appointed the Jagir Enquiry Commission, which recommended the abolition of jagirs. In 1952 the major piece of land reform legislation, the Rajasthan Resumption of Jagirs Act,[104] was passed. This act "resumed" (commandeered) all jagirs, provided compensation for jagirdars, established *khudkasht* (personal cultivation) allotments, created a system of land revenue for all holdings, and—most important—implemented a fixed system of tenurial rights for cultivators. The legality of the legislation was immediately challenged by the jagirdars, and although they tied up the courts for years, they were ultimately unsuccessful. Initially, small Rajput landholders (*bhumiyas*) were excluded from the legislation, but eventually they too were stripped of their land by the Congress Party. The Rajasthan Resumption of Jagirs Act, as well as later legislation that banned zamindari tenures, was implemented statewide. Ajmer came under the ambit of these reforms when the Government of Rajasthan passed the Ajmer Abolition of Intermediaries and Land Reforms Act in 1955.

The implementation of land reforms has been inconsistent across Rajasthan, however, and not every district has experienced the same level of success (Rosin 1978). In Jaipur, on the one hand, postindependence changes to the land tenure system were a continuation of preexisting reforms that had been instituted by the darbar in the early twentieth century. Low-caste cultivators and tribal groups had already been the focus of efforts to reform their land-ownership status and general economic situation. In Ajmer, on the other hand, land reforms were more difficult to implement because British policies had strengthened the position of landlords and stigmatized tribal groups. In Ajmer, as Thomas Rosin (2010: 7–8) writes, "putting a ceiling upon the size of land holdings to shift land to the landless was easily subverted and not applicable to the myriad of smaller holdings. The small land titleholders here seem to have little sympathy for the folks of lower castes whose labor they need to augment their own."

Other efforts at reform did not fare better. An NGO respondent noted that the position of low castes in the state has not changed considerably over time: "The government in Rajasthan has made a lot of promises to SCs, but no one trusts the government to fulfill its promises. The law states, for example, that a certain percentage of the state budget must be put toward programs for dalits. We monitor this. But it never happens."[105]

One major reform deals with the implementation of caste reservations by the Mandal Commission, which was established to study the condition of backward peoples. Along these lines, qualitative work has been done on the viewpoints of SCs toward reservation policies in Rajasthan. Narayan Mishra found that Ajmer was the only district of a number surveyed in Rajasthan where less than 50 percent of SC students agreed that the reservation system set up by Mandal has been "fairly useful" (2001: 240). In Jaipur, by contrast, the highest percentage of students (74.1 percent) agreed that educational facilities provided by the government were "quite useful" (236). Due to the contrasting political cultures that evolved in these districts over time, institutions that are identical on paper function altogether differently across both areas today.

Institutional persistence, coupled with the failure of reforms, has ensured that in both areas caste and tribal violence occurs as it did during the colonial period. The main source of data for violence against SCSTs is usually the Ministry of Home Affairs. However, MHA data are generally considered to be problematic for a number of reasons, the most important being that SCSTs are reluctant to come forward and trust the police to properly report and investigate crimes. Because of these shortcomings, new data on caste atrocities[106] compiled by a local Jaipur organization, the Centre for Dalit Rights (CDR), were utilized. These data unfortunately pertain only to violence against SCs, but they were available for several districts in Rajasthan, including Ajmer.

CDR data on caste violence are superior to MHA data, for a few reasons. First, SC crime victims often believe that the police will not be helpful or will make the situation worse. But the CDR collects data through three avenues. First, victims who are aware of the organization come directly to its offices and report crimes. Second, volunteers (such as witnesses) submit information about crimes (CDR has a network of more than a thousand lawyers and activists). Third, CDR employees use instances of caste crimes recorded in print and electronic media, offer their services to victims by conducting fact-finding missions, and submit reports to government officials if no action is taken. In short, CDR data serve as a critical alternative source of information on caste violence. The results of a comparison between Jaipur and Ajmer district for the year 2009 are detailed in Table 2.7.

TABLE 2.7.

Caste Violence in Rajasthan, 2009 (per 100,000). These figures
are calculated as the number of crimes against SCs divided by the
SC population (2001). Data were available only for the year 2009.

	Jaipur	Ajmer
Crimes Against SCs	9.0	26.0

SOURCE: Data from the Centre for Dalit Rights, Jaipur.

These data show that Ajmer experiences significantly more contemporary
caste violence than Jaipur, even though the percentage of the SC population
in both districts is similar. This information was confirmed by a number
of interviews in the district. On the causes of violence a journalist stated,
"What you will notice is that the situation in the villages has remained the
same. The Shudras [OBCs] have become immensely powerful. They are the
ones who commit violence against SCs, not high-caste Hindus. When a
dalit is killed, a Shudra is usually behind it. They will not allow any of their
gains to go to the dalits."[107] Christophe Jaffrelot (2000) has noted that most
OBCs in north India were landholders during the British period and have
maintained their dominance in the countryside. This is the case in rural
Ajmer today. The SCSTs who bear the brunt of violence in contemporary
Ajmer find themselves targeted by powerful OBCs. An aforementioned
NGO respondent noted the following:

> The main problem, the main cause of the violence, is casteism . . . the strength
> of the caste system. In some areas it is very rigid and in other areas it is not.
> Ajmer has a very rigid caste system, and the dalits there suffer for it. Any at-
> tempts to reorganize the caste system result in violence. A dalit bridegroom can-
> not even mount a horse for his wedding because this is an upper-caste custom.
> If he does, there will be a backlash.[108]

In Jaipur, by contrast, most respondents indicated that caste violence was
not the major problem in the district, citing instead the salience of religious
politics. One journalist noted that "the violence in Jaipur is communal. We
all wait for the next Hindu-Muslim riot. There are some caste issues in the
rural areas outside the city—in the villages—but most of the conflict here
is communal."[109] When asked to compare Jaipur and Ajmer, the respondent
added, "The last major conflagration here in Jaipur was in 2008 when bombs
were detonated in the Old City. If you ask people about violence, this is
what they think of—Hindus and Muslims fighting. But caste violence—you

won't find strong opinions about that. But if you go to Ajmer, you'll find a lot of caste conflict. The issues are very complicated there."

The backward position of low castes and tribals in Ajmer today is a legacy of discriminatory policies instituted during the colonial period. These policies of ethnic stratification increased land inequality, generated tension among caste groups, and ultimately led to increased violence. In Jaipur, however, the position of low castes and tribals was protected, and this has led to a minimization of caste and tribal violence in the district today.

Summary

The neighboring districts of Jaipur and Ajmer in the north Indian state of Rajasthan are in many ways indistinguishable from one another: they share a similar geography, economy, culture, and ethnic demography. In the early nineteenth century, however, the location of Ajmer in the center of the state brought it under the control of British administrators. Jaipur, however, remained an independent princely kingdom. This historical divergence has led to differing patterns of ethnic violence: today Jaipur experiences high levels of religious violence whereas Ajmer experiences more caste and tribal violence.

In Jaipur, on the one hand, Hindu rulers attempted to create a state organized on the basis of religion. They pursued policies of ethnic stratification that divided Hindus and Muslims but protected low castes and tribals. In British-ruled Ajmer, on the other hand, colonial officials increased the salience of the caste system. British policies of ethnic stratification there increased the gulf between high castes, low castes, and adivasis, but a policy of religious neutrality minimized the Hindu-Muslim divide. Considering that as far back as the medieval period Ajmer experienced serious communal violence, the complete absence of it today in the district is a remarkable fact.

The colonial-era pattern of ethnic violence in Rajasthan became embedded in both formal and informal institutions that continue to reflect preexisting social fissures. Likewise, reform efforts have not been successful: Muslims in Jaipur have failed to achieve gains as a community, and in Ajmer low castes and tribals still lag behind in their development. Commonsensical notions of which ethnic identities are salient and how ethnic conflict is organized continue to differ strikingly between districts. Postindependence patterns of ethnic violence in Rajasthan thus derive largely from the colonial period.

CHAPTER 3

Violence in South India
Malabar and Travancore

> The early history of Malabar is inseparable from that of the adjoining
> state of Travancore. Identical in people, language, laws, customs and
> climate, the whole of ancient Kerala is homogeneous in every respect,
> except in the accident of a divided political administration.
>
> —*Imperial Gazetteer of India, 1909*[1]

Kerala may seem a rather odd case for a study of ethnic conflict in India. This
small southern state is arguably the country's greatest success story, having
achieved social development indicators that rival those of many Western nations (Drèze and Sen 1995; Heller 1999). It has avoided the worst of Hindu-
Muslim conflagrations since India's independence, and likewise seems to
experience comparatively little caste and tribal violence. This chapter details,
however, that even in the tranquil state of Kerala there is a discernible pattern of ethnic politics, tension, and occasionally violence across former British and princely areas. The British initially wanted to conquer all of Kerala,
but they were unable to annex the south. This historical "accident" created
a fault line of conflict based on caste and tribal identities in the northern
region of Malabar but on communal identities in the south, in the former
Hindu Kingdom of Travancore. Kerala is also a notable state because, unlike
the other cases examined in this book, it shows that it is possible to implement effective postcolonial reforms that reduce ethnic violence.

The Case Studies

Kerala is a small coastal state in southwestern India, bordered on the north
by Karnataka and separated on the east from Tamil Nadu by the Western
Ghats mountain range. It lies on the extreme southern portion of what is
known as the Malabar Coast. Along with Andhra Pradesh, Karnataka, Tamil

Nadu, and Telangana, it is one of the five states that constitute south India. The local language is Malayalam and the inhabitants of the state are known as Malayalis. Malabar constitutes north Kerala while Travancore forms the south. Prior to independence, the small princely state of Cochin was located in the middle.[2] Map 3.1 depicts colonial south India with Malabar and

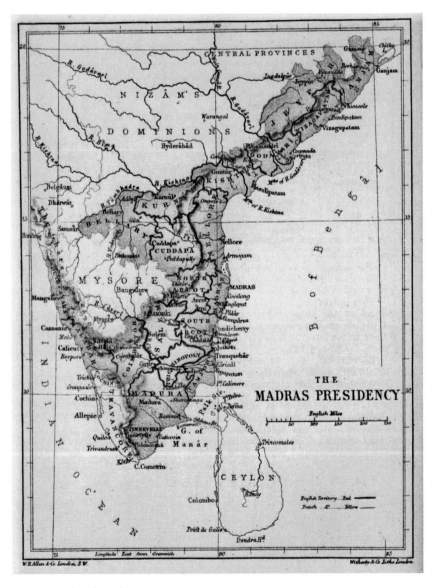

MAP 3.1. Colonial Kerala.
SOURCE: Pope 1880.

Travancore located in the extreme southwest. Map 3.2 shows the Malabar and Travancore districts of postcolonial Kerala (surrounding what are now the Cochin districts). Table 3.1 provides basic comparative figures on both regions from the colonial and contemporary periods. In 1901 the two areas were extremely similar: they had roughly the same total population, both

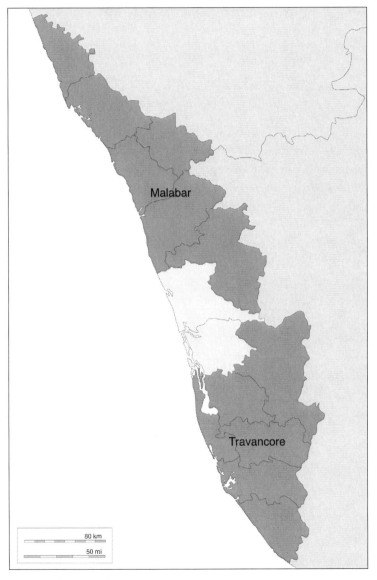

MAP 3.2. Postcolonial Kerala.

SOURCE: Produced by Colm Fox. Original source: http://d-maps.com/carte.php?num_car=8788&lang=en.

TABLE 3.I.
Malabar and Travancore Historical Comparison

	1901		2001	
	Malabar Province	Kingdom of Travancore	Malabar Districts	Travancore Districts
Population	2,800,555	2,952,157	13,515,737	12,245,607
Hindus	68%	69%	53%	62%
Muslims	30%	6%	41%	11%
Christians	2%	24%	6%	27%
SCSTs	–	–	10%	12%

SOURCE: Data from 1901 and 2001 Censuses.

had a Hindu majority, and the combined Muslim and Christian populations of both areas equaled around 30 percent (with Muslims a larger group in Malabar and Christians a larger group in Travancore). By 2001, the figures were slightly more skewed; most important, the Hindu population in Malabar had declined while the Muslim population had grown.

Chapter 2 detailed a comparison of two districts. This chapter details a comparison between two larger regions—a comparison of two areas of the same state. Malabar today consists of the Kannur, Kasargod, Kozhikode, Malapurram, Palakkad, and Wayanad districts, and Travancore comprises the Alappuzha, Idukki, Kollam, Kottayam, Pathanamthitta, and Thiruvananthapuram districts. This broad comparison lacks the fine-grained detail of the previous one, but it has the advantage of allowing various state-level factors to be controlled in the analysis.

In the medieval period, Kerala was a major international center of commerce, especially in the highly lucrative spice trade. The area was known to Greek, Roman, Jewish, and Arab traders for centuries. The intermingling of these groups with the local population over time created enormous cultural diversity in the region. Kerala historically had a close relationship with neighboring Tamil Nadu, and Malayalam itself probably emerged at some point in the sixth century as a variant of the Tamil language. Several ancient dynasties—the Cheras, Cholas, and Pandyas—ruled Kerala in the precolonial period, with each controlling parts of the region at various times.

As Chapter 1 detailed, medieval Kerala was unique in that Islamic supremacy never extended as far south as this region, which meant that the destructive Hindu-Muslim and Sikh-Muslim conflicts that plagued north India did not intrude on Kerala's politics. Although the state had a sizeable Muslim population, they were mostly descended from a distinct Islamic community of Arab traders and merchants who probably first visited Kerala during the seventh century. Consequently, religious divisions never resonated in this region to the same degree as in north India. In fact, the sixteenth-century accounts of Portuguese writer Duarte Barbosa, who lived in northern Kerala, describe communal tolerance between Hindus and Muslims.[3]

Instead, the caste cleavage in Kerala was much more divisive: the state has always been known for its elaborate and uniquely oppressive caste system. Most notable was the pervasiveness of "distance pollution." Throughout India, high castes could be polluted by being touched by low castes (hence the term *untouchable*), but in Kerala even being within a given distance of a low-caste person was considered polluting. The *Imperial Gazetteer of India*, for example, noted that in Malabar "a high-caste man returning from his bath shouts out to warn others of his approach, so that they may step aside into the fields and not pollute him."[4]

The Portuguese were the first European colonial power to arrive in Kerala, when Vasco da Gama landed in Calicut in 1498. They subsequently established several trading outposts during the sixteenth century. They were eventually surpassed by the Dutch, with the Dutch East India Company investing considerable effort to establish trading supremacy in the region. The rising Kingdom of Travancore, however, upended these plans, defeating the Dutch during the Travancore-Dutch War (1739–41). By the end of the eighteenth century, the Dutch in turn were eclipsed by the British East India Company. Much of the later Western competition for influence in south India was intertwined with the Napoleonic Wars that were simultaneously raging in Europe.[5]

In the period immediately prior to British influence, Malabar consisted of a number of small kingdoms ruled by rajas and chieftains, such as Cannanore, Calicut, and Kottayam. In the 1760s, Malabar largely came under the control of the neighboring princely state of Mysore. The Kingdom of Mysore subsequently engaged in four wars with the British (the Anglo-Mysore Wars), and after the final conflict ended in 1799 with Mysore's defeat, the region was annexed by the British. It was named the Malabar district and incorporated into the Madras Presidency.

Prior to the eighteenth century, southern Kerala was much like Malabar: a collection of small, warring principalities. In 1729, however, the young and ambitious Maharaja Martanda Varma (1729–58) came to the throne in Travancore and considerably expanded the borders of what was then a small kingdom through a series of military conquests. His successor, Rama Varma (1758–98), continued this policy of expansion until the state reached its greatest territorial extent. Travancore was a Hindu kingdom and its rulers were Kshatriyas. In 1795 and 1805, the state signed treaties of subsidiary alliance with the British. During the colonial era it was the third-largest princely state by population.

The Kingdom of Travancore did not suffer extensive British interference during colonialism. Robin Jeffrey (1976: 5) notes that from 1800 to 1860 "little attempt was made to tamper with the state's society or local politics," although that changed to some extent when the British forced the maharajas to modernize the polity in the mid-nineteenth century. Still, Travancore was regarded favorably by British officials. It had a nineteen-gun salute, and the last ruler of the kingdom, Chithira Thirunal (1924–47), was designated a Knight Grand Commander of the Order of the Star of India. The state was often the subject of special treatment; for example, in 1907 the royal house had no male heir, but the British did not interfere in princely succession; instead they allowed the family to adopt two girls.[6] The British Resident in Travancore was never very powerful, especially after 1857, and for this reason the office was considered by colonial administrators to be one of the easiest postings in India (Jeffrey 1992: 32). By the early twentieth century, all power in the kingdom resided with the maharaja and his diwan. A British report from 1914 detailed this arrangement:

> The machinery of the administration is of the old world model. The government is conducted in the name, and under the direct control, of His Highness the Maha Raja. The Dewan is His Highness' Chief Minister, with whom all departments correspond in official matters. It is a recognised maxim that no order issues in any official matter from His Highness except through the Dewan. There is no Executive Council; the machinery centres in the Dewan to an extent for which there is probably no parallel just now in any other Native State.[7]

Beginning in the nineteenth century, the cultural and historical similarities that had long defined Malabar and Travancore changed dramatically as the British came to control the north while the south remained independent. The main patterns of ethnic politics, tension, and conflict that are prevalent in contemporary Kerala were forged during this critical historical period.

After the end of colonial rule, the princely states of Travancore and Cochin were joined together into the state of Travancore-Cochin, and Malabar was merged with the new Madras State. Upon linguistic reorganization in 1956, most of Travancore-Cochin, along with a small part of the state of Karnataka, was merged with Malabar and the new state of Kerala was formed, with the southern city of Trivandrum as its capital.

A Historical Accident in Kerala

From the moment of their arrival in India, the British strategically selected areas of the country for annexation. For the most part, they acquired land on the basis of agricultural productivity. When they were interested in a fertile area—Punjab, for example—colonial administrators found a way to justify its annexation. Other areas, such as barren Rajasthan, were of little interest. This strategy creates a clear selection problem: the nonrandom annexation of a territory could bias the study of contemporary ethnic conflict. An ideal way to diminish this endogeneity problem would be to find a state that the British wanted to conquer but were unable to complete the process of doing so. This would allow an examination of the "treatment" of British rule applied to only one part of a state.

One of these special cases is Kerala. There is considerable historical evidence that the British wanted to conquer the entire state but, for various reasons, were able to annex only the north. Most significant was the substantial military threat posed by the neighboring Kingdom of Mysore; if not for that threat the British probably would have conquered Kerala in its entirety. Instead, Travancore fortuitously fell into an alliance with the British and remained an independent kingdom. Comparing north and south Kerala is therefore a powerful way to isolate the effects of colonialism on ethnic violence.[8]

When the British expanded their power into south India, colonial officials were originally intent on controlling the entire Malabar Coast. S. M. Mohamed Koya (1975: 514) notes that "at this time the thinking of the Company's servants was in terms of reaping commercial benefits by acquiring ports like Karwar, Honore and Mangalore. It was hoped that if the Malabar coast were to come under the British . . . it could be restored to cultivation and its products could be exported to Europe." In fact, the first British trading settlement in Kerala was not in Malabar but in the city of

Anjengo in Travancore (Logan 1887: 350). Like Malabar, Travancore was an extremely fertile area. Lord Curzon once lyrically noted about the region:

> Since I have been in India I have had a great desire to visit Travancore. I have for many years heard so much of its natural beauties, its old-world simplicity, and its arcadian charm. Who would not be fascinated by such a spectacle? Here Nature has spent upon the land her richest bounties; the sun fails not by day, the rain falls in due season, drought is practically unknown, and an eternal summer gilds the scene.[9]

The Madras Government similarly documented in a 1907 report that Travancore "is one of the most picturesque portions of South India, containing an extensive hill region, numerous rivers, and a succession of backwaters and vast forests."[10] Most important, Dick Kooiman (2002: 16) adds about the uniqueness of Travancore that most "princely states were located inland (Kashmir, Rajputana, Hyderabad, Mysore) rather than in coastal areas. In that sense, Travancore with its coastal location and sea ports was rather exceptional." There is little doubt that Travancore was exactly the kind of agriculturally productive area that the British had conquered throughout the rest of India. The major puzzle is determining what exactly made Travancore "exceptional." What prevented the British from taking control of this princely state as they had taken control of most other fertile and coastal territories?

A number of factors assisted Travancore in avoiding annexation like Malabar, but the paramount cause was rooted in the mid-eighteenth-century military campaigns of the neighboring Kingdom of Mysore. During this period, the ruler of Mysore, Hyder Ali (1761–82), began a series of military invasions throughout south India. He was succeeded in these efforts by his son, Tipu Sultan (1782–99). These campaigns brought the Kingdom of Mysore into repeated conflict with the BEIC, but it was uniquely successful against the British. Few native powers in Indian history blunted the strength of colonialism like Mysore. Because of the threat posed by this kingdom, the British needed to make an alliance with—rather than annex—Travancore, which ultimately spared the state from British rule and sharply changed its historical trajectory from that of neighboring Malabar.

In 1761 the *dalwai* (commander) of the Mysorean army, Hyder Ali, took control of the state. Although he continued to serve the Hindu Wodeyar dynasty nominally, Ali had effectively usurped the king's authority. Along with his son he began a series of military campaigns throughout south

India.[11] Four subsequent wars involved the BEIC, and Kerala was often a major site of conflict.

In 1766, Ali invaded Malabar and defeated a number of local rajas, making "an easy conquest of the whole country"[12] and bringing it under his rule. The First Anglo-Mysore War began the next year (1767–69). Mysore united with Hyderabad State against the British (who formed an alliance with the Maratha Empire) in order to gain control over large portions of south India. During the Second Anglo-Mysore War (1780–84), Ali, who by this time had allied with the French, declared war against the BEIC after they took over the French port of Mahé. In the midst of this war, Ali died suddenly and Tipu Sultan took control of the Mysorean forces.

Both of these wars were, at the absolute worst, stalemates for Mysore. Many events from the conflict became infamous throughout India. The first war had seen the armies of Hyder Ali reach and prepare to invade the British stronghold of Madras, and the second witnessed Tipu Sultan besiege the British-controlled city of Mangalore and wrest it back under his rule. The Treaty of Mangalore, which ended the Second Anglo-Mysore War, was considered a major embarrassment for the British. Officers in India—Governor-General Warren Hastings especially—were "indignant at the peace" whereas Tipu Sultan "believed himself to have won the war and behaved accordingly" (Dodwell 1934: 592). Arthur Wellesley, the Duke of Wellington and a famed British soldier, was almost killed in a later battle with Sultan, and his troops were badly unprepared for Mysore's use of rocket artillery (Geoghegan 2002: 90). The British had been humbled by their conflicts against Mysore, and after the Second Anglo-Mysore War they came to regard this kingdom, as well as Tipu Sultan, as a formidable enemy.

Buoyed by his successes, in 1788 Sultan began to threaten Travancore's borders, ostensibly because the state had provided refuge to Hindu rajas who had escaped from Malabar. In 1789 Sultan invaded Travancore, triggering the Third-Anglo Mysore War (1789–92). This conflict was different from the preceding two, however, because "for the first time during his reign Tipu Sultan had to fight against the British without any allies, whilst they could rely on the support of several allies, including the Nisam of Haiderabad" (Frenz 2003: 82–83). The conflict ended in 1792 and Sultan had been delivered a major defeat. In the subsequent Treaty of Seringapatam he was forced to cede half his kingdom to the British, including most of the Malabar region.

At the start of the Third Anglo-Mysore War, the various Malabar rajas and chiefs accepted a British alliance: they would unite to defeat Tipu Sultan and afterward they would retain their territory. However, once Sultan was defeated in 1792, the British reneged on their promise and took direct control of the region. The official policy of the British was to "regard [the Malabar rajas] as in the sense of Bengali zamindars, i.e. to strip them of their sovereignty and to seal with them appropriate treaties on tax" (Frenz 2003: 100). Malabar subsequently became a province of British India. Had Tipu Sultan controlled Travancore, the British in all likelihood would have annexed that area as well.

During the Fourth Anglo-Mysore War (1799), the British decisively crushed the Mysorean armies, and Sultan was killed during the siege of the capital city of Seringapatam. After the war, the British took control of the Wayanad region of Kerala, the last portion of Malabar to come under their rule. They subsequently reestablished the Wodeyar dynasty in Mysore.

Before the Third Anglo-Mysore War, the British had an interest in annexing the entire coast of Malabar, yet afterward they signed agreements with Travancore that ensured its political survival. The British were driven by their need for support in order to fight against an exceedingly dangerous rival in Mysore. Barbara Ramusack (2004: 67) confirms that John Shore, governor-general of India at the time (1793–98), made this particular agreement with Travancore due to "the need to protect the districts on the Malabar coast recently acquired from Mysore, and the desire to counter the French."

Correspondence files between British administrators located in the National Archives of India elaborate on this point. In 1789, as Tipu Sultan prepared for war, administrators at Fort St. George, the headquarters of the BEIC in Madras, noted the "advisability of taking the Raja of Travancore under the Company's protection."[13] The *Imperial Gazetteer of India* likewise states:

> In 1778 the Raja [of Travancore] granted a free passage through his territories to the British troops sent to attack the French settlement of Mahé, then much valued by Haider as the base of his military supplies. He had already treated with contempt Haider's proposals to become his vassal, and had openly avowed himself the friend of the British, whom he actively joined in their campaign against the Muhammadan ruler.[14]

If not for this serious threat posed by Mysore, Travancore's colonial history would have unfolded in an entirely different manner.

In addition to the power of Mysore, there are a few additional reasons that help explain why the British made an alliance with Travancore. For example, the British may have made the calculation that defeating the Kingdom of Travancore in military combat was no certainty. The state had already demonstrated its unwillingness to acquiesce to foreign control. William Logan (1887: 393), a famed Collector of Malabar, noted the following colorful story involving Travancore's relationship with the Dutch (whom they later defeated in war), which highlights this point:

> In 1739 Mr. Van Imhoff became Governor. He was a most intolerant man, and directly after he arrived he saw the necessity of curbing the rising power of Travancore if the Dutch were to retain their hold of the trade of the country and not allow it to pass into the hands of the English, who were backing up the Travancore Raja. Van Imhoff, it is said, carried to the Travancore Raja his own protest against the Raja's occupation of the territory acquired in 1734. His protest failed, and Van Imhoff, nettled at this result, spoke of invading Travancore. "The Raja replied that doubtless he might do so, but there were forests into which he could retire in safety." Imhoff retorted that "where Travancoreans could go, Dutch could follow." The Raja then broke up the conference by sneeringly observing, he had "been thinking some day of invading Europe!" Unfortunately for Van Imhoff he had no sufficient force at hand to command respect and obedience to his wishes.

Travancore also benefited from its geography. P. Shungoonny Menon (1878: 7) notes that the state was protected by the Indian Ocean on the west, by the Western Ghats on the east, and by backwaters and rivers on the north, therefore saving it time and again "from the incursions of foreign invaders."

A final factor that worked in Travancore's favor was the state's monopoly control over the trade of pepper—"black gold" to European merchants. Kooiman (1988: 22) notes that the British alliance with Travancore was "built on the exchange of 'cannon for pepper.'" Logan (1887: 350) recounted the words of another colonial administrator who stated that when the BEIC first arrived in south India, Travancore was "in a state which did not favour trade. . . . What the English Company would have liked would have been a despotic monarch who could assign to them monopolies of the produce they came seeking and could enforce the same with a strong arm." Over the next several decades Martanda Varma emerged as that despotic monarch, and in 1788 the British signed with his state what became known as the "pepper contract," which stipulated that Travancore would supply the British with pepper in return for military protection (Assary 2009). Leena More (2003: 236) notes along these lines that the British had long encouraged Martanda Varma's consolidation of power in the hopes that "Travancore's supremacy in the region would create the necessary conditions for them in trade." When the British took control of Malabar, there was no comparable ruler of the region—they encountered instead a multitude of warring rajas and chieftains, none of whom was able to assert hegemony over the others. Malabar was therefore an ideal state for annexation whereas Travancore presented a better opportunity for collaboration.

The glaring question is whether the British could have annexed Travancore even after their wars with Mysore. This was certainly possible, although reneging on their treaties, especially after having already done so in Malabar, was not without risks. But the British did have opportunities. In 1809, for example, Travancore's diwan, Velu Thampi (1799–1809), attempted to mount an insurrection against the British in the region. However, the raja never supported the rebellion and even aided the British in fighting against it. T. K. Velu Pillai (1940: 24–25) notes that, in putting down the rebellion, the British were attempting to "rescue the Raja" from his diwan. They did not hold the prince responsible for the revolt, and they "still treated the Maharaja as an independent ruler and showed considerable respect to the officers of his government." The British had formed a strong relationship with the Travancore royal family and did not wish to disturb the internal workings of a government that provided them with favorable trade policies. In the 1850s the British did threaten Travancore over declining state revenues, after which the princely administration initiated reforms in education and public services. After the Rebellion of 1857, however, annexation anywhere in India was no longer possible; Kooiman (2002: 36) notes that the "timely outbreak of the Mutiny . . . assured Travancore's semi-independent survival."

Ultimately, due to various contingent historical factors, the British found themselves in a position that prevented them from annexing Travancore even though they clearly desired to control it. The princely state subsequently became an important pillar of colonial support in south India in the ensuing decades. The selection of the Malabar-Travancore comparison therefore minimizes the problem of endogeneity. And over the long term, Kerala's "accident of a divided political administration" would fundamentally alter the dynamics of ethnic politics and conflict in both regions.

Colonial-Era Religious Policies in Travancore

Travancore has often been cited by scholars as one of the most religiously tolerant of the Indian states. Susan Bayly (1984: 178), who analyzed Kerala as part of her seminal research on religion in south India, notes that the "Hindu rulers who fought their way to power in the kingdoms of Travancore and Cochin . . . were radical and ruthless; at the same time their religious policies were fluid and syncretic." She notes (1989: 9) that south India as a whole is unique because "powerful and dynamic variants of the three major 'world religions'—Hinduism, Islam and Christianity—have grown, developed and overlapped, all within the comparatively recent historical past, and all within a setting of remarkably rapid social and political change." J. J. Roy Burman (1996: 1214) points out syncretic practices prevalent in Kerala, noting that devotees of the famous Sabrimala Hindu pilgrimage site in Travancore also "visit the temple of Ayyappa to first pay their obeisance to the shrine of a Muslim saint named 'Vavara.'"

To a certain extent, all of this is true. Travancore was more syncretic than many princely areas throughout north India, and it specifically seemed more tolerant than Jaipur State. At the same time, however, for religious minorities, life in the kingdom was hardly as harmonious as the image traditionally advanced in scholarly literature, or in popular conceptions of Kerala. Travancore was a theocratic Hindu state that enacted a number of discriminatory policies toward non-coreligionists. These policies were directed not only toward Muslims—who were a small minority in the kingdom—but also toward the larger Christian community. As a consequence, Travancore experienced some significant episodes of communal violence, especially during the last decades of colonialism.

From its earliest days as a consolidated power, Travancore was an orthodox Hindu state, and the rulers of the kingdom ordered society around religion. In 1750, Martanda Varma dedicated the entire state to the deity Padmanabha, an avatar of Vishnu. The maharajas were thereafter technically *dasas* (servants) of Vishnu and considered themselves protectors of the Hindu faith and its customs (Smith 1963: 94). Because Travancore never came under the control of Islamic rulers, its Hindu character remained unvarnished over time. In his *Historical Sketch of the Native States of India*, G. B. Malleson (1875: 323) of the Indian Civil Service singled out the Kingdom of Travancore as an "example of a territory which, from the earliest tradition, has always been under Hindu rule and governed by Hindu law."

Travancore was also dedicated to the promulgation of Hinduism. The Travancore Administration Report of 1879 to 1880 notes that the fourth largest expenditure of the state (not including the British tribute) was "the Devasom[15] or religious institutions," which cost 572,940 rupees per year.[16] This single expenditure was more than the state spent on the judiciary, police, and education systems combined. The centrality of religion in the kingdom was consistent across many rulers of the state, as was the case in Jaipur. For instance, when Travancore acceded to the Indian Union after independence, one of its central demands was that the new Government of India would subsidize temples at the same level as the princely administration did (Menon 1956: 274).

Though the British generally held up and reinforced the princely states as traditional religious polities, administrators did nevertheless grow concerned from time to time about an excessive focus on religion. This was often the case in Travancore (Kawashima 1998). For instance, a Madras Presidency administrator in the late nineteenth century complained that the "Rajas were as a rule mere puppets in the hands of certain Brahmans of the Trivandrum temple."[17] The British were especially concerned that excessive spending on religious institutions was hampering the state's ability to provide other services. To counteract this effect, British Resident Colonel Munro, who briefly served as diwan of the state in the early nineteenth century (1811–14), brought under the control of the state's central administration the land of 378 Hindu temples that operated independently.[18]

There were two major religious minority groups in Travancore: Christians and Muslims. Christianity has a long lineage in Kerala. According to tradition, Saint Thomas, one of Jesus's Apostles, arrived on the shores of Kerala in 52 A.D. and established its first Christian church. Over time the number of denominations multiplied to include Catholics, Protestants, Anglicans, and Mar Thoma Syrians.[19] The state of Kerala as a whole had a Christian population of roughly 20 percent, although this community was concentrated in the Travancore region, where they formed a fourth of the population. The Muslims of Travancore were a smaller minority, constituting only 6 percent of the population. A distinct Muslim community in India, they were not descended from (or converted by) the various Islamic groups that had invaded north India, and unlike most northern Muslims they spoke Malayalam instead of common northern languages such as Persian or Urdu. They were also separate from the Muslims of Malabar, who were known as *Mappillas*.

Beginning with the conceptualization of Travancore as a Hindu state, the rulers of the kingdom stratified politics on a religious basis. Dick Kooiman (1993: 288) notes that in Travancore there was an "explicit connection between Hindu orthodoxy and state government" that gave "local politics . . . a distinctly communal complexion." Robin Jeffrey (1976: 3) likewise calls Travancore a "staunchly theocratic Hindu state." A number of policies were enacted in the nineteenth and twentieth centuries that were discriminatory toward Christians and Muslims, and in general the Hindu majority in Travancore attempted to suppress their religious rivals.

Travancore's government was traditionally dominated by high-caste Hindus. Muslims and Christians therefore spent much of the late nineteenth century pressing for increased power in the state administration. This demand was couched in a much broader movement for democratization within the kingdom. In 1891, more than ten thousand signatories from a variety of communities presented the government with the "Malayali Memorial," a demand for increased representation in government. This petition also objected to the Travancore government's practice of importing Tamilian Brahmins for upper-echelon posts in the princely administration. Low-caste communities as well as Christians and Muslims were involved in the petitioning. For instance, one portion of the Memorial noted that "there are several Departments in Travancore the doors of which could be left freely open to the Christians, and the comparatively low position occupied by them at present is to a great extent owing to the neglect of their interest by the ruling authorities" (Archives Treasury 2010: 179).

In response, the Kingdom of Travancore established the Sri Mulam Popular Assembly, which allowed semidirect elections beginning in 1905. However, by the 1930s Travancore had made little headway in increasing the representation of minority religious groups. Table 3.2 highlights communal representation in the Travancore government in the 1930s. Muslims were the worst-represented group in the entire administration, and Christians carried a far lower number of seats than their population warranted.

Minority communities were also prevented from holding important positions. For example, Muslims were underrepresented in Travancore's armed forces, which would have been involved in putting down severe communal riots in the kingdom.[20] Most of the diwans of the state were Hindu, and before Travancore finally appointed a Christian named M. E. Watts (1925–29) to the position, a local newspaper wrote disbelievingly, "we cannot conceive

TABLE 3.2.

Communal Representation in Travancore Government, 1930s. Unfortunately the data refer only to the "1930s." The third column indicates the percentage of jobs held by each community (total number of jobs: 20,378); the fourth column indicates the overall population percentage in 1931.

Group	Number of Posts	Percentage of Government Employees	Percentage of Population
Hindus	16,405	80.5	61
Muslims	436	2.1	7
Christians	3,537	17.35	32

SOURCE: Pillai 1940: 754–755.

of it that such an Orthodox State as Travancore would seriously entertain the idea of appointing anyone other than a caste-Hindu as its Dewan in the present state of its social progress."[21]

As the character of Travancore's politics grew more explicitly communal during the nineteenth century, Christians and Muslims pressed for separate electorates. Just as they did in Jaipur, these communities made reference to the separate electorates that existed in British India. The princely administration did not acquiesce to these demands. The principal response of the darbar was that the increased representation of religious minorities in government was not possible in a Hindu kingdom (Nossiter 1982: 77).

This is a crucial point because many scholars suggest that the introduction of separate electorates in British India was a central factor contributing to Hindu-Muslim violence there, or even to the bloody partitioning of the country. Yet in Jaipur and Travancore, neither princely administration created separate electorates and both of these states still experienced more communal violence than neighboring British areas. This puzzle prompts Kooiman (1995: 2130) to ask, "How can we explain the emergence of communalism in Travancore, if there is no government to be blamed for dividing the people by separate electoral arrangements?" The histories of Jaipur and Travancore demonstrate instead that the emergence of communalism in India stems not from supposed divide-and-rule policies imposed exogenously, but instead from the treatment of religious minorities by native rulers.

Communal tension in Travancore continued to build in the early twentieth century. In 1939, at a meeting of the Travancore Muslim Young Men's Association, an advocate named A. K. Bijili noted that although the state had done much to improve the lot of low castes (detailed later), they lagged behind in their treatment of Muslims, which was the cause of growing discord:

> When the present Dewan of Travancore Sir C. P. Ramaswamy Iyer came into power, we thought that his term of office will mark a new era in the history of the State of Travancore. His bold and ready response to the need of the untouchables in being instrumental to throw open the gates of the temples of the State for them and making these temples accessible to them is indeed an act of which any man can justly be proud. The Temple Entry Proclamation of His Highness the Maharaja of Travancore was an eye-opener to many. But the recent [communal] unrest in Travancore is really an unexpected development.[22]

These remarks highlight a clear distinction between how the kingdom responded to low-caste agitation and how it responded to Muslim agitation. Whereas the state was progressive toward the former group, the latter made few advancements as a community before independence.

Muslim protests continued to increase in Travancore during the 1940s. As in Jaipur State, Travancore's discrimination against this community attracted the unwanted attention of the Muslim League.[23] Muslim advocate Mohamed Ismail summarized this situation in a letter to the state's diwan, Ramaswamy Iyer (1936–47), in July 1940:

> Inspite [sic] of the fact that Travancore stands foremost among the Indian States, the position of the Muslims in this country leaves many things to be desired. They have been labouring under various disabilities. Attempts were made in the past to improve their lot and to bring them under the influence and guidance of a centralised organisation; but all of them have met with complete failure owing either to lack of response on the part of the members or want of selfless and efficient leadership.[24]

As was the case in Jaipur, Muslims in Travancore also had to suffer petty indignities on a daily basis. In 1946 a large Muslim conference was planned in Balaramapuram but it was banned by the darbar. The president of a local Muslim agency noted, "It happened that the conference was banned under orders of Government. The Police authorities of Neyyattinkara and Nemom, who for special reasons have their axe to grind against us, were emboldened by this and thought that this was a fit occasion to harass and persecute us in different ways."[25] That same year, Muslim leaders in the kingdom also complained about new rules that made it more difficult to construct mosques.[26]

The situation for Christians in the state was no different. Travancore's Christian community constitutes an important case because they highlight that religious violence in the princely states, though generally occurring between Hindus and Muslims, included other minority religions as well. Throughout the twentieth century, Hindu groups in Travancore worried endlessly about the power of the sizable Christian population in the state, and they periodically "accused [them] of a hidden scheme to take over their kingdom" (Kooiman 1993: 288). The princely government created links with the Hindu Mahasabha in an effort to counter the strength of Christians in the state (Kooiman et al. 2002: 61), and they were active in trying to stop conversions to Christianity.

For a large part of its history, Travancore's Christian community appears to have existed in relative peace and prosperity. However, in the late nineteenth century this began to change dramatically. Susan Bayly documents the increasing tension between Hindus and Christians during this specific period. Many Christians, who previously had not held any kind of inferior position in Travancore society, suddenly came to be considered low caste, or even *avarna* (without caste). Bayly (1989: 294) recounts that "by the mid-1880s the breakdown in ties between Syrians and Malayali caste Hindus had reached its final stage. Syrians were now routinely excluded from Hindu festival rites, and in many temple centres Hindu office-holders levied fines on Christians who tried to uphold their long-standing temple honours."

This development was a drastic change in the perception of Christians within the state. One of its principal causes was that in 1875 the Kingdom of Travancore conducted its first scientific census. The British use of the census, discussed at length in Chapter 1, led to an increase in caste antagonism, but it was not obvious how princely rulers made use of these same data (Ramusack 2004: 89). Once Travancore conducted its first census, Christians were officially relegated to a lower position in society. The princely administration used the census not to promote caste politics, as was the case in British India, but to diminish religious rivals.

Syrian Christians in particular saw a major decline in their fortunes. They had previously been an affluent community with a strong presence in commerce. By the start of the twentieth century their status had completely reversed. As the princely administration in Travancore grew more hardened in its religious discrimination, Syrian Christians became a conspicuous target of these policies. Despite their perceived business acumen, for example, they were suddenly prohibited from making investments in industry (Isaac and Tharakan 1986). Kooiman (1995: 2130) uses this community to point out an important distinction between British India and the princely states on the treatment of religious minorities: "Whereas in British India electoral safeguards to Muslims might help to maintain the empire, in Travancore political concessions to Syrians, the most prominent Christian community, were viewed as threatening the kingdom that became increasingly connected with Hindu orthodoxy."

Many authors argue that Travancore during the colonial period was a state devoid of religious violence. T. J. Nossiter (1988: 45) notes that "Kerala is a unique instance of large numbers of three major world religions living peaceably in one territory." George Mathew (1989: 128) praises Travancore as being "relatively free from communal riots or blood-baths." While it is true that Travancore was not a violent territory—and that it experienced less severe rioting than Jaipur—state discrimination nevertheless led to several noteworthy instances of conflict involving all of the kingdom's religious communities. Consider first the case of Hindus and Muslims. In 1908 there was a major riot in Chalai. T. K. Velu Pillai (1940: 707) notes that this instance of violence, considered one of Travancore's earliest communal eruptions, was in fact only the latest explosion in an increasing trend of violence: "There had been other riots before. . . . One of the earliest occurred at Alleppey. The so-called Pulaya riots in Neyyatinkara taluk and adjacent places, the riot at Talayolapparambu in Vaikam and the riot at Cape Comorin were among the more serious. They had to be put down by the strong hand. . . . these riots had their origin in local disputes or communal tension."

During the 1930s there were two major Hindu-Muslim riots in the kingdom. The first occurred in Manakad in 1930.[27] An article from the *Muslim* noted the following about the incident:

> Taking the side of those parties whose purses are heavy, the Police began to disbelieve the statements of the Mohammedans and rudely dealt with them. Inspector of Police Mr. Karunakara Kartha and his immediate superior were the persons who were responsible for the investigation of this case. In either eyes all the fault lay on the Muslims. As a result, they refused to hear the just complaints of the Muslims.[28]

The second riot occurred in 1939 in Trivandrum during a religious festival.[29]

The state's Christian community also suffered periodic violence. After Travancore subordinated the position of Christians after the 1875 census,

Susan Bayly (1989: 294) notes that during "the 1880s and 1890s there were innumerable riots between Hindus and Syrians. *These outbreaks closely resembled the Hindu-Muslim clashes of north India*" (emphasis added). In 1921 and again in 1922 there were further riots between the two communities (Chiriyankandath 1993: 653). It is also important to note that Christians occasionally clashed with Muslims in the state; for example, a serious riot occurred between the two communities in 1936 (Isaac 1985: 10).

This violence was not due to an inability to maintain the peace. Travancore, on the one hand, had 61 cavalry and 1,442 infantrymen in their police force in the early twentieth century, which means they had one police officer for roughly every 1,964 persons.[30] In Malabar, on the other hand, there were a total of 1,383 officers, meaning one for roughly every 2,024 persons.[31] Both figures are basically equal (and incredibly low), but by the end of the colonial period Malabar experienced almost no religious violence.

The communal riots in Travancore were also not contagion from British India. In fact, the state's politics were quite sealed off from the rest of the country. Even by 1930 Kooiman (2002: 132) notes that Gandhi's independence movement "roused hardly any excitement in Travancore." The princely government also prevented this movement from infiltrating local politics. For instance, when Jawaharlal Nehru arrived in Trivandrum in 1931 with two thousand men, the procession was quickly banned by the darbar from congregating inside the city's fort (Archives Treasury 2010: 384). Most of the communal conflict that occurred in Travancore was in response to specific discriminatory policies instituted by the princely government; it was not due to organizations that originated in the British provinces. And specific communal outfits—the Hindu Mahasabha, for example—to the extent that they operated in Travancore, did so at the behest of the princely government.

By the time of independence, the Kingdom of Travancore was a state that experienced serious communal tension and conflict. The Hindu-dominated government had actively worked to limit the position of both Muslims and Christians, and several communal riots occurred in response to various discriminatory policies implemented by the darbar. The roots of communal animosity in the region today are best understood as the long, historical outcome of forces first unleashed by Travancore's Hindu maharajas during the colonial period. By 1935, Donald Field, the British Resident in the state, summarized that the city's population seemed to be "unhappily stricken with the plague of communal animosities."[32]

Communalism in British Malabar?

One of the central arguments of this book is that, contrary to much existing historical scholarship, communalism was a more significant problem in princely states than in British provinces. The Malabar case, however, poses a considerable challenge to this argument. The various Mappilla uprisings[33] that occurred there in the late nineteenth and early twentieth centuries, culminating in the massive Mappilla Rebellion (or Malabar Rebellion) of 1921, are often taken as clear evidence that British colonial rule promoted religious antagonism between Hindus and Muslims. Many accounts of the Mappilla uprisings, from both contemporaries and modern scholars, emphasize the religious nature of the incidents. Special Commissioner T. L. Strange, appointed to investigate the uprisings, was convinced that they were due to religious fanaticism. Stephen F. Dale (1975: 87) argues that "religious leaders were the single, critical determinant of the Mappilla outbreaks." Steven Wilkinson (2004: 185) concludes that the uprising in 1921 "was one of the worst outbreaks of communal violence ever in British India." Why did British rule in north Kerala produce such violent religious conflict? This question deserves thorough consideration.

The Mappillas formed almost a third of the population in Malabar during the colonial period. There were some critical differences among them: the Mappillas of northern Malabar were a wealthier group, with many involved in business, while those in the south were poorer and worked primarily in agricultural occupations. Most of the agitators during the Mappilla uprisings were from southern Malabar. The British derisively referred to this group as the "Jungle Moplahs."

The violent incidents in which the Mappillas were involved during the nineteenth century—which colonial administrators referred to as "outbreaks" or "outrages"—generally followed the same pattern. Mappillas would kill oppressive Hindu landlords, then take up residence in a public place in order to confront the police in a gunfight. Many Mappillas then committed suicide. These conflicts were considered to be a kind of jihad.

Then, in 1921, a major uprising occurred that came to be known as the Mappilla Rebellion.[34] In the years preceding this insurrection the Indian National Congress had been trying to make inroads among the Muslim population for support in the independence movement. When the British government disbanded the Ottoman Empire after World War I, the position of the caliphate, an international symbol of Islamic power, was placed in jeopardy. The *Khilafat* movement in India formed in response as an Islamic campaign to support the Ottoman Empire. After the war, Gandhi and the Congress Party linked with the Khilafat movement, using the association as an opportunity to unite Hindus and Muslims in their opposition to British rule.

During the first few months of this alliance, Hindus and Muslims in Kerala worked together on the issue of agrarian reform. As the Mappillas grew more aggressive, British authorities in Malabar decided to upend the movement by arresting several of its leaders. They also raided a mosque in Tirurangadi. This action resulted in an enormous backlash. The Mappillas organized and attacked a number of police stations, British camps, courts, and other government buildings. Martial law was declared. For a time the rebels controlled large portions of the region, especially in Ernad and Valluvanad.

Many thousands of Mappillas were involved in the ensuing insurrection. Congress tried to stem the violence but was unsuccessful, and eventually they abandoned the movement altogether. Press reports indicated that the Mappillas attacked the British, landlords, and Hindus whom they suspected of collaborating with the colonial government. The British eventually had to call in reinforcements to counter the rebellion, and after six months the insurrection was defeated. According to official estimates, almost 2,400 rebels were killed and some 1,700 were injured. Thousands more were taken prisoner. The Mappilla community was brutally punished for the rebellion, and many Mappilla prisoners were sent to the Andaman Islands in a penal colonization scheme.[35]

Many scholars describe the Mappilla uprisings as communal violence. Assuming for a moment that they were indeed fundamentally about religion, it should be noted that the first major pangs of Hindu-Muslim unrest in Malabar began not with the British but with Mysore's invasion in the late eighteenth century. During his reign in Malabar, Tipu Sultan—who emphasized Islamic rule much more than his father, Hyder Ali, did—forcibly converted Hindus and smashed several temples. These events marked the first time that the traditional peace between these two religious communities was punctuated (Logan 1887; Miller 1976). In other words, like most princely rulers, Sultan was discriminatory toward non-coreligionists.

In general, however, there are many problems with the traditional characterization of the Mappilla uprisings as communal incidents. To begin with, several scholars consider the movement a large anticolonial struggle. In fact, many British administrators themselves interpreted the rebellion in this way, as a spontaneous uprising against the foundations of colonial power. Congress had linked with the Khilafat movement for the specific purpose of providing a united front against colonialism. In the initial stages of the revolt, one of the prime targets of the rebels was British administrators throughout Malabar. Many of the rebels raised Khilafat flags and openly heralded the end of British rule. In comparison to colonial-era communal violence in Jaipur and Travancore—which was almost always fought by two distinct ethnic communities—the Mappilla Rebellion featured the British state firmly on one side of the conflict. This fact complicates the interpretation of the Mappilla Rebellion as a communal episode because the Hindu-Muslim divide may not have been the main axis of conflict.[36]

A better explanation for the violence addresses the fact that the Malabar region had been rife with conflict around caste identities since the arrival of the British and the implementation of a variety of new agricultural policies (detailed later in this chapter). In the nineteenth century, a major historical event occurred that altered the axis of ethnic conflict in Malabar: a large number of low castes converted to Islam. Like most caste conflict in India, the goals of the subsequent uprisings were largely agrarian. In that sense, the Mappilla uprisings support one of the major arguments of this book: that British rule created low-caste revolt. It just so happened that many of the low castes in Malabar had become Muslim.

Almost all of the participants in the Mappilla uprisings were Islamic, but they were actually recent low-caste converts, mainly from the Tiyya, Cheruman and Mukkuvan castes. Many of the converts had been agrestic slaves: in 1856 there were 187,758 Cheruman slaves, but by 1881 there were only 64,725, a decline attributed to a massive number of Islamic conversions (Dhanagare 1977: 123). Or as British administrator C. A. Innes put it bluntly, Mappillas came from "the dregs of the Hindu population."[37] Conrad Wood (1974: 23) notes that by "becoming a Moplah, a Cheruman labourer or Thiyyan *verumpattomdar* [cultivator] was joining a body that functioned as a self-defence organization of the rural subordinate whose ultimate weapon in this period was the outbreak. Conversion certainly curbed the field of power of the [upper-caste] Namboodiri and Nair landlords."

Precisely because of the strict caste hierarchies that existed in British Malabar, low-caste groups embraced Islam in the hopes of shedding their ritually low status. T. L. Strange noted the effects of mass conversion, writing that the Mappillas in the southern Malabar region suffered from the "absence of any men of learning to instruct them in their new religion."[38] British administrators had noted in 1917 that Mappillas "have been cut off from the rest of the Muhammadan world by difference of language, inasmuch as they know practically no Arabic and have no acquaintance whatever with Urdu and Persian. Their language is a dialect of Malayalam, the speech of the Hindu people of Malabar, with whom they have much in common."[39] Susan Bayly (1989: 11) likewise describes the Mappillas as having become "an exclusive and militantly separatist Indian Muslim Society." Whereas low-caste converts made up most of the Mappillas in southern Malabar, the Muslims of northern Malabar—who were not central to the uprisings—had been converted much earlier and were originally from high castes.

Just as most of the Muslim rebels were low-caste converts, most of the landlords in Malabar were from upper castes—the Nambudhris and the Nairs. Surveying the notes on various Mappilla outbreaks between 1836 and 1919, Wood (1978: 129) notes that of eighty Hindu victims, sixty-two were members of high castes. He writes:

> Malabar, and especially that part where outbreaks occurred, was throughout this period preeminently a land of the big Nambudri jenmi [landlord] and the Nair official. Nearly all the big jenmis were in fact high-caste Hindus. In 1915 Collector Innes gave figures showing that the eighty-six biggest landlord families, owning many hundreds of thousands of acres and paying about a fifth of the total land revenue, were all high-caste Hindus except for two Moplahs, one Tiyyan, and one Goundan.

The Mappilla uprisings can therefore be reconceptualized as a movement of low castes against high castes. This caste antagonism was, as elsewhere in British India, driven directly by new colonial land-tenure policies that increased rural inequality. Prakash Karat (1973: 41) notes that during the period when Mappilla outrages became endemic, religion was not the only prism through which rebels acted: "rumblings of lower castes against upper caste domination became more and more evident." The Servants of India Society endorsed a similar view, writing in a pamphlet after the rebellion, "What right have these lovers of Hindoo nation and protectors of Vedic religion to cry over the Mopla rebellion when they did not try beforehand to . . . remove the cause of distance pollution *which prepared the ground for Mopla atrocities?*"[40]

During the initial uprising against the British, Muslims were not the only rebels; low-caste Hindus were also involved in the rebellion. This is an often misunderstood point. For example, E.M.S. Namboodiripad, the first Chief Minister of Kerala (1957–59, 1967–69), was very cautious about diminishing the impact of religion during the rebellion: "Nambudiripad wanted 'the Marxists' to answer certain simple but relevant questions before asserting that the rebellion was only a 'revolt of the peasants of Malabar.' The questions are mainly about the involvement of Mappilas alone in the rebellion. [Nambudiripad wrote,] 'The oppression and exploitation of the Jenmi and the officials are as bad for the Hindu peasants as for their Moplah comrades'" (Kusuman 2003: 160–61). But the suggestion that low-caste Hindus were not involved in the rebellion is incorrect. Whereas the majority of the rebels were Muslims, Robert Hardgrave Jr. (1977: 82) shows that "reports on incidents occurring during the first weeks of the rebellion frequently implicated Hindus in the rioting, and arrests often included Hindus." Namboodiripad was specifically concerned with the later period of the rebellion, when Hindus abandoned the movement, after which the uprising gained a communal complexion. Furthermore, although most scholarship on this question has focused on agrarian conflict initiated by Muslims, low-caste Hindus were not exempt from generating agrarian violence of their own. In fact, British administrators who had read the reports of William Logan on Malabar noted that he "described the cultivating classes 'as rapidly degenerating into a state of insolvent cottierism' and observed that crime was consequently on the increase."[41] Logan's research showed that between 1865 and 1880—a period in which many Malabar outrages occurred—Hindus were actually the largest group convicted of gang robbery (Dhanagare 1977: 126). This fact further suggests the prominence of intercaste struggles over communal tension.

The Mappilla uprisings also do not match the traditional profile of communal violence in India. Most important, the uprisings were rural, occurring mainly in southern Malabar, especially in the area around Ernad. Varshney and Wilkinson (2006), for example, find that more than 90 percent of Hindu-Muslim riots are urban. The Malabar uprisings would be highly unusual if religion were at the core of the unrest. Similarly, most religious violence in general is not fought over land. It involves other issues such as access to religious sites or competition over jobs. In Jaipur, for instance, one main cause of communal strife has been the socioeconomic backwardness of the Muslim population, but their grievances have little to do with land.

At its core, the Mappilla unrest was agrarian.[42] In fact, the Mappilla Rebellion was at first entirely about land issues such as securing tenancy rights and evicting landlords. K. N. Panikkar (1989: 190) summarizes one major school of existing scholarship on the uprisings by noting that they were "not intrinsically communal." D. N. Dhanagare (1977: 141) adds that "the communal sentiment or 'fanaticism' of the Moplahs was only the symptom and not the disease. The 1921 rebellion, like the uprisings that occurred throughout the nineteenth century, was in essence an expression of long-standing agrarian discontent, which was only intensified by the religious and ethnic identity of the Moplahs and by their political alienation."

Most of the Mappillas, especially those in south Malabar, were poor cultivators, occupying the lowest rung on the rural hierarchy. Investigating the specific discontent of the Mappillas requires an analysis of the changing land-tenure situation in Malabar with the onset of British rule at the end of the eighteenth century. This situation is detailed at length later in the chapter, but a brief explanation is that when Mysore invaded Kerala in the mid-eighteenth century, most of the high-caste Hindu landholders in the region escaped into the surrounding areas, especially Travancore. During the period before the British took control of most of Malabar in 1792, Mysore's ruler Tipu Sultan forged links with the native Muslim population, who in turn increased their control of agriculture in the absence of traditional Hindu landholders. The major problem arose after 1792 when the British came into possession of Malabar. At this time, the exiled Hindus returned home and demanded their land. The British government sided with the Hindus, and the Mappillas were dispossessed in the early nineteenth century. This act was the basis of most of the agrarian discontent that plagued the Mappilla community throughout the rest of the century. The British Resident in Travancore, Atholl MacGregor, summarized it like this: "As to the essential nature of the Malabar Mappilla outrages, I am perfectly satisfied that they are agrarian. Fanaticism is merely the instrument through which the terrorism of the landed classes is aimed." And F. Fawcett (1897: 296), the superintendent of police in Malabar, noted in 1897 that "the Moplahs of E. Malabar . . . are most unfortunate subjects for fanaticism; and more especially so when the land tenures are such as if arranged specially for the purpose of making people discontented."

The obvious question in reframing the Mappilla uprisings as caste-based conflicts is whether or not this reframing could also apply to other communal incidents. For example, Hindu-Muslim riots in Jaipur might just as easily be an expression of underlying caste tensions, and in general it can be difficult to know what ethnic cleavage, if any, is truly responsible for a conflict (Brass 1997). The reason this seems unlikely, however, is that the Muslims and Hindus who have engaged frequently in conflicts in Jaipur are fragmented by caste. The conflicts there do not, for instance, pit high-caste Hindus against low-caste Muslims. Rather, both the Hindu and Muslim populations come from a range of castes. Furthermore, there was no large-scale conversion of low castes to Islam in Jaipur; rather, the Muslim population came from various Islamic groups that had entered north India over the previous centuries. The Mappilla rebels, with their overwhelmingly low-caste convert background, formed a unique community in India.

If the Malabar uprisings were not communal, what role did religion play? In other words, why did agrarian unrest in Malabar take on a communal character? First, most of the low castes who converted to Islam did so in order to escape the ritual injustices of the uniquely oppressive caste system of Malabar. By converting to Islam, they were able to protest the power of high-caste landlords in ways that had previously been inaccessible to them. Second, becoming Muslim meant adhering to a larger ethnic identity, creating, as Ronald Herring (2008: 286) puts it, an "advantage in collective action." For example, mosques served as a type of coordination mechanism against the landlords, and the number of mosques in Malabar nearly doubled from 1831 to 1851 (Dhanagare 1977: 121).

Another important and related question concerns why there were forced conversions of Hindus at the hands of the Mappillas, though it is unclear how many forced conversions actually occurred. Dhanagare (1977: 140) notes, for example, that "the total number of conversion cases . . . appears significantly small in relation to the size of the Hindu population in the disturbed areas." And although attacks on Hindu temples were frequent, powerful landlords were generally the trustees of these temples, so attacks against them were also attacks against the visible symbols of high-caste power (Guha 1999: 74).

Many traditional accounts have emphasized that British policies in Malabar led to communal conflict, though this interpretation is lacking in several key respects. But there is another related point: this book has maintained that the British pursued a policy of religious neutrality that protected Muslims throughout India. Therefore, it is important to note that initially British policies in Malabar were in fact broadly similar to those instituted through-out the provinces. For instance, despite the fact that Hindus greatly outnum-bered Muslims in Malabar, the colonial government's policy of neutrality led to the recruitment of a large number of Muslims into the local government after the British came to control Malabar. In 1792–93 in Ernad (the main site of the future rebellion), for example, two-thirds of all revenue collectors were Mappillas (Wood 1976: 547). But this policy was reversed when high-caste Hindus returned to Malabar after the war with Mysore. The British gov-ernment was then forced to decide between placating either the Mappillas or the former landlords. The debate within the government raged for some time, and there were those who suggested that the Mappillas should retain control of the land (Ibid.: 545). However, when confronted with the choice between supporting high-caste Hindus or Muslim cultivators, the govern-ment sided with the former.

In the 1920s and 1930s, the Muslims in Malabar underwent a complete transformation. At the conclusion of the various Mappilla uprisings, Mus-lim leaders in the region (mirroring the Aligarh movement in north India after the Rebellion of 1857) pushed for the modernization of the community. The Aikya Sangham, an Islamic reform group, led, in the words of U. Mo-hammed (2007: 152), a "Muslim renaissance" in Malabar, especially through the opening of new educational institutions. The Mappillas were also the specific target of a number of British educational reforms in the twentieth century (More 1997: 65). In cities like Calicut, the Muslim middle class built a number of new public works projects and were "doing relatively well under British rule. . . . many 'community leaders' . . . enthusiastically [embraced] colonial-driven modernisation" (Osella and Osella 2008: 334). By the dawn of independence, the Mappillas were far removed from the community that had taken part in rebellion only a few decades prior, and their socioeconomic position had improved considerably. Caste politics had by this time come to dominate Malabar (detailed later in the chapter), and communal tension had eased significantly.

The Mappillas were not the only religious minority group in the prov-ince; there was a small but important Christian minority in Malabar as well. Christians always presented a difficult case for the British. On the one hand, the British were a Christian power and many administrators openly pro-fessed a desire to establish a firm base for Christianity on the subcontinent. On the other hand, the British policy of religious neutrality applied as much to this community as it did to Hindus, Muslims, and people of any other faith. This latter view won out and Christians in Malabar were not given any kind of special treatment by the British government. British policies toward Christians—especially missionaries—could be characterized as standoffish, and many colonial officials worried that aiding the Christian community in Malabar would upset other local religious groups (Mallampalli 2004).

Throughout colonial Kerala, the major center of communal tension was Travancore. The Hindu rulers of the state emphasized religion as the dominant ethnic category and stratified distinctions between the state's three major religious groups. They enforced a number of discriminatory policies against the Christian and Muslim minorities, policies that in turn resulted in increased communal conflict. Across the border in Malabar, the British enforced religious policies that initially strove to create neutrality, and colonial officials were also initially protective of the Muslim minority. But an exceptionally rigid caste system in Malabar led to the large-scale Islamic conversion of thousands of low-caste Hindus. The Mappilla outbreaks in the late nineteenth and early twentieth centuries, often taken as communal violence, were actually bloody expressions of a region plagued with a long history of caste struggle. But just as had been the case in Ajmer-Merwara, by the dawn of independence Hindu-Muslim violence in Malabar had all but disappeared.

Postcolonial Religious Violence in Malabar and Travancore

The colonial-era pattern of communalism in Kerala has not altered since independence. The Travancore region continues to be the area of the state most beset by communal politics and conflict. In contrast, Malabar has remained comparatively peaceful, mirroring the situation of the province since the 1930s. Although religious rioting is not a major problem in the state as a whole, it has not been eliminated entirely—and more important, its occurrence varies considerably from the north to the south.

In Kerala, patterns of religious conflict from the colonial period were embedded and reinforced through local institutions after independence. Formal institutions such as political parties did not alter existing ethnic cleavages. Travancore is the main area where Hindu nationalist groups like the RSS have had success, mainly during a brief spell in the late 1980s and early 1990s. In Malabar, however, Hindu nationalists have failed to make inroads among the electorate. But the Communist Party of India (Marxist)

(CPI-M), which has governed Kerala in coalition governments many times since independence, derives its support primarily from Malabar. By fighting to upend the rigid caste hierarchies that plagued the region, the CPI-M fortified caste as the hegemonic ethnic category in postcolonial north Kerala. Parties—often taken by constructivist scholars as a key agent of change in ethnic cleavages—served only to reinforce ethnic divides in Kerala.

Other formal institutions operated in the same fashion. For instance, the old princely bureaucracy in Travancore remained largely intact after independence (Mankekar 1965: 67). Another key institution was public education, which is an integral part of the story of how Kerala achieved such high levels of social development. In Travancore, the princely family invested heavily in education—from 1866 to 1899 they founded eight colleges in the kingdom. They also had complete discretion over curricula and were keen to emphasize distinctions between their state and British India (Frenz and Berkemer 2006).[43] These schools helped to reinforce among thousands of young students the religious lineage of the kingdom and its royal family.

Similarly, informal institutions enabled existing patterns of ethnic violence to persist in Kerala. Memories of previous conflicts—the degradation of distance pollution and caste-based discrimination in Malabar, for example—still resonate deeply. Individuals across the north and south developed commonsensical notions of ethnic identification and how ethnic conflict should be carried out. Political culture continues to differ substantially between the two regions since colonialism.

A number of interviews were conducted in the state to investigate relations between religious groups as well as the dynamics of conflict across both areas. A university professor in Trivandrum summarized the state of Hindu-Muslim politics across Kerala: "The thing you will notice when comparing Muslims in Malabar and Travancore is that while the Muslims down here [in Travancore] are educated, they are extremely religious. Their religion is very important to them. Muslims in the north, though, have become very secularized."[44] This assessment was confirmed by a professor from a university in the northern city of Calicut: "Travancorean Muslims are not as secular as Malabar's Muslims. Here the Muslims have gone up on the social and economic ladder."[45] When asked about Hindu-Muslim violence in Malabar, the professor continued, "In Calicut, relationships between Hindus and Muslims are quite OK. There are some problems in the periphery, but not in this city. There is no serious rioting here."

The British made great efforts throughout the provinces to expunge religion as a legitimate mode of ethnic classification, seeking instead to establish a secular state. In Kerala, over time—and especially in the aftermath of the 1921 rebellion—the Mappillas became a secularized community, and the Hindu-Muslim divide subsequently became less salient in the north. In Travancore, conversely, religion remained the hegemonic ethnic category.

Kerala is often lauded today as a part of India that is free from communal bloodshed. However, as an article from a state newspaper in 1992 noted, "contrary to the claim by the state's politicians, Kerala has never been immune to communal clashes."[46] This assertion seems surprisingly true of late: from 2005 to 2013, Kerala was the fifth worst state in India in terms of per capita communal violence.[47] But the religious violence that does occur is not uniform throughout the state: most of it has been centered in the former Kingdom of Travancore.

Since independence, southern Kerala has experienced recurrent religious tension and conflict (O. J. 1983; Oommen 1995). Many parts of the city of Trivandrum specifically have seen immense violence, and this city is the center of communal rioting in the state. The Varshney-Wilkinson dataset records Hindu-Muslim riots in Trivandrum in 1961, 1982–83, and 1985. These figures actually understate the amount of violence in the city; additional data collected show that there were also riots in 1968 and 1992.[48] The latter riot is especially telling, because it occurred after the destruction of the Babri Masjid in Ayodhya. Travancore at the time experienced serious violence (thirty-nine deaths and injuries), yet in Malabar—with its significantly larger Muslim population—there was no rioting.[49]

The communal violence in this region is not isolated to Hindus and Muslims, however; the larger Christian minority has also been involved in various incidents. Riots occurred between Muslim and Christian fishermen around Trivandrum in 1972, 1981, 1983, and 1995. A more recent example comes from 2005, when Muslims and Catholics engaged in a high-profile riot in Trivandrum in which two people were injured and more than a thousand lost their homes to arson.[50] This violence has become deeply embedded in the region. For instance, clashes between Muslims and Christians in the coastal areas outside Trivandrum constitute an "almost . . . hundred-year conflict" (Singh 1985: 29).

While Travancore has continued to experience communal animosities, Malabar has experienced less overall conflict. To be sure, Malabar has had some notable instances of communal violence in the postindependence period. December 1971 marked the beginning of a major riot in Tellicherry that, though it produced no deaths, led to a significant number of injuries. More recently, in 2002 there was the infamous "Marad Massacre," in which a group of Muslims attacked and killed nine Hindus in Marad, near Calicut, seriously inflaming tensions in the region. However, despite the occasional outburst of violence, most of the ethnic conflict that has occurred in Malabar—especially since the 1930s—has been related to caste and tribal identities (detailed later in the chapter). A per capita comparison of casualties across Kerala using figures adapted (to include violence involving Christians) from the Varshney-Wilkinson dataset shows slightly more conflict in modern Travancore than in Malabar.[51]

Gopal Krishna's (1985: 67) detailed dataset on Hindu-Muslim riots in the 1960s also highlights that Travancore is still the nerve center of communal tension in Kerala. He notes that "throughout the decade Kerala experienced communal rioting in four places, and each had only one riot. Of the six incidents 3 occurred in Trivandrum, and of the 5 days of rioting Trivandrum accounted for two." Krishna does say that Calicut in Malabar has also experienced riots, although they have all occurred in rural areas of the district.

This almost complete disappearance of religious animosity in Malabar is quite a development, especially considering that most studies of communalism in Kerala focus extensively on the Mappilla uprisings. Assuming that the Mappilla conflicts were communal, why is the area now peaceful? This turn of events bucks a notable historical trend in India: areas that have been violent do not easily become peaceful. Ashutosh Varshney (2002: 144) tackled this transformation in his work, arguing that

> the principal reasons have to do with the pre-existing social hierarchy of Hinduism, its grave caste injustices, and an emerging lower-caste mobilization. India's freedom movement did not introduce mass politics to Malabar. Mass politics there had already taken the form of intra-Hindu struggles over caste, led by lower-caste organizations. Civil rights of the lower castes, especially with respect to pollution, temple entry, and greater access to educational institutions and government employment, were the key issues. Hindu-Muslim issues simply could not match the passions aroused by caste inequalities and injustice.

Accurate quantitative data on communal violence in India are always difficult to acquire. Interviews were used to confirm this pattern of communal violence in contemporary Kerala. The aforementioned university professor from Trivandrum noted the following about riots: "There were riots in Trivandrum in the 1990s. Communal outfits are always ready to act. The coastal regions down here are especially dangerous—and it's not just about Hindus and Muslims, but Christians are also involved in the rioting. They are a major presence here in Travancore."[52] And a local newspaper editor commented on the history of riots in Trivandrum compared to Malabar:

> I recall major riots here [Trivandrum] in the early 1980s. Very often these occurrences happen during religious festivals. At that time the army was even called in. There is periodic violence in this area, and a lot of tension between local religious groups, between Hindus and Christians, and Muslims and Christians. But up north, the major issues are caste issues, issues with depressed castes, those kinds of problems.[53]

This pattern of conflict should be contextualized. The fact that the majority of contemporary communal violence occurs in Travancore is surprising because of a number of factors that might predict otherwise. In terms of Hindu-Muslim riots, the Muslim community constitutes a significantly larger percentage of the population in Malabar than in Travancore. Steven Wilkinson (2004: 32–33) notes that areas in India where the Hindu-Muslim percentage divide is roughly equal should be especially prone to riots. By 2001, Muslims were 41 percent of the population of Malabar whereas Hindus had declined to 53 percent. Based on these factors, one might expect communal riots in Kerala to be significantly higher in the north, but today Malabar is a region of communal peace.

Traditional political science explanations cannot account for this variation in religious violence across the state. Paul Brass's work has focused on the role of Hindu nationalist organizations in producing communal conflict. As Brass's theory would predict, the Travancore region of Kerala is in fact the major part of the state in which Hindu nationalists operate. Kooiman (1995: 2130), for example, writes about the mid-1990s: "Over the past few years Kerala has become a fresh recruiting ground for the Rashtriya Sevak [sic] Sangh (RSS), a communalist party which has established powerful strongholds especially in Trivandrum, the former capital of Travancore." In Travancore, however, Hindu nationalist groups are merely a symptom of the disease, not the disease itself. As Kooiman importantly adds, "These manifestations . . . may be seen as a continuation of the tensions and conflicts that have plagued Kerala, particularly the former Travancore part of it, for a much longer time" (2130). The rise of Hindu nationalism in Travancore is recent whereas communal clashes in the region are not. It is therefore more likely that communal conflict bred Hindu nationalism than the other way around. Moreover, the relative success of the RSS in Travancore in the late 1980s and early 1990s is telling considering that the organization got its start in Malabar right after independence (Menon 1995: 18).

Steven Wilkinson has placed a lot of importance on the case of Kerala in proving his argument about electoral competition and Hindu-Muslim riots. He has argued that Kerala as a whole has seen a smaller number of riots compared to northern states because of the importance of the Muslim voting bloc in coalition governments. He writes (2004: 186), "the reason why the level of Hindu-Muslim violence has been so low, despite the existence in Kerala of antiminority mobilizations similar to those that have led to violence elsewhere in the country, is that high levels of party fractionalization have forced successive governments to order the Kerala police force to prevent attacks on minorities in the state at all costs." However, this argument is pitched at the state level and therefore cannot explain the important variations that exist between north and south Kerala. Whereas Muslims do form a larger portion of the population in northern Kerala than in the south, they are also an important minority in the south. The coalition governments that have controlled the state, led by either the Communists or Congress, cannot afford to ignore Travancorean Muslims. Furthermore, even if politicians did so, it is highly unlikely that northern Muslims—or organizations such as the Muslim League, which are centered in the north—would not be concerned with the plight of Muslims in the south. Wilkinson's argument may explain why Kerala as a whole experiences less communal violence than states in the north, but it cannot explain substate variations in rioting.

Finally, Ashutosh Varshney's argument focuses on the importance of intercommunal networks, and he, like Wilkinson, also places special emphasis on Kerala—specifically the city of Calicut in Malabar—in his book. Varshney (2002: 120) notes that Calicut has not had a single Hindu-Muslim riot in a century, and that the city maintains a "deep intercommunal civic engagement." This intercommunal engagement may be a proximate cause of peace; the deeper cause, however, originates from the decades of colonial rule that followed the Mappilla uprisings. Therefore none of the key existing explanations for communalism can explain why Travancore experiences more religious violence than Malabar.

The communal tension and violence in modern Travancore stem from the fact that it was a princely state during the colonial period. The Hindu maharajas that governed the kingdom emphasized religion and discriminated against Christians and Muslims, creating a deep-seated sense of antagonism between the religious groups. In Malabar, British administrators generally focused on caste, and they enforced a policy of religious neutrality. Over time this policy led to widespread secularized attitudes in the north and to the subsequent minimization of communal violence.

Colonial-Era Caste and Tribal Policies in Malabar and Travancore

The Hindu philosopher Swami Vivekananda once famously described Kerala as a "madhouse of caste," an appellation that has stuck. For example, the 1931 census recorded more than five hundred unique *jatis* (endogamous birth groups), and there were extremely strict, ritual restrictions governing inter-caste contact. Table 3.3 highlights the major castes in both regions during colonialism. In Travancore approximately 60 percent of the population made their living from the land whereas in Malabar the figure was smaller due to a large proportion of the population working as fishermen in coastal areas. The percentage of high castes and "polluting" castes was also roughly the same in both Malabar and Travancore (Jeffrey 1992: 26); a similar potential for caste conflict therefore existed in both regions.

The two major adivasi groups in Kerala are Paniyas and Maratis. Most of the tribes are located in the Malabar region. Wayanad district has the highest

TABLE 3.3.
Composition of Castes in Malabar and Travancore, 1901.

Malabar Province	Kingdom of Travancore
Tiyyas – 661,000	Nairs – 520,941
Nairs – 391,000	Tiyyas – 491,774
Cherumans – 246,000	Pulayans – 206,503
Kammalans – > 100,000	Shanars – 155,864
Nambudhris – < 20,000	Paraiyans, Kuravans, and Asaris – 50,000 to 100,000
	Vellalas, Brahmins, Marans, and Kollans – 20,000 to 50,000

SOURCE: *Imperial Gazetteer of India* Vol. 17: 59 (Malabar) and Vol. 24: 9 (Travancore).

proportion of tribals: in 1991, 35 percent of the tribal population of the state resided there. The only district in the Travancore region with a significant percentage of tribals is Idukki (15 percent of the state total in 1991).

The British administrators who ruled Malabar emphasized caste and tribal identities in the region, which was actually no different from the politics of precolonial Malabar. But it is important to remember that prior to British rule Malabar experienced a brief Mysorean interregnum. Tipu Sultan tried to crush the Hindu rajas in the region and forcibly converted many among the local population. This led only to further desire on the part of the British to depoliticize the religious cleavage in Malabar. For example, a commission established to assess newly acquired British territory after the Anglo-Mysore Wars was led by General Richard Abercromby, who had seen firsthand the dangers of religious fanaticism while leading British forces against Sultan (Frenz 2003: 99).

Like the administrators who ruled the northern province of Ajmer-Merwara, the British in Malabar were foremost concerned with making their new territory profitable. Immediately after acquiring the last portion of the Malabar province (Wayanad) in 1799, Governor-General Richard Wellesley (1798–1805) sent administrators to survey the region, especially its natural resource endowment (Mann 2001: 404). It was above all the desire to generate revenue from Malabar that led to this region experiencing a growth in caste conflict. Major British policy changes occurred in the realm of landholding, and myriad new discriminatory policies against low castes and tribals led to increasing stratification and conflict in the countryside—levels of conflict that dwarfed the caste antagonisms of the precolonial period.

It is unclear what kind of land tenure system existed in Malabar before the arrival of the British. As in the previous chapter's discussion of Ajmer-Merwara, this question is still a source of debate among historians. Most of the evidence suggests that one notable feature of the precolonial agricultural system in Malabar was the absence of private property. D. N. Dhanagare (1977: 116) notes that the "fundamental idea in the Malabar land system . . . seems to have been 'protection and supervision' rather than 'ownership' in the modern sense."

There were three major groups in the agrarian system of Malabar. At its apex were the *jenmis,* or landholders. They were almost always high-caste Hindus—that is, Nambudhris—and they had hereditary control over the land. However, like Rajputs, they did not cultivate the land themselves;

instead they turned it over to other groups for this purpose. Below the jenmis were the *kanamdars* (also known as *kanakkaran*), or land supervisors. They were mostly Nairs, from the middle classes, and were responsible for seeking out cultivators for the land. The cultivators themselves were known as *verumpattamdars* and most of them were Mappillas and from low castes. The uniqueness of this model, known as *Kana-Janma-Maryada,* lay in the fact that the land was held not privately but rather in trust between the three groups. The net produce of the land was shared equally among them (Dhanagare 1977: 116–17). William Logan summarized that "a *kanakkaran* was as much the proprietor of the soil as the *janmi* himself was in former days. They were, in short, proprietors bound together in interest by admirable laws of custom."[54] He further stated, "In order to understand the Malayali land tenures right . . . it is . . . first of all necessary to realise the fundamental idea that certain castes or classes were told off to the work of cultivation, and the land was made over to them in trust for that purpose, and in trust that the shares of produce due to the persons in authority should be faithfully surrendered."[55]

The rise of the British in Malabar led to major disruptions in this existing tenurial model. The critical change occurred in 1801 when, after the Fourth Anglo-Mysore War and the return of exiled high-caste Hindu landlords from Travancore and elsewhere, the government recognized jenmis as having a proprietary right over the land. The kanamdars and verumpattamdars were subsequently relegated to the status of tenants.

It is unclear how the British reached the conclusion that the jenmis had proprietary rights. On the one hand, they may have actually believed that this is how the Malayali land tenure model traditionally worked. Administrator William Thackeray endorsed this view, noting in an 1807 report that "almost the whole of the land of Malabar, cultivated and uncultivated, is private property and held by Janmam [birth] right which conveys full absolute property in the soil."[56] British administrators may have simply been interpreting the Malabar system through the lens of land tenure models that existed in Britain. William Logan, arguing vehemently that the colonial government had badly misunderstood the existing landholding system in Malabar, noted along these lines, "The idea that the janmi is absolute proprietor of the soil, and as such entitled to take as big a share of the produce as he can command . . . is founded on error, and has been brought about by engrafting on the customary Malayali law usages which spring from

European ideas of property having a totally distinct origin and history."[57]
He went further, stating that before the arrival of the British "the Janmi was
simply a man exercising authority within a certain defined area, and entitled
as to a well-defined share of the produce . . . of the land lying within that
area. But in view of the new rights he secured, the Janmi became the *lord of
the soil.*"[58]

On the other hand, it is possible that the British did not misunderstand
Malabar's land tenure system but rather worked out a deal with the high-
caste Hindus who had returned from exile and demanded back their land.
K.K.N. Kurup (1976: 430) writes:

> The analysis of the revenue policy adopted by the Company in Malabar at the
> close of the eighteenth century reveals that it was a policy more or less borrowed
> from its previous experience under the 'Diwani' in Bengal. Even the administra-
> tive structure initiated by the Company consisting of a supervisor and the native
> revenue collectors who were the traditional Rajas in Malabar, was a part of the
> administrative plan worked out in Bengal.

In either case, the results of this new British policy were devastating for the
peasantry. Aside from tearing apart the traditional agrarian system, the power
of jenmis increased steadily at the expense of other groups, thereby increasing
caste stratification. Logan collected figures on the rise in evictions during the
late nineteenth century, detailed in Figure 3.1. Despite seemingly clear evidence of increasing evictions, in 1928 the Malabar Tenancy Committee came
to the curious conclusion that "the materials at the disposal of the Committee do not prove that evictions are either so numerous or so unjustifiable as
has been represented to us by the advocates of the tenants' interest."[59]

A second major disruption to the existing agricultural system came in
the introduction of a vast array of new taxes. Precolonial Malabar was a
highly unique territory in that taxes were, according to the observation of
visiting Dutch Commander Hendrik van Reede in 1677, "unknown among
the people of Malabar. . . . the Nayars [Nairs] are unacquainted with taxes
on house, head, land or cattle."[60] Because power in precolonial Malabar
was highly decentralized, over time kings and chiefs became unable to collect revenues from areas other than their own private lands. C. K. Kareem
(1977: 583) explains:

> Unlike in any other part of the country the rulers or Kings of Kerala had no right
> over the landed property held by the individuals. As a result of this, land revenue

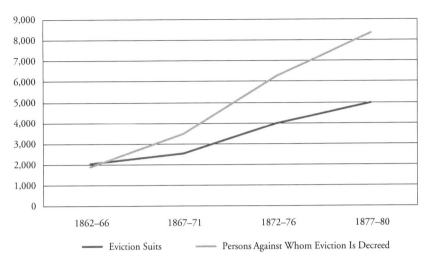

FIGURE 3.I. Evictions in Malabar, 1862 to 1880. All figures are averages. The figures are probably too low because many evictions occurred without the knowledge of colonial authorities, or landlords were able to evict tenants without invoking any laws.
SOURCE: Panikkar 1984: 180.

was unknown to the people of Kerala. . . . From the very early days of the history of this country the land was owned by those who actually cultivated the land. . . . There was no authority to check the ryots [peasants] from ploughing and cultivating the land they held. Unrestricted, they enjoyed the fruits of their labour.

Even British administrators in Malabar held this view, noting that "the Hindu rulers [of Malabar] appear to have levied no regular land revenue, but to have contented themselves with customs and tolls and with the occasional levy of special contributions."[61]

However, colonial officials were endlessly in pursuit of new sources of revenue; therefore taxation came to exist for probably the first time in Malabar. That alone might have been a sign of development except for the fact that these taxes were heavily regressive. The Assistant Collector of Malabar noted in 1829:

The fact is that the gardens of all Adhikaris and Menons [castes] and their relations are shamefully under-taxed. The same remark is applicable to those belonging to opulent individuals who were able to purchase the favour of the public servants. Whilst, on the contrary, the gardens of all the poorer classes are assessed so high that these poor creatures cannot pay the public revenue out of the pattom or proprietor's net rent without the sale of some of the household furniture.[62]

British administrator M. Moberly summarized it best when he noted that under colonial rule Malabar became "the most rack-rented place on the face of the earth."[63] At the risk of idealizing precolonial Malabar, it seems that it was the rare example of a territory in which agricultural taxation did not exist and different groups in society equally shared the land. Only with the arrival of the British did the situation change considerably. As land became concentrated in the hands of the jenmis, caste stratification and antagonism in the region grew.

As was the case in Ajmer-Merwara, later British administrators in Malabar tried their best to overcome initial mistakes and reverse wrongheaded policies. Logan himself undertook this task, although with little success. His Malabar Compensation for Tenants' Improvement Act of 1887, which tried to provide compensation for evicted tenants, proved ultimately ineffective. Many landlords shuffled tenants for higher rents, a practice known as *melcharths,* and high-caste landlords managed to prevent the implementation of a later bill that banned this practice. The Madras Government was generally unconvinced that those who tilled the soil needed any legislation to secure their tenure (Hardgrave 1977: 64). D. A. Washbrook (1976: 40) notes that "repeated attempts by Fort St. George to raise the position of untouchables . . . were rendered nugatory for its predominantly high-caste executive refused to enforce them: land set aside for panchama [dalit] resettlement disappeared from the records and a High Court ruling of 1917 revealed that slavery still existed in Malabar, eighty-four years after it had been outlawed."

Alongside these changes to the existing land tenure system in Malabar was the increasing importance of the courts in providing legal justification for new policies. The jenmis were assisted time and again by court decrees in their actions against the peasants, a situation that had not previously existed. Westernized courts were a new feature of British rule in the region and their rulings tilted the power balance even further in the direction of jenmis.

Policies toward adivasis in Malabar were also, on the whole, very similar to the policies instituted by the British in Ajmer-Merwara, and the same as those instituted generally throughout India. These policies were implemented through the machinery of the Madras Presidency, which was in control of Malabar. Some members within the administration in Madras were actually more liberal about tribal policy than those within other governments throughout the rest of India. In fact, a few tried to fight several injurious policies regarding adivasis that were handed down from the British central government. Forests in Malabar, as in Ajmer, were deemed to be officially the property of the state. One administrator, the Deputy Collector of Nellore, wrote to the government in response that "there were originally no Government forests in this country. Forests have always been of natural growth here; and so they have been enjoyed by the people."[64] However, the British government disregarded this and other similar objections and dispossessed the adivasis.

The British also pursued Criminal Tribes legislation in Malabar. Again, several voices within the Madras Presidency objected. Before the Criminal Tribes Act of 1871 was passed, the Inspector General of Police in Madras wrote to the British government, arguing that there was no problem with criminality among tribes in the region (Radhakrishna 2001: 158). However, the central government again ignored these complaints and implemented the legislation.

The result of these two policies was the gradual deterioration of adivasi livelihood in the region. In a postcolonial report from 1955, a Government of India administrator noted the many problems with structuring policies for Malabar's forests:

> There were some agrarian disturbances in the Koothali estate in Malabar in 1954 and the Madras Govt. asked Sri W.R.S Sathianathan, at that time Member, Board of Revenue, Madras, to enquire into the matter and submit a report. In his report on the situation . . . Sathianathan expressed the view that the agitation in that estate was only a symptom of a disease which was spreading rapidly over the whole of Malabar Dist. and added that it was necessary for the Govt. to adopt a bold and comprehensive policy for the treatment of private forests and unoccupied private and Govt. lands.[65]

Various British policies that dispossessed the adivasis and opened up forests to a host of new groups combined to depress severely the state of tribal groups in the region.

British policies in Malabar undermined the position of low castes and adivasis. New landholding policies dispossessed peasants throughout the region, led to skyrocketing eviction rates, and sharply increased caste antagonisms. Tribals were also cut off from forests and dispossessed. The roots of caste and tribal violence in contemporary Malabar can thus be traced back directly to the arrival of British administrators in the late eighteenth century.

Malabar has come to be considered a notable area for agrarian conflict in contemporary India, but this was not always the case. In fact, T. K. Ravindran

(1978: 126) notes that "Malabar was . . . remarkably free from agrarian unrest in the pre-British period." This is a critical point because by all accounts an extremely rigid precolonial caste system existed in Malabar. Yet it was only after the implementation of a series of British colonial policies that caste conflict began to increase significantly.

The rise of low-caste mobilization began in Malabar during the colonial period, especially throughout the 1930s. Although low castes such as the Tiyyas were integral to organizing in various ways against their caste disabilities, the Nairs (middle castes) also formed an important part of the movement (Jeffrey 1992). During the decade a number of major political organizations were formed: the Kerala Congress Socialist Party was founded in 1934, the first all-Malabar peasants meeting occurred in 1936, and the Communist Party of Kerala was created in 1939 (Menon 1992). Over the next several decades, these groups would use countless marches, protests, and strikes to attempt to upend the nature of caste relations in Malabar.

The situation for low castes and tribals in the neighboring Kingdom of Travancore was remarkably different. At the outset, the land tenure system in Travancore differed considerably from that of Malabar. In fact, it was very different from the princely state of Jaipur examined in the previous case study. In Jaipur and in many of the other Rajput states, hereditary jagirdars limited control of the land by princes. In Jaipur State specifically, the raja controlled less than half the land. In Travancore, however, the maharajas controlled a much larger portion of the land. By most estimates, almost 75 percent of the cultivable land (excluding wastelands and forest areas) was controlled by the Travancore royal family (Somarajan 1983: 131).

Land in Travancore was basically broken up into two overarching categories: private land was called *puravaka* and crown land was called *pandaravaka*. The princely administration had a large amount of power and discretion over land policy in Travancore because it was the preeminent landholder in the state. Furthermore, puravaka land in Travancore was not concentrated in the hands of big landlords as it was in Malabar. Land ownership in south Kerala was significantly more diffuse. George Kristoffel Lieten (1975: 455) notes that

> a notable feature of the size of distribution were the regional differences. The Northern Malabar districts had very huge estates while the Travancore region was mostly characterised by its small peasant proprietors. This is evidenced by the Census of Land Holdings and Cultivation, 1956: while the number of owned

holdings of over five acres constituted in Travancore-Cochin only 5% of the total, in the three Malabar districts this percentage went up to more than 30%[,] comprising almost 85% of the land.

In the mid-nineteenth century, as the earliest spasms of agrarian revolt began to take hold in Malabar, Travancore embarked upon a series of significant land reforms. These reforms were the main mechanism through which the rigid caste structure of Travancore began to break down. First, in 1818, the government instituted a ryotwari settlement, although by this point the ryots were still tenants-at-will. Despite this designation, their existence was much better than that of the peasants of Malabar. Scottish chronicler of India Francis Buchanan-Hamilton described Travancore's peasantry at this time as "contented and prosperous."[66] In 1826 and 1829, laws were enacted that prevented the arbitrary eviction of tenants from their land. A few decades later the princely administration enacted the Pattam Proclamation of 1865, which has often been called the "Magna Carta of Travancore ryots" (Somarajan 1983: 133). This proclamation created land tenure rights for those who inhabited pandaravaka lands, and a proclamation two years later established the same system for puravaka lands. These major changes led a British administrator in a 1914 report to remark that "the policy of the Darbar has been throughout one of *marked* consideration towards the agricultural classes."[67] A 1928 report added, "The Indian States of Travancore and Cochin, where conditions are similar to those in Malabar, have solved the tenancy problem, so far as it relates to kanamdars."[68]

Aside from its progressive land tenure system, the Kingdom of Travancore also instituted other policies that assisted the amelioration of low-caste groups. The traditional narrative about Travancore (similar to the state of Kerala as a whole) depicts a territory of extremely strict caste restrictions. Beginning in the late nineteenth century, however, the rulers of the kingdom began to enact several pathbreaking policies designed to improve the condition of low castes, especially untouchables.

An example of this change in attitude is a controversy over women of the Shanar caste that brewed throughout the early nineteenth century. The tradition in Kerala had been that Shanar women were not allowed to cover their upper bodies in the presence of Brahmins. In the early nineteenth century the maharaja of Travancore had upheld this policy, but by 1859 he reversed his position. The diwan, Madhava Rao (1858–72), explained to the British Resident, W. Cullen, that "His Highness now proposes to abolish all rules prohibiting the covering of the upper parts of the persons of Shanar women and to grant them perfect liberty to meet the requirements of decency any way they may deem proper with the simple restriction that they do not imitate the same mode of dress that appertains to the higher castes."[69] It was not the British who pushed for this policy. On the contrary, F. N. Maltby, a later Resident at Travancore and Cochin, wrote about the issue: "On the whole, the opinion which I have formed, and I trust the Government will consider it a just one, is that the question is one in which it is not desirable, or in any way necessary, that the British Government should put any pressure upon the Native State."[70] Furthermore, the British did not seem inclined to enforce progressive caste issues in Travancore. Only a few years earlier, in 1853, they had recommended to the princely state that it abolish a festival held specifically for low castes, arguing that it was "endangering the Public Peace."[71] In general, many low-caste reforms that occurred in Travancore were opposed by the British (Singh 2010: 285). As Robin Jeffrey has noted, for British administrators the ideal prince was "progressive but not too progressive,"[72] and the Travancore government was often accused of being too progressive on issues concerning low castes.

Besides the well-known Shanar clothing issue, there were other, smaller changes that the rajas of Travancore enacted to improve the condition of untouchables and break apart the highly rigid regional caste system. Maltby noted some of the progress in an April 1862 report sent to the Madras government:

> Two important measures . . . have been commenced, tending to break down caste distinctions. His Highness the Rajah has signified to me his determination to build suitable Courthouses for his Courts instead of their being held, as is now often the case, within religious precincts to which the lower classes are not admissable [sic], and also of directing the preparation of a form of address to the Courts, proportioned to the rank of the Court addressed and not to the grade of the addresser. At present the Christian Converts have just cause to complain that they are compelled to use a form of address expressive of low origin and degraded position.[73]

The single largest step taken by Travancore was the Temple Entry Proclamation of 1936, which allowed untouchables for the first time to enter Hindu temples. This was considered a seminal event throughout India, even earning lavish praise from Gandhi. The proclamation was issued in November of that year by Maharaja Chithira Thirunal, and the effort was pushed aggressively by his diwan, C. P. Ramaswami Iyer. The text of the proclamation was as follows: "We have decided and thereby declare, ordain and command that, subject to such rules and conditions as may be laid down and imposed by Us for preserving their proper atmosphere and maintaining their rituals and observances, there should henceforth be no restriction placed on any Hindu by birth or religion on entering or worshipping at the temples controlled by Us and Our Government."[74] This act, in the words of A. Sreedhara Menon (2001: 27), "ushered in a bloodless social revolution." There was no area of British India, for example, that had done anything similar; in fact, only after the proclamation in Travancore did some other British territories follow suit and pursue similar legislation, although Malabar did not completely open up its temples to untouchables until after independence.

In a circuitous way the Temple Entry Proclamation was actually in keeping with Travancore's reputation as a theocratic state. Ramaswami Iyer and the maharaja understood that pressure from Christian groups and the possibility of mass low-caste conversions (as in Malabar) threatened the character of the Hindu kingdom. Rather than lose these groups, Travancore struck first and brought them into the Hindu fold. In fact, upper-caste groups were instrumental in urging the government to open schools for low castes, because they were afraid that missionaries would use their schools for conversion. Scholars have rightly noted that the Hindus of Travancore were not a unified community, but growing attempts to proselytize among low castes began to foster the emergence of a more unified Hindu bloc. It is also vital to recognize the importance of Christian missionaries in pushing for ameliorative policies for low castes, albeit somewhat inadvertently. Missionaries in Travancore were active in converting low-caste groups to Christianity, and "even stimulated caste insurgency" (Desai 2005: 463). It is partly in response to this practice that the Travancore princely administration issued the Temple Entry Proclamation. This action does not, however, diminish the importance of the leaders of the kingdom themselves, in whose hands lay the ultimate authority to decide how to respond to low-caste mobilization. Menon (2001: 28) notes that Travancore "produced in the nineteenth century a galaxy of social reformers who championed the cause of the eradication of untouchability . . . [such as] Chattampi Swamikal . . . Sri Narayana Guru . . . Kumaran Asan . . . T. K. Madhavan . . . and Ayyankali."

In the Kingdom of Travancore, as in Jaipur, adivasis occupied a completely different position in society than their counterparts in British Malabar. Most important, many of the seminal land reforms initiated by the princely administration in the mid-nineteenth century had provisions attached specifically for adivasis. For example, they were given rights over officially designated tribal lands, and these areas were closed to nontribal immigration. Moneylenders were also banned from these regions (Mohanty 2006: 178). Christoph von Fürer-Haimendorf (1985: 27) cited Travancore as an example of a princely state with progressive policies on adivasis: "In the former princely state of Travancore the rights of such tribes to cultivate free of tax in forest areas was clearly laid down and compact blocks of land of an acreage seven times of that required in any one cultivating season enabled them to continue cultivation permanently in a cycle of rotation."

Overall, the distinctions between Malabar and Travancore in terms of their policies on low castes and adivasis were stark. In Malabar, British administrators, much like in Ajmer, pursued a host of policies that led to the deterioration of the peasantry. Perhaps the most important new policy was the recognition of jenmis as lords of the soil. This singular act dislocated tenants and cultivators from the traditional landholding system that had been based on supervision rather than ownership. The result was a sharp rise in the number of evictions, as well as high levels of caste antagonism. British policies on adivasis were no better: the forests of the Malabar region were taken over by the state while tribal groups were dispossessed and some were criminalized. By contrast, the Kingdom of Travancore pursued the opposite set of policies. A number of reforms in the late nineteenth and early twentieth centuries radically altered the position of low castes, foremost of which was the Temple Entry Proclamation. In addition, a number of new land reforms were advanced by the administration. Adivasis also benefited from these progressive policies as Travancore prevented them from losing access to forests and cultivable land.

Postcolonial Caste and Tribal Violence in Malabar and Travancore

Today there is still a clear divergence in the pattern of caste and tribal violence between northern and southern Kerala. Whereas Malabar after independence became synonymous with simmering caste and tribal tensions, similar violence in the Travancore region never materialized. Formal and informal institutions reproduced and transmitted the legacies of the past into contemporary Kerala.

At the outset it is clear that caste is still the hegemonic ethnic category in contemporary Malabar. Consider formal institutions in the state such as political parties. The CPI-M has always had its strongest base in Malabar (Menon 2007). Communist-led coalition movements have governed the state repeatedly since independence, and most of their support comes specifically from Malabar. Donald Zagoria (1971: 145) writes, "It is, for example, well known that Communist electoral strength is considerable in three Indian states—Kerala, West Bengal and Andhra. But it is less well known that communism is much stronger in certain identifiable parts of these three states—the Malabar portions of Kerala." The success of the communists in Malabar is a strong indicator of the salience of caste and tribal identification because the party derives most of its strength from low castes and tribal groups (Jeffrey 1978; Menon 2007).[75] At the same time, the party does not make religious entreaties to voters.[76] Partly due to the religiosity of Travancore, the communists have been unable to derive the same level of support from this region.[77] They have also failed to achieve the same level of success in Travancore because the princely government preempted the potent message of low-caste equality by passing several progressive policies for these groups in the nineteenth and twentieth centuries.

Another formal political organization is the Indian peasant movement, specifically the Kisan Sabha (Peasants Union), which also has a regional stronghold in Malabar (Karat 1973: 24). Both the communists and the Kisan Sabha have made social justice for depressed castes a primary focus of their work. The story of informal institutions in Kerala is similar; in Malabar, cultural practices revolve around caste, but in Travancore they are still centered on religion.

When India achieved independence, and by the time it was about to linguistically reorganize its states, the differences between agrarian conditions in Malabar and Travancore were immense. In 1956, once the two areas were joined together to form Kerala, the new state's Planning Department undertook a comparative analysis (which included the former princely state of Cochin), the results of which are detailed in Table 3.4.

These data starkly highlight the deleterious effects of British rule in Malabar. By 1956 it lagged behind Travancore-Cochin on almost every single agricultural indicator. The British and their various agricultural policies had significantly retarded the development of the region. Similarly, Figure 3.2 highlights that when the postindependence period began in Kerala,

TABLE 3.4.
Agricultural Statistics for Kerala, 1956

	Malabar	Travancore-Cochin
Proportion of cultivated area to total area	45.20%	48.20%
Proportion of irrigated area to total area	2.60%	29.20%
Average paddy yield per acre	1,092 lbs. of dry paddy	1,754 lbs. of dry paddy
Proportion of villages electrified	6.50%	26.00%
Power generation — kilowatts per lakh of population	Nil	810
Mileage of roads per square mile of area	.38 miles	.70 miles

SOURCE: Kerala State Archives, Confidential (1954–1956), 36394, 1956, #960.

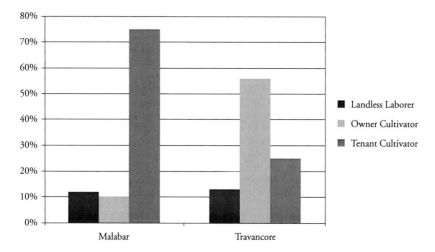

FIGURE 3.2. Land Tenure System in Kerala, 1957 to 1958.
SOURCE: Nossiter 1982: 16.

cultivators in Malabar were in a much less privileged position than those in neighboring Travancore. The power of landlords was entrenched in Malabar, whereas in Travancore the position of low castes and tribals had undergone a sea change in the nineteenth and twentieth centuries, and by independence they were already significantly ahead of their Malabari counterparts. As late as 1988 B. A. Prakash (1988: 51) surveyed the situation in Malabar: "Though Malabar had been a major exporter of a wide variety of agricultural products to Europe for more than two thousand years and consequently exposed to influences from abroad, it still remains an under-developed region with a backward agricultural sector."

Contemporary Kerala does experience some serious caste violence, most of it occurring at the margins of the caste system. In 2013, for example, the state led India with the highest per capita crime rate against SCSTs.[78] Unfortunately there is no state-level dataset with reliable figures on caste and tribal violence that can allow a clear comparison of Malabar and Travancore. Interviews and qualitative data collection were therefore conducted in the state in order to shed a light on caste and tribal relations and conflict throughout the region. The aforementioned university professor from Trivandrum noted that "caste conflict is concentrated in the north, but it happens all over the state. Caste politics is big in Kerala. But the adivasis, the Naxalites, they were only operating in the north. This was before 1977, and they lost some support over time."[79]

Caste antagonisms run high in modern Malabar. In their Kerala Development Report of 2007, the Planning Commission notes that the caste system in Malabar is much more rigid than that of Travancore, and they make reference to the past in explaining this fact: "[In Travancore] the institution of attached labour began to wane and that of wage labour, expand. These developments led to the decline of the rigidities of the caste system in Travancore. But in Malabar, the caste system remained entrenched in the prevailing agrarian system" (2007: 56). Similarly, the intensive work of P. Radhakrishnan (1989: 126) in selected villages in Malabar in the 1970s highlights the continued salience of caste, as well as the existence of widespread caste inequality:

> While the pattern of tenancy . . . clearly reflected the virtual dependence of certain social groups on the Nambutiris because of the latter's dominance in the village land system, certain other social groups were reduced to even greater dependence as agricultural labourers, homestead tenants, household servants, and so on. Such dependence in turn had led to the social subservience of all the dependent groups[,] which was perpetrated by the Nambutiris by insisting on strict adherence to traditional caste-practices and caste-based socioeconomic relations.

Overall, these pieces of evidence highlight the tension that exists between caste groups in Malabar, a kind of antagonism that does not exist in neighboring Travancore.[80]

Tribal violence has also been a much larger problem in contemporary Malabar than in Travancore. The Malabar region is in fact the part of Kerala in which Naxalites were ever a serious force. In the late 1960s a Naxalite faction of the CPI-M in Kerala organized coordinated attacks against police stations and wireless stations in Malabar, specifically in Tellicherry and Pulpally. Wayanad district has been the heart of tribal conflict in the state. While Naxalites have not been extremely successful in the region, they have continued to carry out sporadic attacks in the decades since their founding. In contemporary India, the Wayanad area in Kerala is now considered by the Indian government to be "Naxalite-targeted." In contrast, there has been almost no Naxalite activity in Travancore.

Even in the past several years, tribal conflict has been evident in Malabar. A famous recent incident was the government-initiated attack in 2003 against protesting adivasis in Muthanga (Bijoy and Raman 2003), located in Wayanad. In response to numerous failures by the state government to distribute land to adivasis, a small contingent of tribals protested by entering and taking up residence in the Wayanad Wildlife Sanctuary. A brutal crackdown by the government soon followed. For Kerala's tribes the present still bears the indelible stamp of the past: by the late 1970s the average percentage of landlessness among tribals in Malabar was 40.3 percent whereas in Travancore it was only 7.93 percent (Kunhaman 1985: 467).

Summary

When British power expanded into south India, the fertile coastal region of Kerala immediately attracted the interest of colonial officials. While the northern Malabar portion of the state came under direct British rule, due to various factors—most important, the military threat from the neighboring Kingdom of Mysore—the southern Travancore region remained independent. This "accident" of history, as British officials described it, offers a striking opportunity for comparative analysis. Because the British wanted to control the entire state but were unable to do so, it is possible to isolate the effects of colonialism on ethnic conflict by comparing Malabar and Travancore.

In Malabar, British administrators emphasized the centrality of caste and implemented a host of new discriminatory policies—for example, the empowerment of landlords and increased rural taxation—that decimated the low-caste and tribal populations. In the late nineteenth and early twentieth centuries, many low castes in Malabar converted to Islam in order to escape the confines of the rigid caste system, an act that briefly changed the ethnic divide from one of caste to one of religion. Over the long term, however, Malabar remained an area ridden by caste and tribal conflict, and as happened in Ajmer-Merwara, religious violence receded over time.

In Travancore, however, the Hindu rulers of the kingdom created a theocratic state that limited the position of the Christian and Muslim minorities. They were blocked from freely practicing their religion and from access to government jobs, and they generally held a subordinate position in society. These policies resulted in increased communal tension and periodic riots within the state, especially in the early twentieth century.

The postindependence era in Kerala mirrors the colonial period because formal and informal institutions reinforced ethnic divides. Perhaps the clearest indicator of the persistence of colonial-era patterns of ethnic conflict in Kerala is the fact that Naxalites have mainly been concentrated in Malabar while Hindu nationalist groups have mainly been concentrated in Travancore. Even almost seventy years after the dawn of independence, the pattern of ethnic violence across contemporary Kerala reflects its colonial origins.

A final and important note about Kerala deals with postindependence reforms. In Rajasthan, a number of reforms that targeted the Muslim community in Jaipur and low castes and adivasis in Ajmer were stymied. As the previous chapter showed, reform efforts there have had little success in changing the past. In contrast, the governments of postcolonial Kerala implemented a number of successful reforms. In the postindependence period, for example, the communists worked tirelessly to mobilize low castes throughout Kerala, especially in Malabar (Nossiter 1982, Menon 2007). This ultimately resulted in their historic election in 1957. Over the next several decades, they implemented a number of reforms—especially land reform in 1969 (Herring 1983)—that had a remarkable effect on raising overall levels of social development. Despite a continually sluggish economy, Kerala's high life-expectancy rates, low infant-mortality rates, and almost universal literacy rates have been a model to developing countries around the world. Perhaps as a consequence of this development, Kerala has experienced significantly less overall ethnic violence than most areas of north India.

Even though these varied reforms did not completely eliminate ethnic violence in the state, or alter the pattern of ethnic violence inherited from the colonial period, this south Indian case study details that postcolonial reforms did not fail everywhere. The political leaders of postindependence Kerala have shown that successful changes to the colonial past are possible and, more important, can have a considerable impact in promoting peace.

CHAPTER 4

Explaining Violence in East India: Bastar

> The Pax Britannica is so firmly established that the idea of overt rebellion is always distant from our minds, even in a remote State like Bastar.
>
> —B. P. Standen, *Chief Secretary to the Chief Commissioner,*
>
> *Central Provinces, 1910*[1]

Patterns of ethnic violence in contemporary India are driven by historical factors that stem from the colonial period. British administrators in the provinces organized society around castes and tribes, but native rulers in the princely states—continuing practices prevalent during the precolonial period—organized their kingdoms around religion. Both sets of rulers then instituted disparate policies of ethnic stratification. In the provinces, the British favored high castes, protected religious minorities through a policy of neutrality, and discriminated against low castes and adivasis. In the princely states, native kings did the opposite: their policies favored their coreligionists, protected the low castes and tribals, and discriminated against non-coreligionists. Local institutions coupled with the failure of postindependence reforms transmitted these patterns of ethnic violence into contemporary India. Today, former British provinces such as Ajmer and Malabar experience primarily caste and tribal violence whereas former princely states such as Jaipur and Travancore suffer considerable religious violence.

This chapter considers the single largest outlier for this historical theory of ethnic conflict in India: the princely state of Bastar, now located in the eastern state of Chhattisgarh.[2] From the mid-nineteenth century onward, this tiny and remote Hindu kingdom was the bloodiest battleground for tribal conflict in colonial India. After independence, violence in Bastar only intensified as it became the front line of India's tribal-led Naxalite rebellion. Although there are other cases that deviate from the central theory of this book—for example, British cities like Bombay experience serious communal rioting[3]—no region compares to the per capita violence of Bastar, which accounts for more than *one-third* of all Naxalite casualties in contemporary India. Why has this small kingdom, which never came under British direct rule, experienced such horrific tribal violence?

The original cause of Bastar's tribal rebellions was, beginning in the early nineteenth century, an enormous amount of British intervention in the princely administration—a level of colonial interference that outstripped that of any other princely state of similar size in India. As the British came to control the kingdom, they implemented the same discriminatory policies toward adivasis that had led to tribal revolts throughout provincial India. Unlike Kerala, postcolonial Bastar has not changed at all: postindependence governments have refused to implement reforms of the past and have even exacerbated many colonial-era policies. These decisions have led to the extraordinary growth of Naxalite violence in the state.

The Case Study

During the British period, Bastar State covered more than thirteen thousand square miles—approximately the size of Belgium. In 1901 it had a population of 306,501. To British administrators it was one of a number of "jungle kingdoms"—so named because of its lush, dense forests and its large population of adivasis. In fact, the majority of the population was tribal—specifically, members of the Gond tribe. The rulers of the state were Rajputs who had fled Warangal (in the present-day state of Telangana) sometime during the fourteenth century to escape Muslim invaders. The local tribes consider the raja of Bastar to be the high priest of Danteshwari, a local goddess. The power of the raja is embodied in the Sword of Danteshwari, held by the royal family. The princely state was known for a historically close relationship between adivasis and their king. This bond is perhaps best exemplified by the kingdom's unique celebration of the Hindu Dussehra festival, which marks the triumph of Ram over Ravana. The raja is "abducted" by tribals on the eleventh day of Dussehra, then officially returned to the throne the next day (Gell 1997).

During the precolonial period, Bastar was incorporated into first the Mughal and then the Maratha Empire. On account of its geographical inaccessibility, however, it always managed to retain a special level of isolation from external forces. The Deputy Commissioner of the Central Provinces and Berar, Wilfrid Grigson, remarked that the state constituted a "backwater in Indian history."[4] The kingdom is situated in one of the most heavily forested areas of India, part of the Dandakaranya forest region. Map 4.1 shows colonial Bastar located in the south of the Central Provinces. Map 4.2 highlights the location of the Bastar districts within the contemporary state of Chhattisgarh.

In 1818 the British finally broke the power of the Marathas in central India and subsequently entered into a political relationship with Bastar State (which was also around the time that colonial officials took control of Ajmer and signed a treaty of subsidiary alliance with Jaipur). Bastar was then incorporated into the Central Provinces. Over the next several decades, British influence in the state steadily increased, to the point that by the middle of the nineteenth century colonial administrators essentially governed the kingdom directly and the raja ruled in name only.

The most important consideration here is whether Bastar was actually unique in its high level of British interference. As Chapter 1 noted, one school of historians of colonial India has treated princely rulers as powerless

MAP 4.1. Colonial Bastar.

Bastar

MAP 4.2. Postcolonial Bastar.

SOURCE: Produced by Colm Fox. Original source: http://d-maps.com/carte.php?num_car=16466&lang=en.

and ultimately subservient to the British. However, several key facts illustrate that the level of colonial interference in Bastar was quite uncommon compared to that of other native states across India.

First, during the nineteenth and twentieth centuries the British dismissed three consecutive rajas of the state under the pretext of "incompetence" (detailed later in the chapter). Princes were occasionally dismissed on these grounds, but few native states in India suffered this degree of repeated intervention. Second, during the fifty-six-year period from 1891 to 1947, the British governed Bastar directly through colonial administrators for forty-two years. During this time the British even governed the state through Englishmen—a highly unusual practice because they generally preferred to use British Indians from the provinces (Ramusack 2004: 196). Finally, Bastar was not given any gun salute. In 1922 the Chief of Bastar requested a dynastic salute of nine guns but was refused whereas four smaller states in the region—Mayurbhanj, Patna, Kalahandi, and Sonpur—received a nine-gun salute.[5] In fact, Bastar was almost as large as Jaipur but still received no formal colonial designation. The amount of British interference in Bastar State was significantly different from that in other areas during the post-1857 period; whereas the rest of the princely states experienced a gradual loosening of control, by the dawn of the twentieth century, Bastar had experienced the opposite.

After independence, Bastar State was incorporated into Madhya Pradesh and eventually, in 2000, into the new state of Chhattisgarh. The kingdom now comprises the present districts of Bastar, Dantewada (South Bastar) and Kanker (North Bastar).

Colonial-Era Tribal Violence in Bastar

Once the British began political relations with Bastar State, they interfered in its internal administration almost immediately, at first under the pretext of preventing the adivasi tradition of human sacrifice. However, in 1855 an official inquiry showed that human sacrifice had never actually been a local tradition. The reporting British officer wrote that it was "pleasing to find that there did not exist . . . a tradition of human sacrifices. In the low country it was said that these hill tribes never sacrificed human beings and for once the account was strictly true."[6] The actual cause of British interference was likely the fact that Bastar had extremely large iron ore deposits (10 percent of the country's total), as well as other abundant precious minerals and forest produce. The British proceeded to lay a direct claim on the forests of Bastar, something they did not do in other princely states (Sundar 1997: 92). In Jaipur and Travancore, for example, the British indirectly placed new commercial burdens on princely forests but did not take them under direct control. This was a major disruption of tradition in Bastar. Alfred Gell (1997: 435) notes that during the Mughal period "the tribal population enjoyed the benefit of their extensive lands and forests with a degree of non-exploitation from outside which would hardly be matched anywhere else in peninsular India." And Nandini Sundar highlights that prior to British rule there was not even a recorded state forest policy in Bastar (2001: 24).

As British influence grew in central and eastern India during the late eighteenth and early nineteenth centuries, the first recorded spasms of tribal conflict occurred in and around the Bastar area—for instance, the Halba Rebellion in 1774 and the Paralkot Rebellion in 1825. D. Banerjea (2002: 12) notes about the first uprising that "the presence of Maratha forces and the terror caused by the East India Company . . . precipitated the rebellion." About the subsequent Paralkot Rebellion, he adds, "The presence of the Marathas and the British threatened the identity of the Abujmarias [tribe] and they resisted this through organising the rebellion."

Bastar State experienced two tribal revolts during colonial rule: in 1876 and 1910. The first rebellion began innocently enough with the arrival of the Prince of Wales in India. The diwan of Bastar attempted to arrange a meeting between the prince and the raja, Bhairam Deo (1853–91). The adivasis, however, interpreted this action as an attempt by the British to abduct the raja, and within hours they had mobilized in large numbers and prevented him from leaving the state. Though traditionally considered a rebellion, the 1876 conflict was actually relatively minor and featured very little bloodshed. W. B. Jones, Chief Commissioner of the Central Provinces (1883–84), summarized the incident in a confidential report from 1883:

> In March of 1876 a disturbance broke out at Jugdalpur [the capital], the origin of which has never been quite satisfactorily explained. The immediate occasion of the outbreak was the Raja's setting out for Bombay to meet . . . The Prince of Wales. The people assembled in large numbers and compelled him to return to Jugdalpur. Their ostensible demand was not that he should not go, but that he should not leave behind the then Diwan Gopinath Kapurdar (a Dhungar, shepherd by caste) and one Munshi Adit Pershad (a Kayeth in charge of the Raja's

Criminal Court), whom the people charged with oppression. . . . They simply demanded that the two men mentioned above should be sent away.[7]

The British were skeptical of the idea that the adivasis were rebelling against the raja. An officer sent to investigate in 1882 disconfirmed the idea, noting that "relations between Raja and subjects generally [were] good, very good."[8] Commissioner Jones also noted that "the insurgents committed no violence and professed affection for the Raja."[9] Rather, it seems that the adivasis were upset with the raja's choice of appointees. But another main cause of the disturbance was creeping British influence in the state. For example, Jones noted that earlier in the year the adivasis had felt antagonized by new Christian missionaries who arrived in Bastar.[10] In addition, new traders, immigrants, and colonial policies combined to create a rising sense of embitterment among the tribal population in the state.

After the death of Raja Bhairam Deo in 1891, the British began to penetrate the princely administration more steadily. Because the raja's son, Rudra Pratap Deo (1891–1921), was only six years old at the time, the British directly administered the state for the next sixteen years. This direct control over Bastar continued after Rudra Pratap Deo became raja in 1908. Extra-Commissioner Rai Bahadur Panda Baijnath acted as superintendent during the last four years that the king was a minor, then continued to act as diwan after the raja took the throne. E. A. De Brett, Officer on Special Duty in Bastar, wrote about Rudra Pratap Deo's lack of power, noting that he was "bound in all matters of importance to follow the advice of his Diwan and has never taken an active part in State affairs."[11] The Chief Commissioner of the Central Provinces later wrote that "the Diwan was the virtual ruler of the State."[12]

The 1910 rebellion was much more violent and widespread than its predecessor, earning the moniker *bhumkal* (earthquake). One of the chief instigators of the conflict was Lal Kalendra Singh, first cousin of the raja and a former diwan himself. He had been angling for a return to power after he had been removed by the British, also due to "incompetence." He mobilized the adivasis by declaring that if he were returned to the throne he would drive the British out of Bastar completely. A contemporary report from a Christian missionary living in Bastar, Reverend W. Ward, sheds some light on this rebellion:

In the second week of February we first heard of the unrest among the Aborigines south of Jagdalpur. Vague rumours were afloat but none of a very serious nature. On the 18th a Christian living among the Prajas—Aborigines—came to me with the story that the Prajas were all armed and were moving toward Keslur, where the Political Agent, Mr. E. A. DeBrett [sic], I.C.S. [Indian Civil Service], was camping, to make known their grievances. . . . A branch of a mango tree, a red pepper, and an arrow were tied together, and sent to all villages in the State. The mango leaves stand for a general meeting; the red pepper, a matter of great importance is to be discussed and that the matter is necessary and urgent; the arrow, a sign of war.[13]

The entire state rose in rebellion and the initial British force of only 250 armed police was quickly overwhelmed. For weeks, looting, robbery, and arson plagued the entire kingdom. By the end of February additional troops from Jeypore and Bengal had arrived and the rebellion was finally put down. Hundreds of prisoners were taken, including Lal Kalendra Singh, who was expelled from the state and later died in prison.

The British conducted several inquiries into the causes of the 1910 rebellion. The Chief Commissioner of the Central Provinces summarized the British government's position in a December 1910 report that bluntly stated, "from an examination of the evidence before them the Government of India were [sic] of opinion that a *too zealous forest administration* might not improbably be the main cause of the discontent of the hill-tribes."[14] B. P. Standen, Chief Secretary to the Chief Commissioner, wrote at the same time that "the alleged grievances of the people are . . . the result of a weak rule combined with gradual over-elaboration of the administration—a combination which must sooner or later give rise to dissatisfaction."[15] De Brett also conducted an inquiry into the rebellion and discerned eleven main causes, chief among them "the inclusion in reserves of forest and village lands."[16] L. W. Reynolds, another officer stationed in Bastar, noted the following:

> The proposal to form reserves was not finally sanctioned until June 1909 and action giving effect thereto must therefore be nearly synchronous with the rising. In his telegram of the 17th March 1910 the Chief Commissioner stated that one of the objects of the rising was the eviction of foreigners. I believe it to be the case that in connection with the exploitation of the forests Messrs. Gillanders, Arbuthnot and Company, who have a contract in the State, have introduced a large number of workmen from Bengal. . . . the [tribes] resent the introduction of these foreigners. It is not unnatural.[17]

All of the contemporary reports pointed to the same causes—the excessive influence of the British and, more specifically, new forest policies. Sundar also found that most of the main participants in the 1910 rebellion were from areas that suffered the most under new colonial land revenue demands (1997: 98). Despite the British admission to having an "overzealous" forest administration, colonial policy in Bastar did not change substantially in the wake of rebellion. The British continued to sign various forest mining agreements and renewals of previous agreements—in 1923, 1924, 1929, and 1932. These agreements continued to encroach on forest lands and steadily displaced the adivasi population. The government also continued to reserve forests; as late as 1940 the administrator of the Bastar State wrote to the political agent of Chhattisgarh States that "most of them [adivasis] dislike the proposals for forest reservation. . . . However[,] if these areas are not reserved it will be impossible to reserve any good teak forests in the Zamindari. (It is a most unfortunate fact that the best teak areas and the thickly populated, well cultivated Maria [Gond] villages coincide.)"[18]

The British also continued to govern the state directly through various machinations, although this too had been disastrous prior to 1910. In 1921, Rudra Pratap Deo died without a male heir, and his daughter, Profulla Kumari Devi (1921–36), was placed on the throne as a child. One British administrator noted, "She is about eleven years of age and no reference is made as to her eventual fitness to rule, but this is unimportant as she could always rule through a Manager or Dewan."[19] Bastar thus experienced another *minority administration,* a term that referred to periods when a minor was on the throne. In 1936, when the *maharani* (queen) of Bastar died suddenly in London of surgical complications, the British installed her eldest son, Pravir Chandra Bhanj Deo (1936–47), on the throne although he was only seven years old at the time. The maharani's husband, Raja Prafulla Bhanj Deo, first cousin of the ruler of the nearby Mayurbhanj State, had been passed over as a possible successor. This was an attempt by the British to continue ruling the state directly instead of turning over power to the queen's consort. R.E.L. Wingate, joint secretary to the Foreign and Political Department of the Government of India, noted that passing over Prafulla for the throne was against the queen's wishes: "It is her [the Maharani's] desire that Prafulla should have the title of Maharaja and that he should share her role as Ruling Chief, being co-equal with her and succeeding her as Ruler in the event of her death before him, her son not succeeding to the gaddi [throne] until his death."[20]

Despite the queen's preference, Prafulla—who had been educated with high marks at Rajkumar College in Raipur[21]—was deemed "exceedingly vain and filled with self-conceit. . . . he is a man of very questionable moral character and completely unstable,"[22] and he was denied the throne. Prafulla had also been very popular with tribal groups in Bastar. The administrator of Bastar, E. S. Hyde, noted a meeting between adivasis and Prafulla in 1936 after Prafulla had been passed over for control of the kingdom: "First of all the Mahjis told Prafulla that they had confidence and trust in him and that he was their 'mabap' [mother and father]; to this he replied that he could do nothing for them, that he had no powers. He was willing to do anything for them but . . . he could do nothing."[23]

Even before the death of the maharani in 1936, there had been a movement to install Prafulla as the hereditary raja in "joint rulership" of Bastar with his wife. Later there was an attempt to at least establish a Council of Regency and make him the regent.[24] Both movements were quashed by the British, who believed that Prafulla was responsible for several anti-British pamphlets that over the previous several years had appeared in newspapers throughout India. Administrators noted with some reservation, however, that "there is no actual proof as the printer's name is absent from the pamphlets."[25] The British eventually removed Prafulla as the guardian of his children and deemed that he should not be allowed to enter Bastar State.[26] When Pravir Chandra was placed on the throne, the colonial administrators in charge of his guardianship were themselves confused as to the justification behind his minority administration. E. S. Hyde commented, "I am not altogether clear what is meant in this case by guardianship. . . . It would, however, be of assistance to me and my successors if our position could be defined. It is certainly an unusual and somewhat delicate one, for normally when a Chief is a minor his father is dead."[27]

The British found fault one way or another with almost all of the occupants of the throne of Bastar. Lal Kalendra Singh was removed as diwan because the colonial authorities came to realize that he was "totally unfit to be trusted with any powers."[28] Rudra Pratap Deo was a "very weak-minded and stupid individual . . . considered unfit to exercise powers as a Feudatory Chief."[29] Prafulla Bhanj Deo was an agitator, unstable, and even needed to be removed from his children. And by the dawn of independence, the colonial administrators were already beginning to have serious doubts about the abilities of his son, Pravir Chandra, heir to the throne.

The policies that British administrators instituted in Bastar—the reservation of forest lands, heavy immigration into these areas, and new revenue burdens—mirrored policies that had been implemented throughout British

India, including in provinces such as Ajmer and Malabar. In Bastar, however, these discriminatory policies toward adivasis were even more severe, primarily because the state had such abundant natural resources. These policies implemented in the nineteenth century were the original cause of tribal rebellion in Bastar.

Postcolonial Tribal Violence in Bastar

The achievement of Indian independence in 1947 provided little relief to the adivasis of Bastar. Institutions continued to reinforce the past. For example, informal institutions, such as memories of previous conflicts—the 1910 bhumkal is a story well-known to all adivasis in the region—have hardened ethnic identities and created long-term tension between adivasis and the government. More than anything, however, postcolonial Bastar is a story about the failure of reform. In states like Jaipur, reform efforts were instituted but largely ineffective. But in Bastar, postcolonial governments hardly attempted reform at all, and in this case they exacerbated many policies from the colonial past.

The new Congress Party government that came to power in Bastar after independence almost immediately began agitating against the ruler of the state, Pravir Chandra, exactly as the British had done against Bastar's erstwhile rulers. By this time, Pravir Chandra occupied a purely ceremonial role in the state, but he remained immensely popular with the kingdom's adivasis. The first step came in 1953 when the Madhya Pradesh government had the prince's property taken from him and placed under the Court of Wards. They argued that this was necessary because Pravir Chandra was insane. To be sure, the prince was by most accounts a bizarre man. As early as 1936 his British caretakers noted that "he has always been delicate."[30] In 1960, Home Minister G. B. Pant (1955–61) wrote in a letter to a Madhya Pradesh minister, "Some people say that he was almost an idiot. I cannot say if that is absolutely correct; but there is no doubt that he is erratic and whimsical."[31] His father, Prafulla, described him as a "young puppy whom the British have ruined."[32]

Despite making some seemingly legitimate complaints against Pravir Chandra due to his strange behavior, the new Indian government also made numerous petty claims against him. The Secretary of the Ministry of States complained in May 1953 that "the Maharaja had now grown an enormous beard and his hair had come down right up to his waist. The nails of his fingers are very long. He looks just like a Sanyasi [renouncer]. . . . His is not a presentable appearance."[33] This description was taken as further evidence of Pravir Chandra's mental instability. About a subsequent meeting the Secretary wrote, "He [Pravir Chandra] said that he has taken to the practice of Yogic exercises. I suggested that he was too young for that and that he had better marry and live a decent family life."[34]

Pravir Chandra was embittered by losing his property. In 1955 he formed the Adivasi Kisan Mazdoor Sangh (Tribal Peasants Workers Association), a political organization that was created partly to help restore his land but also pressed for better policies for villagers in the state. In 1957 he was recruited by the Congress Party (despite his insanity) to stand for election. He viewed this situation as another opportunity to have his property returned. However, Congress would not return his property and the shaky alliance ended quickly. After that, the Indian government began to work toward removing Pravir Chandra from the Bastar throne, and they intended to replace him with his brother, Vijay Chandra. In their internal memos about pursuing this line of action they make a clear link to the past:

> The adivasis have seen and read the articles appearing in certain news-papers regarding the Maharaja's derecognition. They have taken a serious view and are stirring up agitation. . . . There was a similar move at the time of the death of his grand-father Shri Rudrapratap Deo and the adivasis stirred up a violent agitation, but the British Government was wise enough to put his mother on the Gaddi. History will repeat itself now.[35]

The policy of declaring those whom they did not like insane was a tradition among the British. It was certainly the case for several of the preindependence rulers of Bastar. In a letter to Lord Curzon in 1899, Secretary of State Lord George Hamilton (1895–1903) wrote, "I felt that, if ever it became necessary to take so strong a step as deposition [of a prince], you would be less likely to frighten the Native Princes generally if you took that step, not on a plea of misgovernment but of insanity."[36] The Indian government was not above using the same methods. Even the evidence of insanity that the postindependence state used mirrored that of the British. For instance, in 1920 Raja Rudra Pratap Deo was accused of mental instability and "mal-administration," and was even briefly banned from entering his state when he returned from a trip abroad. The main reason was that on three occasions he refused to meet with the British Resident stationed in Bastar. He apologized, stating that a member of his family had been sick at the time.

He was also surprised by the British overreaction.[37] The postcolonial Indian government similarly attacked Pravir Chandra for the same reason. The Secretary of the Ministry of States recounted a conversation with the king in 1953: "I told the Maharaja that he had acted very improperly in not paying due respect to the President of India when the latter had visited that part of Madhya Pradesh. The Maharaja in reply disowned any desire whatsoever to be disrespectful but said that his inability to be present at the President's arrival was due to his illness. He was then down with high fever."[38] Pravir Chandra's refusal (whether legitimate or not), like that of his grandfather, to meet the president was taken as further evidence that he should be removed as the ruler of Bastar. Congress finally succeeded in doing that in 1961, when he was replaced by his brother, Vijay Chandra.

The new Indian government also did not reverse many relics of the previous British administration. Foremost among these was forest policy. The reservation of forest lands was a major cause of preindependence rebellions, but the postindependence government actually accelerated this policy. From 1956 to 1981, one third of the forest felled in the Bastar district was intended for development projects (Sundar 1997: 198). Devindar Nath (1972: 1), an IAS officer and Collector of Bastar district in the 1950s, relates a story from 1955 in which he notes that in the early postindependence period adivasis were often cheated out of these lands:

> Each of the tenure-holders found himself in possession of property worth several thousands of rupees, but in their ignorance and illiteracy, they were neither conscious of their rights of property, nor had they any realisation of its value. Timber merchants belonging to different parts of the country made their appearance in the villages and purchased timber from the Adivasis for small sums. Gangs of labourers were employed to fell trees in the cultivators' fields, and transport of teak on a large scale started. The Adivasis were not paid even a small fraction of the value of their teak. . . . the stage was set for complete denudation of the Adivasis' fields.

On the surface there were many attempts at reform in Bastar. An absurd number of overlapping organizations were created in the area: Community Development Programme, Community Area Development Programme, Whole Village Development Programme, Drought Prone Area Programme, Hill Area Development Programme, Intensive Rural Development Programme, Tribal Area Development Programme, Intensive Tribal Development Programme, and the Bastar Development Authority. These development schemes undoubtedly generated revenue for the Indian government and private corporations, but adivasis reaped few benefits. By the late 1980s—despite all of the development efforts just listed—only 19 percent of the villages in Bastar were electrified, and there was only one medical dispensary per 25,000 villagers (EPW 1989: 40). Similarly, only 2 percent of land in the Bastar region was irrigated (Navlakha 2010: 43). Even today some fifty million rupees is spent on development programs in Bastar every year, but natural resource extraction in the region generates ten times as much for the government (Sundar 2001: 24).

Due to this failure of reform, there were two notable postcolonial conflicts in Bastar in the decades after independence. They both featured the raja and the adivasis on one side and the new Indian government on the other. The first incident occurred in 1961. After his deposition in that year, Pravir Chandra was briefly arrested for antigovernment activities, which led to the adivasis besieging the police station where they believed he was being held (though he was not actually being held there). For several days Bastar was gripped by a state of panic. Huge protests rocked the state, and the new raja was unable to quell the disturbances because the adivasis refused to accept him as their king. Thousands of signatures were collected to restore Pravir Chandra to power, and G. B. Pant bemoaned that the "Adivasis still continue to cherish their traditional feelings of respect and loyalty to the erst-while Princes."[39]

The second conflict occurred in 1966. On March 25th of that year, Pravir Chandra Bhanj Deo was gunned down by Jagdalpur police on the steps of his palace. Sundar (1997: 218–19) recounts the tale:

> Police guards [trying to prevent a procession by the adivasis] armed with rifles, instead of the usual lathis, were posted at the four main entrances of the palace. . . . An incident with a prisoner who was under trial and being escorted to the police lock-up in the palace premises accidentally sparked off an encounter between the people assembled in the palace grounds and the police, with the people shooting bows and arrows and the police responding with tear gas and bullets. One policeman died from an arrow wound and another was injured. . . . The police then chased the adivasis through the gardens and fired at them in front of the two palaces. Pravir Chandra, who had come out to see what was happening, was shot and killed along with other people. By about 12:45 pm, most adivasis had taken shelter inside the two palaces.

A subsequent investigation by Justice K. L. Pandey found the police to blame for this conflict (Ibid.). This so-called "police action" is still highly controversial, and it is widely believed that Pravir Chandra's death was a political assassination. Though probably only a small number of adivasis died, rumors still abound that hundreds or even thousands were killed.[40] Today the adivasis in the former Bastar State continue to venerate Pravir Chandra. March 25th has since been styled *Balidaan divas* or "Day of Martyrdom."[41] Both the British government and the new Congress Party government had made innumerable complaints about one ruler of Bastar after another, but the only group not to complain was the adivasis they ruled.

It is due to the continuation of colonial-era policies and the failure of reform that a political space was created for the Naxalites in Bastar. Understanding the extent of tribal violence in Bastar today requires a brief introduction to the Naxalite insurgency. The Naxalites come from the long and complicated history of the communist movement in India. The Communist Party of India (CPI) abandoned violent revolution and adopted parliamentary politics in 1951, which subsequently led to the creation of a more leftist faction, the Communist Party of India (Marxist) (CPI-M). In 1967 another split occurred and the far-left Communist Party of India (Marxist-Leninist) (CPI-ML) was established. Most contemporary Naxalite groups descend from the CPI-ML. These groups are considered Maoist because they draw on the insurgency tactics that Mao Zedong used during the Chinese Civil War.

There are generally considered to be three phases of the Naxalite movement in India. During the first phase, from 1967 to 1975, an uprising began in West Bengal and spread to its surrounding regions. The beginning of the conflict is dated to a revolt of peasants against landlords in 1967 in the West Bengali village of Naxalbari (hence the name of the movement). The uprising was led by former CPI-M member Charu Majumdar, founder of the Naxalites, and most of the peasants involved in the revolt belonged to the Santhal tribe. By 1975 the initial rebellion was put down. From that time until the early 2000s, the various Maoist groups became severely fragmented and had limited success in carrying out attacks against the Indian government. Over the past decade, however, the movement reorganized successfully under new leadership and has now come to pose a major threat to Indian political stability. The culmination of the rebirth of the movement came in 2004 when two of the largest Naxalite factions, the People's War Group and the Maoist Communist Centre, joined together to form the Communist Party of India (Maoist). By 2006 Prime Minister Manmohan Singh stated that Naxalites were "the single biggest internal security challenge ever faced by our country."[42]

The Naxalites became an important force in Bastar when they entered the area in the early 1980s and began mobilizing villagers around their economic grievances. Many of the earliest Naxalites came from the movement in Andhra Pradesh and they began a "Go to the Village" campaign in Bastar to enlist tribal support (Navlakha 2010). The two main groups operating there now are the CPI-ML and the People's War Group. Two of the main initial recruiting grounds for the Naxalites in Bastar were hostels and schools, especially special schools for adivasis.

Dantewada, the capital of the Bastar region, is today the deadliest area for Naxalite violence in India. According to figures from the WITS, Dantewada suffered 516 deaths and 472 injuries in Naxalite violence from 2005 to 2009. During this period, the three districts that compose the former Bastar State (with a total population of slightly more than two million people) experienced 1,171 casualties from Maoist violence, or a staggering 35 percent of the total number of casualties in India.

To further examine this brutal violence in the region, as well as to gain insight about the causes of the conflict, a number of interviews were conducted in Raipur, the capital of Chhattisgarh. First, respondents were asked about the composition of the modern Naxalite movement. A local newspaper editor summarized the situation as follows: "Only a small number of tribals are Naxalites, but the Naxalites are almost all tribals. They are mostly Scheduled Tribes. Scheduled Castes might be involved, but they are not the major part of the movement—it is mostly tribals. These groups have provided a fine hunting ground for the Naxals."[43] There are no precise figures on the composition of the various Naxalite groups in the region. A *Hindustan Times* piece on Chhattisgarh from 2005 notes that tribal groups are "considered the backbone of the ultra-left movement."[44] Another respondent from the Chhattisgarh Tribal Development Program confirmed this view: "They are all STs, but . . . the leaders of the movement are not actually from this region. They come from Andhra Pradesh, Bengal, or Delhi."[45]

Respondents were also asked about the causes of contemporary violence. Almost all of them were uniform in their explanation of the Naxalite conflict in the region. The aforementioned newspaper editor noted, "The points that the Naxalites make are valid. They talk about underdevelopment and poverty, and that is all valid. Everyone knows that development [projects have] filled the coffers of big business and the government."[46] A local Congress Party politician voiced a similar view: "It is about revenge. The main cause of the violence is that tribals are seeking revenge for the way they have been treated historically. Many historic injustices have occurred here in Chhattisgarh."[47] A Forest Department respondent commented, "Under-development is the main cause of the violence. If you go to Bastar, if you go talk to the police, you will see that. The adivasis here are quite backward economically."[48] A professor who taught at a local agricultural college added: "The Naxalites are mainly fighting against the police and the Forest Department. Those are the two main groups that they really hate. They want to control the forests without interference."[49]

Ultimately, the history of Bastar was similar to that of many British provinces. As in those territories, colonial administrators implemented policies in Bastar that discriminated against adivasis, who constituted the majority of the population. This led to a series of tribal rebellions and created the dominant fault line for ethnic conflict in the region. Contemporary interviews highlight that this pattern of ethnic violence based on tribal identities has not dissipated since independence. The failure of reform in Bastar has been a major contributor to the enduring violence in the region. Considering how little has changed from the colonial past, it is not surprising that today the name of the main Naxalite front organization in Bastar is Adivasi Kisan Mazdoor Sangathan, almost the exact name of Pravir Chandra's tribal organization formed in 1955.

One corollary of this historical argument—that Bastar was in many ways indistinguishable from a British province—is that the state should therefore experience lower levels of religious violence today. And it is true that contemporary Chhattisgarh experiences almost no communal violence. The Varshney-Wilkinson dataset records only thirteen casualties in Chhattisgarh over forty-five years, and none in the former Bastar State. But this is not unexpected, because only a minuscule percentage of the population (2 percent) is Muslim, so it is an extremely unlikely area for communal animosity in any case. This was also true for the colonial period, because Bastar did not experience any major communal riots during British rule. Nevertheless, it should be noted that British religious policies in Bastar, as elsewhere in provincial India, focused above all on the policy of neutrality.

The rajas of Bastar perceived themselves in religious terms, operating like princes throughout the rest of India. For example, as late as 1961 Pravir Chandra "wanted to form a new Chamber of Princes which would work for the establishment of a Hindu State in India."[50] During the colonial period, British administrators also worried repeatedly about a "small clique of influential Hindus in Jagdalpur."[51] Perhaps in response to this fear, when the British came to control the state they appointed Muslims to high positions within the Bastar administration. As noted earlier, the British had been appointing Englishmen as diwans—a fact that highlights the exceptional level of control they had in Bastar. But in the early twentieth century they appointed two Muslims to the position: Khan Bahadur Mahdi Hassan and Khan Bahadur Hafix Walayatulah.[52] Even in Bastar, a state where Muslims had almost no representation at all in the local population, they were appointed to senior positions within the colonial administration.

Summary

This book presents the central argument that the colonial period created long-term patterns of ethnic violence in contemporary India. Due to different conceptualizations of ethnic politics, former British provinces today experience more caste and tribal violence whereas former princely states experience more religious violence. Chapters 2 and 3 offer evidence for this pattern across the modern states of Rajasthan and Kerala. This chapter has considered the major case that deviates from this historical theory: the tiny Hindu kingdom of Bastar, which is the foremost battleground for Naxalite conflict in India today.

The long history of tribal conflict in Bastar began with an enormous amount of British interference in the state—a level of interference that was different from that in any other princely state in India. Bastar was essentially a British province, and the cause of tribal conflict in the kingdom was akin to the causes of tribal conflict in any other province. British administrators enforced a number of discriminatory policies against the tribes of Bastar, including reserving forests, implementing crushing new taxes, and displacing adivasis from their land, all of which led to two rebellions during the colonial period. These policies were embraced, even exacerbated, by the postindependence Congress Party that came to control the area, leading to another two postcolonial rebellions, as well as the subsequent rise of the Naxalite movement. Most important, the tiny state of Bastar highlights that where British administrators governed, tribal rebellion ultimately followed.

CHAPTER 5

Patterns of Ethnic Violence Across Contemporary India

All we want is our hills.

—*Orissa adivasi, to anthropologist Verrier Elwin*[1]

This book began in Chapter 1 by laying out an historical theory of ethnic conflict in India, and Chapters 2 to 4 then detailed extensive archival and interview evidence for this argument gathered from five cases drawn from various regions of the country. Controlled historical comparisons from the northern state of Rajasthan and the southern state of Kerala highlight that former British provinces such as Ajmer and Malabar have historically experienced significant caste and tribal violence, whereas former princely states such as Jaipur and Travancore have experienced higher levels of religious conflict. The previous chapter explained the key deviant case for this theory: the tiny Hindu kingdom of Bastar, the deadliest battleground for tribal conflict in India.

Despite detailed qualitative evidence for the central theory of this book, five cases may nevertheless give a false impression of broader trends occurring across a country as a whole, especially a country as enormous and diverse as India. In order to provide an additional test of this theory, this chapter details the results of a quantitative analysis of ethnic conflict patterns across 589 contemporary Indian districts.[2] Using multiple methods can offer a more triangulated and convincing account of Indian ethnic conflict. The results of this analysis provide additional evidence that ethnic violence patterns in the country originate from the colonial period: former British districts experience more contemporary caste and tribal conflict, but former princely districts experience more religious violence.

Data Sources on Ethnic Conflict in India

One of the major problems confronting scholars of ethnic conflict in India (and throughout the developing world) is a broad variety of data limitations and insufficiencies. For example, the standard metric for caste and tribal violence in India is "SCST crimes," a measure compiled by the Ministry of Home Affairs. These data and their shortcomings were discussed in Chapter 2. Both reporting bias (the failure of the police to investigate and register crimes) and enforcement bias (variation among states and their enforcement of SCST legal protections) seriously undermine the value of these data. Compiling figures on religious violence is even more difficult. Most important, the Indian government does not make publicly available information about communal riots at the district level. As the fieldwork for this book was being conducted, governments in Rajasthan and Kerala refused to provide district-level figures.[3]

This chapter employs two strategies in order to counteract these data problems. First, it draws on a new dataset[4] of caste and tribal violence in contemporary India that is based on information from the Worldwide Incidents Tracking System (WITS) (Wigle 2010). Second, this chapter also utilizes an existing (and widely cited) dataset on Hindu-Muslim riots compiled by Ashutosh Varshney and Steven Wilkinson (2006).

The WITS conflict data were created during the decade from 2004 to 2012 by the US government's National Counterterrorism Center. The database aggregates national and international press reports of violence throughout the world. The specific kinds of events recorded in the WITS database include a range of armed conflict such as terrorism, arson, assassinations, and bombings. Each incident of violence is geocoded, so events were retrieved that could be matched to specific states and districts within India. In terms of caste and tribal violence, the WITS data were used for information about the Naxalite movement, discussed in the previous chapter. Most of the Naxalite rebels are adivasis and low castes; therefore, data on the Naxalite conflict is a good proxy for contemporary caste and tribal violence in India. Though Naxalism is a distinct subset of caste and tribal conflict, it is the most threatening form of this type of violence. Furthermore, in the absence of better data on nationwide caste atrocities, Naxalite violence stands as the best alternative. The resulting dataset is a comprehensive account of caste and tribal violence in India from 2005 to 2009.

The Varshney-Wilkinson dataset focuses on Hindu-Muslim riots across India from 1950 to 1995. Because the Indian government does not make information about communal riots readily available to researchers, Varshney and Wilkinson carefully constructed a catalogue of riots from *Times of India* (Bombay) newspaper reports covering almost the first five decades of post-colonial India. This dataset was then used in their work (Varshney 2002; Wilkinson 2004) as well as in subsequent studies of communal violence (Bohlken and Sergenti 2010).

The Statistical Models

The major dependent variables in the quantitative analysis are broken down into two overarching categories: those pertaining to caste and tribal violence (WITS data), and those pertaining to religious violence (Varshney-Wilkinson dataset). All of the dependent variables in both datasets are count (or event) variables that record the number of attacks, deaths, or injuries. Therefore, a negative binomial regression model was ideal for this analysis.[5] There are two main reasons for using this particular model rather than alternatives.[6] First, the distribution of events count data is not linear, so traditional linear models are inappropriate. Second, the negative binomial model includes a dispersion parameter (unlike Poisson models), which is appropriate here because the dependent variables in this analysis are highly overdispersed; some districts in India have had hundreds of deaths from caste or religious violence whereas others have had none.

Contemporary ethnic conflict patterns are examined at the district level of analysis. Districts were chosen for a number of reasons. A state-level analysis would be problematic because present-day state boundaries have changed, often considerably, from the colonial period. Whereas some colonial and contemporary state boundaries match up almost perfectly, others do not. The colonial territory of Rajputana, for example, has roughly the same borders as the present-day state of Rajasthan, but the princely state of Hyderabad is now strewn across the modern states of Andhra Pradesh, Telangana, Karnataka, and Maharashtra. British rulers, however, placed an importance on district-level administration, and this has persisted into modern times. Paul Brass (1994: 138) has noted that "the entire system of British district administration, which . . . concentrated authority at the district level . . . was retained virtually intact, particularly the central importance of the District Magistrate and the district courts and the police." Princely rulers also often divided their states into districts, adopting this administrative model from

British India. Therefore, using districts as the level of analysis for the quantitative study is most appropriate for matching colonial and postcolonial boundaries. Also, in terms of coding, it was relatively easy to match these districts because many of their names did not change after independence.

This district-level strategy, however, was not without its own complications. The number of districts in India has expanded considerably since independence. By 1971 there were 356, and as of this writing there are well over 600. Because most of the control variables for this study are taken from the 2001 census, the list of 2001 districts was used. A total of 589 districts were included in the analysis; several Union Territory districts (small administrative regions under the control of the central government) were excluded.[7] This study therefore includes almost every area of the country instead of simply selecting a number of states or a random or representative subset of districts from each state. This approach can ultimately provide a more complete picture of ethnic violence throughout India.

All of the dependent variables in the subsequent regression analyses record the total number of *casualties,* which is defined as combined deaths and injuries. This specific measure was chosen rather than the number of attacks, for example, for a few reasons. In some districts a number of attacks occurred in which there was actually very little violence (deaths or injuries). These incidents might officially be recorded as riots but they were mostly benign. More important, the total number of casualties from conflict more accurately and comprehensively reflects the human suffering that occurs during ethnic violence.

The key independent variable of interest in these analyses is colonial rule—specifically, the type of colonial rule. Every district in India was coded as having belonged to either a British province or a princely state. The historical information used for this coding process came from a variety of sources: the *Imperial Gazetteer of India,* various District Gazetteers, and district websites maintained by the Indian government.[8] Two measures of the independent variable were constructed. The main measure is a dummy variable for each district (coded 1 if a contemporary district was a former British territory).[9] Then, a second variable coded the number of years each territory was under the control of the British (all princely state values were 0). This second variable can help capture some of the heterogeneity of British provinces: the earliest areas came under direct rule in the seventeenth century (Bombay) whereas other provinces were annexed nearly two hundred years later.

Colonialism and Contemporary Caste and Tribal Violence

The first regression analyses pertain to contemporary caste and tribal violence in India—specifically, the Naxalite movement. Several district-level control variables were included in the analysis to account for alternative explanations for caste and tribal violence.[10] Because the Naxalite conflict can be described as an ethnic (adivasi) insurgency, a number of insights were incorporated from the well-known Fearon and Laitin (2003) study of ethnicity and civil wars around the world from 1945 to 1999.[11]

First, a log of the population of each district, compiled from the Indian census, was coded. Districts with larger populations will presumably have higher levels of conflict because rebels will be more difficult to defeat in populous areas. A log of the area of each district, taken from the census, was recorded to account for the size of a state. A third variable that measures the percentage of each district's SCST population, compiled from the census, was also coded. SCs and STs are the two main groups engaged in Naxalite conflict, so districts with larger SCST populations may be more prone to violence.

The fourth and fifth variables deal with geographical factors. The fourth control variable measures the percentage of the district population that lives in designated rural areas, compiled from the census. Most caste and tribal violence in contemporary India occurs in the countryside. A fifth variable was included to account for forest cover, because rough terrain is often a factor presumed to aid rebels in fighting against the state (Kocher 2004; Scott 2009). This variable measures the percentage of each district covered by forest, compiled from IndiaStat.[12] This is a key variable for the Naxalite conflict because throughout eastern India battles often occur in heavily forested areas.

The sixth through eighth variables deal with broad socioeconomic explanations for violence. Because insurgencies could be caused by poverty or lack of socioeconomic development, these variables may be correlated with violence. The sixth variable accounts for the argument that the Naxalite movement is driven by the natural resources of a region (Miklian and Carney 2010). A dummy variable for whether or not a district contains mining operations was coded, compiled from IndiaStat. Specifically, this variable records the presence of coal, iron ore, or bauxite mining. The seventh variable is the literacy rate (percentage) per district, compiled from IndiaStat. The eighth and final variable is a measure of poverty: the percentage of households per district who claim no economic assets, compiled from IndiaStat. Examples of economic assets include televisions, radios, cars, and access to banking.

Descriptive statistics for all variables are displayed in Table 5.1. The results of the first set of regression analyses are displayed in Table 5.2. The first two models are basic regressions that use only two control variables: population and area. The third and fourth models include the full battery of controls. The dependent variable in all models is Naxalite casualties—the total number of individuals killed and injured in Naxalite attacks per district from 2005 to 2009 (the data are cross-sectional but not time-series). All of the regression models were run using robust standard errors clustered by state to account for potential heteroscedasticity.

The results show that British rule across all models correlates positively and significantly with the number of casualties from Naxalite attacks. Determining the substantive effects of variables (that is, interpreting the coefficient) is

TABLE 5.1.
Descriptive Statistics.

Variables	Obs.	Mean	Std. Dev.	Min.	Max.
Dependent Variables					
Caste/Tribal Violence Casualties	589	5.657046	43.52806	0	988
Hindu-Muslim Riot Casualties	589	13.00679	113.7783	0	2429
Independent Variables					
Province	583	0.6638079	0.4728112	0	1
Years British	578	92.09343	71.79932	0	286
Control Variables					
Population (Log)	579	14.03742	0.9692225	10.41103	16.00541
Area (Log)	573	8.262106	0.9857156	2.197225	11.70212
% SCST	576	33.88229	22.53614	0.7038926	98.4724
% Muslim	569	11.64926	15.31336	0.0513504	98.49425
% Rural	580	76.61807	19.50783	0	100
% Forested	574	21.99394	24.39197	0	95.66
Coastal Districts	589	0.1154499	0.3198358	0	1
Mining Activity	588	0.1513605	0.3587051	0	1
Literacy Rate	578	63.90348	12.75276	30.17	96.51
% No Assets	554	0.3714494	0.1562206	0.0577348	0.7736033
Rainfall (Log)	486	6.925094	.600822	5.065754	8.844961

TABLE 5.2.
Colonialism and Caste/Tribal Violence Casualties, 2005 to 2009.

	Model 1	Model 2	Model 3	Model 4
Province	1.404*		0.871**	
	(0.723)		(0.388)	
Years British		0.0154***		0.00843***
		(0.00431)		(0.00324)
Population (Log)	−0.0568	−0.404	2.766***	2.659***
	(0.382)	(0.450)	(0.549)	(0.596)
Area (Log)	1.678***	2.179***	−0.373	−0.243
	(0.389)	(0.435)	(0.533)	(0.523)
% SCST			0.0102	0.0178
			(0.0215)	(0.0206)
% Rural			0.0916***	0.0890***
			(0.0194)	(0.0197)
% Forested			0.0744**	0.0751***
			(0.0295)	(0.0289)
Mining Activity			0.828	0.691
			(0.529)	(0.513)
Literacy Rate			−0.0181	−0.0133
			(0.0599)	(0.0503)
% No Assets			4.123	3.749
			(5.970)	(5.208)
Constant	−13.03***	−13.10***	−46.32***	−46.34***
	(4.795)	(4.896)	(7.095)	(6.949)
Lnalpha				
_cons	3.177***	3.068***	2.785***	2.728***
	(0.395)	(0.390)	(0.405)	(0.398)
Observations	564	555	521	512

Negative Binomial Regressions
Robust Standard Errors in Parentheses, Clustered by State
* $p<0.1$, ** $p<0.05$, *** $p<0.01$

not straightforward in a negative binomial model. Therefore, the "percent change coefficient" of all independent variables was calculated.[13] Put in substantive terms, Model 1 in Table 5.2 shows that a former province experiences *93 percent more Naxalite casualties* than a former princely state, whereas Model 3 shows that a former province experiences *51 percent more Naxalite casualties* than a former princely state, holding all other variables constant. These results provide strong evidence for a link between British rule and contemporary caste and tribal violence.

Several other factors also play a role in producing Naxalite conflict. The existence of large populations is correlated with violence. More important, a variety of geographical factors matter; for example, rural districts with forest cover are especially prone to Naxalite violence. These results are not surprising and they reinforce a number of existing studies that highlight similar causes for Naxalism in South Asia (Bohara, Mitchell, and Nepali 2006; Joshi and Mason 2008; Do and Iyer 2010).

Colonialism and Contemporary Religious Violence

The second major component of the quantitative study deals with the effect of colonialism on contemporary religious violence. The only existing comparison of British and princely areas and communal conflict comes from Ian Copland (1998), whose work was discussed in Chapter 1. Copland finds that if you take into account population disparities, British India during the period from 1920 to 1940 experienced between 15 to 18 times more violence than princely India. The following analysis considers the postcolonial period but includes a host of additional variables not covered in Copland's work that may affect violence outcomes.

The major symbol of communal bloodshed in India is Hindu-Muslim riots. The next set of regression analyses were conducted using the Varshney-Wilkinson dataset of Hindu-Muslim riots across India from 1950 to 1995. However, the analysis here is restricted to the period from 1990 to 1995. This is done because all of the pertinent control variables collected are from 2001, whereas some of the major controls do not exist for the 1950s or 1960s. For example, poverty is considered a major cause of Hindu-Muslim violence, but district-level poverty measures are not available for any period prior to 2001. Using conflict data from 1990 to 1995, however, still covers one of the most important periods of communal politics in India—the run-up to and aftermath of the Babri Masjid demolition, which occurred in 1992.

A number of control variables were carried over from the previous analysis. A log of the population and a log of the area of a district were included. A third variable measures the percentage of the district population that is Muslim. There are a number of areas in India where the Muslim population is minuscule (like the Bastar districts) and violence would be unlikely in these regions. Also included is the percentage of a district that is rural, which should be negatively related to religious conflict because communal violence tends to be concentrated in urban areas. Including this variable can also account for the argument that ethnic violence patterns in India are purely geographic: caste and tribal violence are concentrated in rural areas, religious violence is concentrated in urban areas.

The fifth through seventh variables account for socioeconomic explanations of communal violence. For example, Anjali Thomas Bohlken and Ernest Sergenti (2010) highlight the potential importance of economic factors by showing that a 1 percent increase in the growth rate of a state reduces the likelihood of a Hindu-Muslim riot by more than 5 percent. The literacy rate and the percentage of households with no assets are therefore used again in these regressions. One final control for coastal districts (dummy variable) is included. This is added in order to consider Saumitra Jha's (2013) recent argument that medieval port cities created economic links between Hindus and Muslims that reduced the likelihood of violence over the long term. The results of this analysis are displayed in Table 5.3. The dependent variable in all models is Hindu-Muslim riot casualties—the number of individuals killed and injured in Hindu-Muslim riots per district from 1990 to 1995.

British rule is now negatively and significantly correlated with contemporary Hindu-Muslim violence across all models. Models 5 and 6 are basic models that use only population and area as controls, whereas Models 7 and 8 include the full battery of controls. Put in substantive terms, Model 5 shows that a former princely state experiences *61 percent more Hindu-Muslim riot casualties* than a former province, and Model 7 shows that a former princely state experiences *92 percent more Hindu-Muslim riot casualties* than a former province, holding all other variables constant.

These results are intriguing for a number of reasons. The three most violent cities in the dataset for Hindu-Muslim violence from 1990 to 1995 are all British cities: Bombay, Surat, and Ahmedabad. The most violent princely city (fourth overall) is Bhopal. Perhaps most important, these results highlight the danger of looking only at absolute figures for Hindu-Muslim violence. When all districts are included with a variety of controls, former provinces actually experience less Hindu-Muslim violence than former princely states in contemporary India, a result starkly at odds with the conventional wisdom about British rule and its effect on communal violence.

A number of alternative factors also matter in Models 5 through 8. The presence of large Muslim populations is positively correlated with violence.

TABLE 5.3.
Colonialism and Hindu–Muslim Riot Casualties, 1990 to 1995.

	Model 5	Model 6	Model 7	Model 8
Province	−0.952** (0.441)		−2.491*** (0.538)	
Years British		−0.00568* (0.00315)		−0.0171*** (0.00364)
Population (Log)	2.685*** (0.429)	2.700*** (0.428)	3.218*** (0.535)	3.298*** (0.575)
Area (Log)	−1.369*** (0.289)	−1.385*** (0.289)	−0.992** (0.483)	−1.186** (0.509)
% Muslim			0.102* (0.0582)	0.0923 (0.0606)
% Rural			−0.0196 (0.0208)	−0.0256 (0.0206)
Literacy Rate			0.0540 (0.0426)	0.0411 (0.0434)
% No Assets			1.399 (1.573)	1.612 (1.764)
Coastal Districts			1.380 (0.843)	1.764** (0.897)
Constant	−24.85*** (4.491)	−25.01*** (4.478)	−38.99*** (9.444)	−37.26*** (9.760)
Lnalpha				
_cons	3.376*** (0.153)	3.369*** (0.157)	3.138*** (0.171)	3.137*** (0.176)
Observations	564	555	518	509

Negative Binomial Regressions
Robust Standard Errors in Parentheses, Clustered by State
* p<0.1, ** p<0.05, *** p<0.01

Rural areas experience less conflict, which is not surprising. One surprising result from these models, however, has to do with the presence of coastal districts. This variable is positively correlated to Hindu-Muslim riots, suggesting that areas near the coast are prone to violence.

Endogeneity: How British India Became British India

The major underlying problem with these analyses is endogeneity (Geddes 1990; Collier and Mahoney 1996). That is to say, are patterns of ethnic violence in the country a product of colonial rule or were they already established prior to colonialism? This issue is tied together with the question of how the British (nonrandomly) selected areas of India for annexation (Iyer 2010). If they selected areas that already had high levels of caste and tribal violence, for instance, then colonial rule is not an important variable in explaining these conflict outcomes.

At the outset, the qualitative work in Chapters 2 through 4 made clear that the preexisting level of ethnic violence in a region did not matter to British administrators when considering its annexation. There is no historical evidence that they had a master plan to annex either violent or peaceful regions, and there are plenty of examples of both kinds of territories coming under their control.[14] Rather, the main selection criterion for annexation was fertile land. Therefore, the British were not selecting cases on the specific dependent variable of interest: ethnic violence.

It is still possible, though, that the actual selection factor—the availability of productive land—might in some way be related to ethnic violence. As a hypothetical example, productive land may have been heavily rack-rented, meaning that levels of caste violence in these regions may have already been high prior to British conquest. However, the relationship between the availability of productive land and caste violence is not obvious—it is difficult, based on the value of land, to infer anything concrete about caste relations in a given area.[15] Ultimately, the British selection of areas for annexation does not appear to be directly related to ethnic violence, nor does the real selection factor (fertile land) indirectly influence ethnic violence outcomes. In general, the reasoning behind the British annexation of a territory seems divorced from the causes of ethnic conflict.

The most common way to deal with endogeneity problems in quantitative models is through the use of an instrumental variable analysis.[16] A classic instrument for colonial expansion is rainfall: the British were attempting to control fertile land where rainfall was plentiful. Dry, barren areas (such as Rajputana), by contrast, were not of interest to colonial rulers. The key to using an instrumental variable analysis, however, is justifying the "exclusion restriction"—that is, ensuring that the instrument is not related to the dependent variable (ethnic conflict). It is unlikely that rainfall is related to Hindu-Muslim riots, which occur overwhelmingly in cities and rarely have to do with water (or agricultural issues). Therefore, rainfall is a good instrument for the study of communal violence (detailed shortly). However, rainfall could be related to contemporary Naxalite violence because these adivasi rebels want to control fertile land. Therefore, an instrumental variable analysis cannot be used for the study of caste and tribal violence.

To consider the endogeneity problem for Naxalite violence, an alternative strategy of nearest neighbor propensity score matching was utilized.[17] This strategy is a method of determining the propensity of observations to be treated on the basis of observed covariates, and then matching treatment and control cases with the closest propensity scores to create a balanced set of comparable observations. In this case, the observations are districts and the treatment is colonial rule. Princely states were matched with British provinces annexed prior to the Doctrine of Lapse in 1848. The vast majority (95 percent) of provinces were annexed prior to this period, and the logic of expansion radically altered from 1848 to 1856, leading up to the Rebellion of 1857.

The analysis used the following control variables to condition the match: the area of a district, the percentage of its population that is SCST, the percentage of the district that is forested, the presence of mining activity, and the percentage of households with no assets. The default model for propensity score matching is logit, and the dependent variable is a dummy that codes districts with Naxalite casualties above or below the all-Indian mean (5.65 casualties). The results of the matching analysis are detailed in Table 5.4.

The results indicate that in the matched sample, British areas annexed before 1848 are 9.5 percent more likely to experience Naxalite casualties greater than the mean in India, which is a significant effect. A matching design, however, does not solve the problem of endogeneity because cases can be matched only on observable covariates (Miller 2013: 8–9). There is still the possibility of an unobserved factor driving the results. Therefore, a sensitivity test was conducted (Becker and Caliendo 2007) using Rosenbaum's (2002) criteria for determining the potential strength of unobservable ef-

TABLE 5.4.

Matching Analysis, Colonialism and Caste/Tribal Violence, 2005 to 2009.

	Likelihood of Experiencing Maoist Casualties > Mean (5.65)		
Sample	Province (pre-1848)	Princely State	Difference
Unmatched	.10915493	.092741935	.016412994
Matched	.10915493	.014084507	.095070423***

Propensity Score Matching, Logistic Treatment Model

* p<0.1, ** p<0.05, *** p<0.01

fects.[18] The results indicate that an unobserved variable would have to make British areas 50 percent more likely than princely states to experience more than the mean number of Naxalite casualties in order to eliminate statistical significance (that is, the results would then no longer be significant at the 95 percent level). Because the analysis in Table 5.4 already paired treatment and control cases on a number of key covariates, it is unlikely that some unobserved variable has an effect this strong.

An instrumental variable analysis was used to consider the endogeneity problem for Hindu-Muslim violence. The results are displayed in Table 5.5. A variable was coded for the log of the average millimeters of rainfall per district from 2004 to 2009. This instrument justifies the exclusion restriction for communal violence because rainfall is unlikely to be correlated with riots. Because the negative binomial model cannot be used for an

TABLE 5.5.

Instrumental Variable Analysis of Hindu–Muslim Riot Casualties, 1990 to 1995.

Variables	Model 9	Model 10
Province	−1.275* (0.723)	
Years British		−0.00993* (0.00569)
Population (Log)	0.687*** (0.227)	0.794*** (0.205)
Area (Log)	−0.235 (0.168)	−0.330 (0.203)
% Muslim	0.0167** (0.00769)	0.0159** (0.00682)
% Rural	−0.00951 (0.00605)	−0.00975 (0.00619)
Literacy Rate	0.0142 (0.0112)	0.00948 (0.0104)
% No Assets	−0.524 (0.937)	−0.394 (0.829)
Coastal Districts	0.165 (0.215)	0.378 (0.301)
Constant	−8.591** (3.653)	−9.009*** (3.082)
Observations	438	434

IV Probit Regressions using Rainfall

Robust Standard Errors in Parentheses, Clustered by State

* $p<0.1$, ** $p<0.05$, *** $p<0.01$

instrumental variable regression, the analysis was run using an instrumental variable probit model. The dependent variable was a dummy coded 1 if Hindu-Muslim riot casualties per district exceeded the mean casualty rate of 13.00.

British rule is still negatively and significantly correlated with riot casualties in Models 9 and 10, although only at the 90 percent level. The rainfall variable is strongly correlated with British rule (at the 99 percent level) in both first-stage regression models, suggesting that it is in fact a good predictor of colonial expansion in India.[19]

Both of these robustness checks help in minimizing the endogeneity problem inherent in this study. They both also show that even when taking into account the critical fact that the British were nonrandomly annexing territory in India, the effect of the colonial period is strong in producing modern violence patterns. British rule promoted caste and tribal violence in the form of the Naxalite insurgency, but it reduced the long-term likelihood of Hindu-Muslim conflict.

Summary

Over the past three chapters, qualitative case studies from northern, southern, and eastern India showcased that British rule engendered caste and tribal violence whereas the rule of native kings promoted religious conflict. Cases from Rajasthan, Kerala, and Chhattisgarh all highlight the role that bifurcated colonialism played in producing contemporary patterns of ethnic violence. This chapter builds on this qualitative work to test this historical theory of ethnic conflict in India across the entire country. It rigorously analyzed the impact of colonialism on modern ethnic conflict using a quantitative study of 589 Indian districts. This statistical analysis utilized a wide variety of data sources and a number of regression models. The results provide further evidence for the primary argument of this book.

British colonialism promoted higher levels of contemporary caste and tribal violence throughout India. Using the Naxalite insurgency as the main proxy for this kind of violence, this chapter shows that being a former British province considerably increased casualties from Naxalite attacks. These results were highly significant even when controlling for a number of alternative explanations. Conversely, another set of regression results highlighted that princely rule promoted contemporary religious violence. While again controlling for a number of alternative explanations, the analysis showed that being a former princely state considerably increased Hindu-Muslim riot casualties. Both of these results were sensitive to robustness checks: a matching design and an instrumental variable analysis.

This clear dichotomy in violence outcomes highlights that the legacies of colonial rule play a key and underaddressed role in explicating why ethnic conflicts in India revolve around one identity rather than another. The five case studies in Chapters 2 through 4 highlight the role of colonialism in producing patterns of ethnic violence, but the analysis here covers 589 districts. In every region, bifurcated colonial rule had an important long-term effect on conditioning and structuring violence outcomes. On the one hand, British policies that emphasized caste—benefiting high castes while discriminating against low castes and tribals—led ultimately to more insurgency in the countryside. However, British religious neutrality and protective policies for Muslims decreased communal conflict over the long term. On the other hand, the policies of princely rulers that emphasized religion—benefiting coreligionists while discriminating against non-coreligionists—increased communalism in the native states. But the protective policies of princely rulers toward low castes and adivasis minimized the Naxalite movement in these territories.

CHAPTER 6

The Indian Model of Colonialism

Surely the oddest political set-up that the world has ever seen.

—*Francis Wylie, Political Advisor to the Viceroy,*
on bifurcated colonialism in India, 1970[1]

The loss of Britain's New World territories in the late eighteenth century signaled the end of the "First British Empire," but the subsequent conquest of India formed the beginnings of a "Second British Empire," one based largely in the east (Armitage 2000; Marshall 2005). In the decades after the Rebellion of 1857, British administrators came to realize the value of utilizing both direct and indirect rule in a colony—what they began calling the "Indian model" of colonialism. Using India as a foundation, the British expanded their power throughout Asia and Africa in the late nineteenth and early twentieth centuries, exporting variations of this Indian model to several new colonies located on the periphery of the Indian Ocean. Drawing on the Indian case, this chapter offers a preliminary investigation of ethnic politics and conflict in three colonial states heavily influenced by the British Raj: Burma, Malaya, and Nigeria.

Creating an Indian Model

British power was relentlessly expanding across India in the early nineteenth century. An ever-increasing number of native states were brought under the control of the British East India Company, most controversially during the period when Lord Dalhousie's Doctrine of Lapse was in effect. The whole country would most likely have been conquered had a number of sepoys and native rulers not banded together and launched a major uprising against colonial rule (Copland 2002: 15). Any grand British dreams of controlling the entire subcontinent abruptly ended with the Rebellion of 1857.

Although the uprising failed, British authorities were afterward forced to abandon the policy of annexing princely states, and the haphazard boundaries between British and princely India became fixed for the rest of the colonial period. More than six hundred native states continued to exist, and one-fourth of the country's population resided in these territories. This hybrid model of colonialism was unique[2] among British colonies because before India most of them had been ruled directly (Lange 2009: 31).

The Rebellion extinguished British plans for the complete control of India, but over the next several decades administrators slowly came to realize that the resulting system of bifurcated rule had a number of benefits that were hardly foreseeable during the darkest days of the uprising. Administrators in time came to champion this new Indian model of colonialism as highly advantageous for the British government. There were a few key reasons for its popularity, which were discussed in Chapter 1 but are worth mentioning again here.

Most important, using indirect rule lowered the chances of rebellion against colonialism. The British experience in India demonstrated that princes, if kept happy, would not unite and attempt to overthrow the colonial state. After 1857, princes were devolved substantial internal autonomy, and the British began to think of them not as an obstacle to colonialism but as an important tool for its continuation (Hutchins 1967; Fisher 1991). Keeping native elites in power provided them with a form of legitimacy that European officials did not have. As Sir John Malcolm, the Governor of Bombay, put it, "If we made all India into Zillahs [British districts] it was not in the nature of things that our Empire should last fifty years; but that if we could keep up a number of native states without political power, but as royal instruments, we should exist in India as long as our naval supremacy was maintained."[3]

Bifurcated rule was also cheap. Rather than investing heavily in controlling an entire colony (especially India, with its hundreds of millions of inhabitants), the British were able to rule with a minimal drain on their treasury. They relied on native authorities to share in the burden of governing: princely rulers were responsible for financing their states, and they paid hefty tributes to the British for their autonomy. Moreover, the areas that came under direct colonial control were usually fertile (which assisted commercial exploitation), whereas the hinterland was left under the discretion of native elites.

Finally, many colonial states, especially India and more generally those in Asia and Africa, had sweltering climates, rough terrain, and tropical diseases, and for all these reasons they were not easily inhabitable by Western settlers (Acemoglu, Johnson, and Robinson 2001). Therefore, making large investments in manpower in these kinds of colonies was impractical and risky.

Chapters 2 through 5 highlight that bifurcated colonialism had a major effect on patterns of ethnic violence across contemporary India. But this model also had an impact outside the subcontinent. With India firmly under their control by the late nineteenth century, British administrators gained access to the entire Indian Ocean region. By controlling these vast waters, they opened up a massive new set of markets and commercial opportunities (Bose 2006). Without India, British expansion into a number of states could not have occurred. In 1911 the *Times* explained to the British public the singular importance of the Raj: "India stands right across the greatest highway in the world; it is the centre of the East. Through its possession we secured our great predominance in Eastern trade, and from its shores we extended our interests to Australasia, the Malay peninsula, the Pacific Islands, and the Chinese coast. . . . It is, therefore, in a special and peculiar sense the centre of Imperial defence" (*Times* 1911: 3).

After the British conquered India, they did turn their ambitions eastward toward Southeast Asia—but also westward in the "Scramble for Africa," which occurred at the end of the nineteenth century. Three states colonized by the British during this period of expansion were Burma, Malaya, and Nigeria. Colonial officials had learned an important lesson from the Indian experience that they would take abroad with them into these new states: incorporating traditional rulers[4] was a necessary component in the process of state-building and governing (Fisher 1991; Mamdani 1996; Metcalf 2007). The importance of this lesson only intensified during the twentieth century as cracks appeared in British imperial power amid the Great Depression and two world wars. The application of the Indian model to new colonies abroad was led by British administrators who had served in India, as well as by thousands of Indian bureaucrats and workers themselves. For example, Lord Lugard, considered the father of indirect rule in Nigeria, was born in India, served in a number of South Asian military campaigns, and witnessed bifurcated colonial rule in practice.

There are some important caveats to note, however, before considering how the Indian model influenced other British states in Asia and Africa.

The most pressing concern is the problem of conceptual stretching (Sartori 1970). The direct-indirect rule distinction, for example, has an entirely different connotation in African historiography. There the comparison has generally been between French (direct) and British (indirect) styles of colonialism (Asiwaju 1970). Along these lines, indirect rule by the native princes of the subcontinent may bear no actual resemblance to native rule by chiefs in Africa. It should not be assumed that traditional rulers in Burma, Malaya, and Nigeria had the same level of internal autonomy as the Indian princes (discussed later in the chapter). When the Indian model was exported to a new British colony, it was never implemented wholesale. On the contrary, local histories, the particular constellation of ethnic groups in a state, and a number of other factors ultimately determined British policy. In the ensuing sections of this chapter, therefore, the similarities and differences between India and the style of colonialism in other cases are detailed in order to clearly bound the comparison.

Second, the expectation in examining additional cases is not that patterns of ethnic violence will exactly mirror such violence in India (although there were in fact some very clear similarities). For instance, tribal violence may not always be heightened in former areas of British direct rule. There was naturally a high degree of variation in the way the British colonized different territories across their vast empire. The main expectation is only that because the Indian model was exported to these colonies, there will be some discernible pattern of ethnic violence across directly and indirectly ruled areas.

A final and related issue has to do with the data on ethnic violence in these three countries. In researching Indian ethnic conflict, this book utilized a number of data sets; some were compiled personally while others were collected by different scholars. But the information here about patterns of ethnic violence in Burma, Malaya, and Nigeria are drawn from secondary sources. It is therefore not possible to calculate the per capita violence figures that would be necessary to make an adequate comparison across British and native areas. The analysis that follows should therefore be considered more suggestive than definitive. More research and data collection on these states, however, could rigorously test the argument that the exporting of the Indian model created disparate patterns of ethnic violence abroad.

Despite the risk of extending the analysis too far, there is still an alluring comparison to be made between India and other cases across Asia and Africa. In the broadest sense, British officials during the late nineteenth century shared power with native rulers in a number of new colonies, just as they had shared it with the princes in India. It began with the princes in India, then continued in Burma with the *sawbwa*,[5] in Malaya with the sultans, and in Nigeria with the emirs.

Ethnic Conflict in Burma

In the immediate precolonial era, most of Burma was ruled under the Konbaung dynasty. In the course of the first half of the nineteenth century, this kingdom fought and lost three wars with an expanding British Empire. The First Anglo-Burmese War began in 1824, after which the British received a number of new territories on the western front of Burma. The Second Anglo-Burmese War occurred in 1852, when the British annexed the fertile Lower Irrawaddy Delta, or what is known as Lower Burma. The Third Anglo-Burmese War began in 1885, after which the remainder of the country came under British control. The last ruler of the Konbaung dynasty, King Thibaw, was exiled in 1885 (Lieberman 1984; Taylor 2009). From 1886 until 1937, Burma was officially a province of the British Raj, and therefore shared several similarities with India.

Like the British Raj in India, Burma experienced a bifurcated model of colonialism (Lange, Mahoney, and vom Hau 2006: 1430). Roughly two-thirds of the state and the vast majority of its population lived under the rule of British administrators. The rest were governed by native rulers. The areas that constituted the former (sometimes known as Ministerial Burma) included the Arakan, Irrawaddy, Pegu, and Tenasserim Divisions. Native Burma (also known as the Scheduled or Frontier Areas) consisted of the Chin Hills, Kachin State, and Shan States. Map 6.1 shows some of these divisions between British and native Burma (shaded areas depict high elevation and cover most of native Burma).

The British, much as they had in India, directly controlled the fertile areas of Burma, such as the Irrawaddy plains. Native Burma was generally considered to constitute less agriculturally productive land (Stevenson 1945: 2; Brown 1994: 41). A final similarity with India was that the native rulers of Burma had high levels of internal autonomy (Lintner 1984: 405). Henry Dodwell (1932: 446) notes about the sawbwa, for example, that "major chieftains in the Shan States retain powers of life and death, and administer their native customary law, not the English codes." This internal

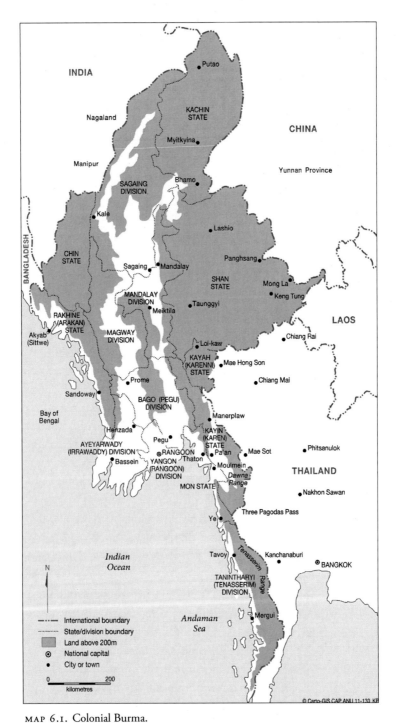

MAP 6.1. Colonial Burma.

SOURCE: Used with the permission of CartoGIS of the Australian National University.

autonomy was due in part to the fact that native areas in Burma were very remote and difficult for the British to control. Even precolonial rulers exercised little sovereignty over these regions (Selth 1986: 486).

During the colonial period, Burma was a highly plural society, consisting of a variety of ethnic groups. The dominant group was Burmans, a term distinct from *Burmese,* which refers to a national identity. There were also a number of ethnic minority groups such as Chins, Kachins, and Karens.[6] The majority of the population spoke Burmese, and close to 90 percent were Buddhist. These two identities—Burman and Buddhist—have been closely intertwined throughout the history of the country. After the British conquered Burma, a number of Indians also immigrated and settled there.

Colonial rule in British Burma mimicked in many ways the processes of state-building that were simultaneously occurring in neighboring India. For example, in their Burmese provinces the British had an overarching goal of de-emphasizing the religious cleavage. They abolished the Buddhist monarchy and removed Buddhism as the official state religion. Colonial administrators then reorganized the entire system of primary education that had hitherto provided religious instruction via monasteries. In doing so, the British sought to create a new educational system that they hoped would produce a modern, secular population. Colonial officials also stopped drawing on Buddhist monks to fill major administrative positions within the country. In general, British ethnic policies in directly ruled areas of Burma were very similar to policies implemented in the Indian provinces, where colonial officials tried to expunge the importance of religion (Brown 1994: 41–43).

Native Burma, by contrast, remained under the control of indigenous rulers, and ethnic politics was organized quite differently in these areas: indigenous rulers ordered politics around distinct groups of ethnic minority identities. Native Burma was itself named for these minority groups—the Chin resided in the Chin Hills, the Shan in the Shan States, and the Kachin in the Kachin State. These were three of the major groups, but a number of other ethnic minorities also resided in these areas.

Once the rulers of native Burma had ordered politics in a certain fashion, they then began to institute their own policies of ethnic stratification. These leaders generally implemented ethnically chauvinistic policies that benefited their own group over native Burmans. As one example, in the Shan States the sawbwa passed laws that barred Burmans from entering or settling in their territories (Lintner 1984: 405).

Bifurcated rule created different types of ethnic politics throughout Burma. Colonial officials in British Burma tried to de-emphasize religion in the hopes of creating a secular state. In native Burma, traditional rulers reinforced the cleavage of minority ethnic categories. These different ways of organizing and stratifying ethnic politics in both regions subsequently led to disparate patterns of ethnic violence (Walton 2008).

Peasant revolts in Burma occurred primarily in British areas, which, given the history of British India, is not surprising. The major peasant revolt—led by the Buddhist monk Saya San in 1930 through 1931—began in the directly ruled Tharrawaddy district (Ghosh 2000). Although this rebellion was instigated by a number of monks, it was not religious in character. In fact, the causes of the violence mirrored the discontent of peasants in British India. Robert H. Taylor (2009: 199) notes, for example, that "[San] developed peasant support for opposing the state's restrictions on the use of timber and bamboo by the villagers, a traditional privilege that the colonial state had appropriated as a monopoly." Similarly, Chapter 4 of this book highlighted a major source of tribal discontent in Bastar: the British monopoly over access to forests and forest produce.

British Burma, however, was not immune from experiencing religious violence, especially between Buddhists and Muslims in the Arakan region (Smith 1994: 54–57). Initial attempts to curb the power of religion in Burma led to the *sangha* (monkhood) becoming politically active in the 1920s—an initial response to secularization similar to what had occurred in India. However, by the end of the colonial period, the leader of the Burmese national movement, General Aung San, was firmly committed to secular politics (Von Der Mehden 1961).

In native Burma, hostility and violence occurred largely between different ethnic minority groups. Conflict along ethnic lines still plagues these regions of the country today and has led to a number of localized ethnic separatist movements (Lintner 1984; Smith 1994: 22–23). Many of the ethnic minorities in these areas are hostile toward Burmans, and none of these groups have been integrated into contemporary Myanmar. As David Brown (1994: 33) puts it, "Since [the 1950s], virtually all of the minority linguistic groups in Burma has [sic] been involved, at one time or another, in insurgency against the state. While some of this dissidence has taken a communist direction, ethnic disaffection has remained a central factor."

The British experience in Burma was heavily influenced by the history of India. British Burma and native Burma existed side by side, but ethnic politics in these regions was conducted and organized in highly contrasting ways. British administrators and native rulers pursued policies in their respective regions that benefited and harmed different sets of ethnic groups; the result is that the former areas have experienced widespread peasant discontent whereas the latter have experienced separatist violence organized around ethnic minority identities.

Ethnic Conflict in Malaya

In the fifteenth century, most of Peninsular Malaysia[7] was brought under the control of a centralized power called the Malacca Sultanate. More than a century earlier, Islam had become the dominant religion in the region. Beginning in the sixteenth century, Malaya came to the attention of a number of European colonizers—first the Portuguese, then the Dutch. The earliest British influence in the region occurred through the British East India Company, which signed a lease for the territory of Penang with the Sultan of Kedah in 1786. The Anglo-Dutch Treaty of 1824 was a key historical development because it settled the central issue of competing British and Dutch influence in the East Indies. This treaty enabled the British to take control of Malaya while the Dutch took control of what became Indonesia.

During the colonial period, Malaya was divided between systems of direct and indirect rule. One area, the Straits Settlements, was placed under the direct control of British administrators. This territory consisted of the coastal areas of Malacca, Dinding, Penang, Singapore, and Labuan. The Straits Settlements were first governed by the BEIC, but in 1867 they became crown colonies. Afterward, a centralized system of British administration was created that included setting up the office of the Governor (responsible to London), a variety of councils, and a large civil service.

The Federated Malay States (FMS), consisting of Selangor, Perak, Pahang, and Negri Sembilan, and the Unfederated Malay States (UMS), consisting of Johor, Kedah, Kelantan, Perlis, and Terengganu, remained under the control of native sultans (Emerson 1937; Zainal 1970). Map 6.2 indicates these divisions across colonial Malaya. Adopting the practice from the Indian princely states, the British dispatched officials (Residents-General) to the courts of these native rulers. There is a debate among historians of Malaya as to the level of political power enjoyed by the sultans. Some scholars suggest that they were figureheads with merely symbolic power (Emerson 1937; Fisher 1991) while other accounts stress the ways in which the sultans continued to exercise real political authority (Gullick 1965; Milner 1982, 2011). But one area of agreement seems to be that the rulers of the UMS had more internal autonomy than the rulers of the FMS (Milner 2011: 10). This was probably due to two factors: first, the FMS was a centralized political entity, unlike the loose confederation of the UMS; and second, the FMS came under British control in 1895 whereas the UMS did so later, in 1909.

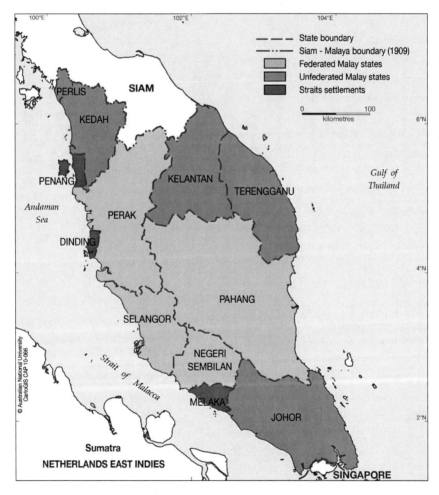

MAP 6.2. Colonial Malaya.
SOURCE: Used with the permission of CartoGIS of the Australian National University.

Like Burma, Malaya was a very plural society during colonialism. The main language spoken in the country was Malay, and Islam was the dominant religion. Unlike Burma, the primary ethnic divisions in the country were based on racial categories. The largest ethnic group in the country was the Malays, and most of them were considered to be sons of the soil (*bhumiputra*). Under this designation were also a large number of indigenous groups. In the nineteenth and twentieth centuries—during the period of colonial rule and due to colonial administrators—a massive influx of Chinese and Indian immigrants further increased the diversity of Malay society, although both of these groups had already been living in Malaya before colonialism.

British officials in Malaya organized the colony around the ethnic category of race. In directly ruled regions, the British conducted the first modern census in 1871. However, it was not conducted in the FMS until 1901 and in the UMS until 1911 (Hirschman 1987: 559). The fact that official colonial policies toward ethnicity in areas of direct rule were crafted decades before any such policies occurred in indirectly ruled areas had important historical ramifications. The census helped to prioritize and cement racial relationships in British Malaya. In the Straits Settlements, the British also employed the same policies as they had in India and Burma that aimed at depoliticizing the religious cleavage. This included limiting the scope of Islamic law and replacing religious instruction with a new system of secular education (Aziz and A.B. 2004: 345–48).

Unlike in India, the census was not a major determinant of violence in British Malaya. Instead, it was the widespread use of immigrants from other parts of the empire that led to rising ethnic antagonism. Thousands of Chinese and Indian workers were brought to the colony to work in the burgeoning tin and rubber trade. The use of immigrants was also bolstered by the fact that many British administrators in the region held the opinion that Malays were a lazy race (Shoup 2008: 46). Therefore, administrators in British Malaya enforced policies that were generally favorable to immigrants but viewed as discriminatory by Malays themselves. Because of this growing tension, during the colonial period directly ruled areas such as Singapore experienced a number of racial riots (Leifer 1964).

Ethnic politics took on a very different character in areas of Malaya where the sultans remained in power. Like the princes of India, the sultans were religious rulers and they kept religious identities salient in their territories. In these kingdoms religion and politics were deeply intertwined. Also as in India, this relationship was further reinforced by British administrators, who sought to uphold the sultanates as artifacts of traditional Malay society. In contrast, Islam was not the state religion in the crown colonies (Fernando 2006: 253). This focus on religion in the indirectly ruled areas did not change after the end of colonialism. Shanti Nair (1997: 133) notes that "in contemporary times, Malay royalty . . . have continued to be regarded by some parts of the Malay community as protectors of its privileges and special rights, and as the upholders of Islam." Similarly, Frederik Holst (2012: 46) has described the sultans as "a common reference point for ethnicized religious policies." For instance, as late as 2010 the Sultan of Selangor issued a law (with the prodding of the Islamic religious establishment) declaring that non-Muslims could not use the word *Allah* (Mohamad 2010: 522).

On the other hand, in native Malaya the salience of racial categories was comparatively muted. In the period prior to British colonialism, levels of immigration into these sultan-ruled areas had been much lower, as were the tensions that erupted from immigration. There had even been increasing rates of intermarriage between Malays and immigrants during this time (Christie 2012: Chapter 11). This is additional evidence that ethnic politics in the FMS and UMS revolved around religion, not racial categories.

Most ethnic conflicts that occurred in the country after colonialism were concerned with race, and it has been argued that "the residue of racial ideology continues to haunt contemporary Malaysia" (Holst 2012: 570). A major ethnic clash, the 1964 race riots, occurred in Singapore, a former directly ruled area, which ultimately led to its expulsion from Malaysia. In areas that were ruled by sultans, however, racial tensions were minimized in comparison. While race riots in 1969 began in Kuala Lumpur,[8] which had been a part of indirectly ruled Selangor, violence occurred all over the country, including in former directly ruled Malacca and Penang (Snider 1968). During that time, another round of racial riots broke out in Singapore, which by then had become an independent nation.

Malaysia is also an important comparative case because since 1969 the country has done an admirable job of limiting major spasms of ethnic conflict (Collins 1998; Sriskandarajah 2005). Compared to Indonesia, for example, which has experienced intermittent bloody flare-ups of ethnic violence, Malaysia has been a model for managing ethnic tensions. The country and its leaders may have differed from India's politicians in tackling widespread reform of colonial-era ethnic policies. The major exception to that rule is

Kerala, and Donald Horowitz's work (1993) notably singles out Malaysia and Kerala for special mention as highly plural states that have nevertheless limited ethnic violence.

Ethnic Conflict in Nigeria

The Niger Delta had always been an area of interest for British officials in Africa. This region was at the time known as the Oil Rivers, due to its abundant production of palm oil. Some of the earliest British influence in the area occurred through the Royal Niger Company, just as the BEIC had played the earliest role in advancing British interests in India. One of the first areas annexed was the coastal city of Lagos, on the western fringe of Nigeria, which then became a crown colony in 1861. By the end of the nineteenth century, British power had expanded eastward to control most of what is known as Yorubaland. This development led to the creation of the Niger Coast Protectorate, which eventually became the Southern Nigeria Protectorate. The British finally brought the entire country under their control when they completed taking over the north in 1900, creating the Northern Nigeria Protectorate.

The colony of Nigeria is considered to have been the archetypal case of British indirect rule (Fisher 1991; Falola 2001: 17; Lange 2009: 170–72) beginning in 1914, when the southern and northern protectorates were unified under the direction of Lord Lugard. But prior to 1914, Nigeria was governed in a manner similar to India, by combining forms of direct and indirect rule. Areas like the Sokoto Caliphate and Kano in the north and Oyo and Benin in the south remained under the control of native rulers. The British did not interfere extensively in these native administrations. The emirs of Sokoto, for example, retained 75 percent of the revenue in their kingdom (Carland 1985: 72). In fact, British political officers throughout the north, especially from 1906 to 1912, adopted a strong noninterventionist stance (Bull 1963; Carland 1985: 66–79). As John Wood noted about the Residency system in India, officers in northern Nigeria seemed more interested in the prerogatives of native rulers than in those of the colonial administration (1984: 71).

In parts of the south, however, a direct rule regime was implemented. C. K. Meek writes about these directly ruled areas: "Indirect rule . . . had not been considered possible, as no framework had been discovered on which Native Administrations could be erected. There were not chiefs with substantial territorial jurisdiction. Indeed, in most areas there were no chiefs at all, and there was no higher unit of government than the commune or small group of contiguous villages. The British system of administration had therefore been direct."[9] Similarly, when the northern and southern protectorates were to be united in 1914, Lugard himself was of the opinion that British officials had been governing southern regions of the country too directly (Falola and Heaton 2008: 117).

For example, although southeastern Nigeria was never officially under direct rule, many scholars argue that it was in reality governed by British administrators,[10] because colonial officials did not find a set of authorities comparable to emirs who could govern these territories. Instead they created "Warrant Chiefs"—named for the warrant that made them members of the Native Court system—to rule these areas. Because these rulers did not actually exist in the southeast, this form of governance can be called direct rule (Jones 1973). Similarly, in Yorubaland in the southwest, the initial system of indirect rule fared so poorly that British officials eventually also had to establish more direct control over this territory.[11] Prior to 1914, then, the colony of Nigeria looked very similar to India, with some areas under direct rule and others under indirect rule. Map 6.3 indicates the broad colonial divisions across the country.

Nigeria was also an ethnically diverse colony. In the north the major ethnic groups were the Hausa and the Fulani; in the southwest it was the Yoruba and in the southeast it was the Igbo. This is only a broad overview of the complex ethnic demography of the region; other important ethnic groups, such as the Ijaw and Tiv people, also resided there. The Hausa and Fulani were overwhelmingly Muslim, whereas many Yoruba had converted to Christianity, as had a large number of Igbo. English became the official language of Nigeria, but Hausa, Yoruba, and Igbo were three other major spoken languages.

In areas where the British had more direct control, such as Yorubaland, colonial officials ordered politics around ancestral city membership, an ethnic category that relates back to Yoruba mythology. According to legend, the sons of Oduduwa, the founder of the Yoruba, created a number of city-kingdoms. A group's attachment to an ancestral city is reinforced through a number of cultural practices, such as yearly rituals that bring Yorubas back to their home.

British officers in Yorubaland chose to emphasize ancestral city membership in order to expunge the salience of religion, because there was a clear

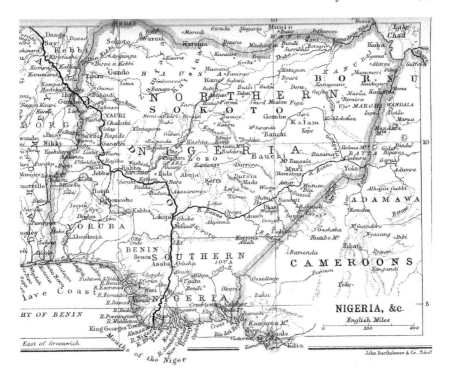

MAP 6.3. Colonial Nigeria.
SOURCE: John Bartholomew and Company, Edinburgh, c. 1914.

Muslim-Christian divide in the area. David Laitin (1986: 154) details these ethnic policies: "The British strategy was to defuse religious antagonism rather than to divide Yoruba country by religion. A major reason for their gingerly treatment of potential religious conflict was that British administrators, due to their recent experience with the Sudanese Mahdi, feared the revolutionary implications of religious fanaticism. . . . British colonial rule, then, politicized one cleavage (between ancestral cities) and depoliticized another (between religious groups)."

In areas of indirect rule, native rulers ordered ethnic politics very differently compared to British administrators: in many areas they prioritized rather than minimized religion. This was not surprising considering the influence of religion even before the British arrived; in parts of the north, for example, Islam had been established as the state religion as early as the fifteenth century (Ibrahim 1991: 120). Political culture revolved around Islam in the territory of Kano (Paden 1973). Likewise, in the Sokoto Caliphate the sultan continued to prioritize Islam as the foundation for local politics and the legal system (Korieh and Nwokeji 2005: 113).

Despite the fact that Nigeria was unified under a system of indirect rule in 1914, there is still a discernible pattern of ethnic organization and conflict in the country today that dates from the earliest British political experiments in the colony. The northern portion of the country has experienced a long-standing history of religious identification and violence. For example, the 1987 elections throughout the north were marked by strong religious voting (Ibrahim 1991: 131), and since 1999 most of the north has implemented Sharia law. Because religion has taken on such salience in the north, many northern areas have seen bloody and recurrent waves of religious violence (Bienen 1986; Ukiwo 2003).

In the southern parts of Nigeria, patterns of violence were and continue to be very different. In southwestern Yorubaland, the salience of religious cleavages has been minimized; Sharia rule has not been implemented and this area tends to be more secular. Conflict has instead revolved around the category of ancestral city membership (Laitin 1986).

Summary

After the Rebellion of 1857, the British in India were forced to allow the existence of hundreds of princely states, areas over which they had limited control. This outcome was initially considered a major blow to British ambitions on the subcontinent, but the system of bifurcated colonial rule eventually became popular among British officials, mainly because it diminished the chances of future rebellions against their authority. Political officers began to call this bifurcated system of governance the Indian model of colonialism.

In the nineteenth and twentieth centuries, the British exported the Indian model to a number of new colonies throughout Asia and Africa, including Burma, Malaya, and Nigeria. In all of these states, British officials in directly ruled areas shared power with native authorities in indirectly ruled areas. In Burma the British relied on native rulers to control the country's most remote regions, in Malaya they relied on sultans, and in Nigeria the emirs controlled areas throughout the north.

Bifurcated rule in these states led to different conceptualizations of ethnic politics across directly and indirectly ruled areas. One striking similarity is that in all cases the British sought to minimize the salience of religion, a policy first pursued in India after the Rebellion. They crushed the Buddhist monarchy in Burma, limited the power of Islamic courts and schools in Malaya, and expunged religion by privileging ethnic categories derived from ancestral cities in Yorubaland in Nigeria. In all of the directly ruled areas of these colonies, the British tried to create a new, secular citizenry. Native rulers in these three states, however, pursued different kinds of ethnic policies; in Burma, they prioritized ethnic minority status, but in Malaya and Nigeria they reaffirmed precolonial cleavages based on religion.

As different conceptualizations of ethnic politics were structured during the critical period of colonial rule, patterns of ethnic violence began to emerge in each country, and these patterns are still discernible today. In the modern states of Myanmar, Malaysia, and Nigeria, there are long-lasting patterns of violence across former areas of direct and indirect rule. Though further research must be done to collect systematic data and more rigorously study these patterns, this chapter has offered a preliminary investigation. If these cases are any indication, the legacies of British rule—and the specifics of the Indian model of colonialism—may be central to understanding patterns of ethnic violence in a wide array of multiethnic states that surround the waters of the Indian Ocean.

Conclusion

> Historians of South Asia seem still obsessed with the British, with colonialism and postcolonialism, overlooking ways of interpreting the past and present that do not make colonial rule responsible for all that has happened. Indirect rule and the so-called princely or native states of India provide opportunities for comparative investigation of modern South Asian cultural configurations.
>
> —*Karen Leonard*[1]

Political theorist Tom Nairn (1977: 317) once remarked that nationalism was the great historical failure of Marxism. The assumption that national identities would recede as a source of conflict was violently disproved by the events of the twentieth century. Especially after the end of the Second World War, ethnic identities such as those based on national, religious, linguistic, or tribal categories have been one of the principal sources of conflict around the world. Horrific bloodshed during the breakup of Yugoslavia, the Rwandan genocide, and countless other examples testify to the enduring importance of ethnicity in generating violence.

This book has endeavored to explain one central and puzzling aspect of this ethnic conflict that plagues much of the world: why it revolves around one cleavage rather than another. Though this question may be important for theoretical reasons that relate to the study of ethnicity within the social sciences, answering it is not purely an academic exercise. The mobilization of particular ethnic categories—such as religious identities—has been shown to be more violent than other kinds of mobilization (Wilkinson 2008). Along these lines, if ethnicity can be manipulated, then some divided societies may desire to emphasize an identity that is nonconflictual over one that incites violence. Understanding why some identities become salient relative to others can also generate important insights into how ethnicity is constructed, and how it persists or changes over time.

As one of the most populous and ethnically diverse countries in the world, India is an ideal location for studying patterns of ethnic violence, a natural laboratory of sorts for this topic. Hinduism, Buddhism, Sikhism, and Jainism all emerged from India, and adherents of world religions such as Islam, Judaism, and Christianity can be found in almost every corner of the country. India is likewise home to thousands of distinct castes and indigenous tribal groups. Despite its rich and overlapping ethnic demography, the country experiences some clear patterns of ethnic violence. In some regions this conflict occurs around a dominant religious cleavage, primarily between the Hindu and Muslim communities. In the southern city of Trivandrum in Kerala, for instance, communal conflict among Hindus, Muslims, and Christians has been a problem for more than a century. But in other areas—often those that have an identical ethnic demography—conflict instead occurs between different castes, or between the state and adivasis. This is the case in the northern city of Ajmer in Rajasthan, where caste factions dominate local politics and where Hindu nationalists have tried but failed to create a divide based on religion. What explains these patterns of ethnic violence in India?

Summary of the Book

This book has argued that patterns of ethnic violence in India stem from legacies of colonial rule that were reinforced over time through institutions. India is well known as having been the "jewel in the crown" of the British Empire; less well known is that the British never controlled the entire country. Most of the areas that were already British colonies prior to the conquest of India had been brought under direct rule, but the Rebellion of 1857 prevented the subcontinent from being entirely annexed. Afterward, roughly one-fourth of the Indian population lived in princely states ruled by largely autonomous native kings. This key historical divide forms the colonial origins of ethnic violence in contemporary India.

Both the British administrators and the princely rulers governed heterogeneous populations, but they had very different conceptions of how to manage this ethnic diversity. In the provinces, British administrators emphasized the centrality of caste. Colonial officials chose this particular identity after the Rebellion of 1857, which they perceived as a religious (primarily Islamic) uprising, because they were intent on de-emphasizing religion.

Caste (along with tribal identities) was promoted as the central organizing principle for a new, modern society. During the latter half of the nineteenth century, the caste system was divorced from its Hindu origins and became largely a system of social categories. It was subsequently viewed as scientific in character, bearing resemblance (depending on the administrator) either to race or to the class structure of Victorian England.

Beginning with this assumption, British administrators then stratified ethnic groups by enforcing policies that benefited high castes but discriminated against low castes and tribals. High castes such as the jenmis in Malabar, for example, gained a new proprietary right over the land, while low castes and adivasis in the region suddenly became tenants-at-will. At the same time, in the interests of promoting secularism, the British embraced a policy of religious neutrality, or what Peter Hardy (1972) has called "balance and rule." In effect, this policy meant that groups such as Muslims, a small minority in the country, were protected under colonialism. In provinces such as Ajmer, Muslims came to form almost half of the local administration, and a culture of religious cooperation between Hindus and Muslims was gradually fostered. The outcome of these policies in the provinces was intense caste and tribal violence, but over the long term communal conflict was minimized.

In the princely states, ethnic politics was organized altogether differently. Native kings had always derived their legitimacy from religion—even in the precolonial period—and they had constructed theocratic states. Many territories were explicitly religious kingdoms; for example, Travancore, in the south, was officially dedicated to the Hindu god Padmanabha. In these areas, politics was organized around the centrality of religious legitimation, laws, shrines, customs, and rituals. Religion was inherently central to the princely states, but the British also reinforced this ethnic category: they believed that religious rule had been native to India, and some administrators relished the opportunity to highlight a divide between modern provinces and "backwards" princely states.

In their territories, native kings constructed policies of ethnic stratification that were the mirror image of British India; these policies benefited dominant religious groups but discriminated against minority religious groups. Even in states such as Kashmir, where most of the population was Muslim, the Hindu rulers of the kingdom brutally repressed them and enabled Hindus to dominate local politics. At the same time, many princes protected low castes and adivasis. This was because, respectively, cultivators had a hereditary right to the land in many princely kingdoms, and certain tribes—like the Bhils in Rajasthan—were viewed as the earliest inhabitants of these states. These policies of ethnic stratification in turn created a pattern of intense religious violence, but minimal violence among castes and tribes. Thus, across India's provinces and princely states, different conceptions of ethnicity led to different political cultures, then different policies of ethnic stratification led to different fault lines of ethnic violence.

This central theory—a new interpretation of British Indian history—is supported by extensive qualitative and quantitative evidence. The qualitative component is derived from fifteen months of fieldwork in India in which primary source research was conducted in six archives and dozens of elites were interviewed in five carefully chosen case studies. The first two pairs of cases were controlled historical comparisons of two neighboring areas that were similar in most regards except that one was a British province and the other was a native state. Chapter 2 detailed a comparison of the districts of Jaipur and Ajmer in the north Indian state of Rajasthan. Jaipur was a Hindu kingdom and Ajmer was selected by colonial officials to be their lone outpost in the area then known as Rajputana. Chapter 3 then detailed a state-level comparison between the northern portion of Kerala, known as Malabar, and the southern region of the state, known as Travancore. These two cases constitute a "historical accident," because the British wanted to bring all of Kerala under their control but a variety of contingent factors enabled them to conquer only the north. The south consequently remained under the control of a powerful Hindu dynasty.

In both Ajmer and Malabar, extensive primary source evidence showed that the British emphasized the centrality of caste and tribal identities. Colonial officials who descended on Ajmer in the early nineteenth century were among the first administrators to codify the designation "untouchable," and the effect of census operations in the area was the heightened salience of caste identities. New landholding and forest policies instituted in both provinces enhanced the power of zamindars but dispossessed low-caste agriculturalists and tribal groups. For example, in pre-British Malabar, there was most likely no system of private property, but British administrators misinterpreted the existing agricultural system and granted proprietary rights to jenmis. This new policy resulted in skyrocketing eviction rates and, subsequently, the earliest political mobilization of low castes and adivasis in the region.

Colonial administrators in Ajmer and Malabar also sought to minimize the salience of religion, and minority Muslim communities were protected by the British policy of religious neutrality. In Ajmer, Muslims constituted a large share of the government administration, and equality between Hindus and Muslims led to the religious divide slowly receding over time. In Malabar, although Muslims were responsible for a series of uprisings against the government in the late nineteenth and early twentieth centuries, the vast majority of rebels were actually recent low-caste converts, and the history of this region since the advent of colonialism included repeat episodes of intercaste tension and violence. By the end of the British period, however, Malabar, like Ajmer, experienced almost no communal conflict.

The colonial histories of Jaipur and Travancore, by contrast, were quite different. Hindu rajas ruled these theocratic states, and they emphasized the centrality of religion. The rulers of Travancore governed a state that, unlike most areas of northern India, had never come under the control of Muslim armies; these rajas were therefore particularly staunch defenders of Hinduism. The leaders of both areas heavily favored the Hindu majority while restricting the rights of Muslims and, in Travancore, Christians. In Jaipur, for instance, newspapers from the early twentieth century described the kingdom as one of the worst areas for communal violence in the entire country.

In both Jaipur and Travancore, however, the same rajas instituted a number of protective policies toward low castes and adivasis, which in turn prevented the growth of caste and tribal violence in these areas. The rulers of Jaipur acknowledged, for instance, that the Meena tribe ruled most of the state in the medieval period and therefore guaranteed them a ceremonial position in the kingdom and a certain allotment of government jobs. Similarly, land policies toward adivasis in Travancore were among the most progressive in India. The rajas of Travancore also pushed aggressively for low-caste uplift after the mid-nineteenth century, opening the doors of Hindu temples to untouchables before any other region in India.

Across these four cases the patterns of history are clear: British administrators emphasized the centrality of caste and enforced policies that stratified ethnic groups along these lines, but they simultaneously protected religious minorities. In these areas, caste and tribal identities became hegemonic, and violence centered on these identities; the religious divide, however, receded over time. Princely rulers, for their part, emphasized the centrality of religion and enforced religious policies of ethnic stratification, but they protected low castes and adivasis. Religious violence increased, but caste and tribal violence was minimized. These four cases drawn from such different geographical regions of India—regions with sharply contrasting cultural and historical attributes—highlight that bifurcated colonial rule created clear fault lines of ethnic conflict.

Many aspects of the argument presented in this book challenge traditional historical work on the colonial era in India. For example, the dominant view on religious violence in colonial India can be summed up as "princes good, British bad." The controlled comparisons in Rajasthan and Kerala demonstrate the opposite. Similarly, the area that experiences the most immense tribal conflict in contemporary India is not a former British province but a former princely state. To consider some of the limitations of the theory presented in this book, Chapter 4 examined the theory's key deviant case, focusing on Bastar, a small, remote former princely state that is the single deadliest battleground for Naxalite conflict in modern India. An analysis of this kingdom has shown that tribal revolt began in Bastar in the mid-nineteenth century precisely because of creeping British influence in the state. Bastar was unique among Indian princely kingdoms in terms of the sheer amount of British interference in its administration: for almost half a century it was ruled directly by colonial officials. Therefore, Bastar is the exception that proves the rule: where the British were in power, tribal rebellion soon followed.

Disparate sets of ethnic policies across provinces and princely areas created very different patterns of ethnic violence in India. In the postindependence period, these patterns have not dissipated. Dozens of elite interviews spanning Rajasthan, Kerala, and Chhattisgarh were conducted to study the modern period. Respondents drawn from district- and state-level government departments, NGOs, ethnic organizations, political parties, police administrations, newspapers, and universities all showcased that patterns of ethnic violence have not changed in postcolonial India. In Ajmer and Malabar, respondents detailed that conflict still revolves around caste and tribal identities. In Jaipur and Travancore, however, respondents highlighted the central role of religion in fomenting political violence. For example, after the destruction of the Babri Masjid in 1992, mentioned at the beginning of this book, there were riots in both Jaipur and Travancore—but no corresponding riots occurred in neighboring Ajmer or Malabar.

Patterns of violence established during the colonial period persisted into postcolonial India for two overarching reasons. First, they became embedded in both formal and informal institutions. Political parties in Jaipur and Travancore, for instance, did not create new ethnic cleavage structures; instead they built on the religious divide inherited from princely rule. Likewise, the Communist Party that has been so central to Malabar's politics emphasized caste (then class) because of a long history of low-caste agitation in the region. Institutions as informal as the collective memories of different ethnic groups continued to structure ethnic conflict in one form or another. Patterns of violence became self-reinforcing; every riot hardened ethnic divides, built histories of animosity, and kept communities apart. Even major events did not alter these conflict patterns. For example, Partition caused much of the Muslim population in Ajmer to leave for Pakistan, but many of Jaipur's Muslims also left. Partition affected both districts in similar ways, but in postindependence India, Jaipur continues to experience much more communal violence than Ajmer.

Second, the new postcolonial governments failed to implement effective reforms of the past. For example, at the dawn of independence, agricultural reforms in Ajmer and Bastar began from a weakened position due to the power of British-backed zamindars, and new policies largely failed to improve the lives of landless low-caste and tribal laborers. One of the few exceptions was the state of Kerala, where the communists in Malabar used low-caste mobilization to come to power, implement a number of impressive reforms, and decrease the amount of ethnic violence in the state compared to most other regions.

Evidence from the case studies showcases a clear pattern of ethnic violence across contemporary India, but even five in-depth cases can potentially provide a misleading portrait of the entire country. Chapter 5 therefore provided statistical evidence from almost six hundred Indian districts that similar ethnic conflict patterns exist across the country, even when controlling for a variety of alternative explanations such as poverty, geography, and levels of social development. British rule correlates strongly with contemporary caste and tribal violence, but negatively with religious conflict.

The British experience in India after 1857 deeply influenced colonial administrators in London. They began to extol the virtues of what became known as the "Indian model" of colonialism. Colonial officials realized that combining direct and indirect rule was less expensive, less intrusive, and less likely to produce violent backlashes among native populations than outright direct rule. As the British Empire continued to expand in the late nineteenth and early twentieth centuries, the Indian model was exported (in one form or another) to a number of new colonies across Africa and Asia. Chapter 6 provided an overview of ethnic politics and conflict in three such colonies: Burma, Malaya, and Nigeria. In all of these states, the British ruled certain areas directly but left other regions to be controlled by kings, sultans, or emirs.

In the directly ruled parts of these colonies, the British tended to implement a policy of de-emphasizing religion, no doubt drawing on the Indian experience. In Burma, for instance, the Buddhist monarchy was dismantled, and in Nigeria the religious divide in Yorubaland was replaced by a concerted effort to make ancestral city membership salient. In some indirectly ruled areas, however, native rulers—often with the encouragement of British officials—continued to emphasize religion. The sultans of Malaya, for instance, became the defenders of Islam in their states. Bifurcated rule in these colonies created different fault lines of ethnic conflict. Even in the contemporary states of Myanmar, Malaysia, and Nigeria, there appear to be patterns of ethnic violence that descend from the British period. In northern Nigeria, religious violence has been a major problem, but not in Yorubaland. Racial tensions plague directly ruled Malaysia, but religious identification is still much stronger where the sultans once reigned. Chapter 6 provides evidence of the analytical power of drawing on the Indian model for insights in explaining contemporary ethnic violence in states around the Indian Ocean.

The arguments presented in this book contribute to several current debates within social science research. This project has aimed to advance work on the causes of ethnic violence in contemporary India, on the determinants of ethnic salience, and on the broader impact of colonialism on ethnic conflict. It is worth revisiting these three literatures to consider how the Indian case may provide answers to several of these important puzzles.

Ethnic Violence in Contemporary India

An impressive literature within political science has examined the causes of ethnic conflict in India, specifically the recent and widespread occurrence of Hindu-Muslim riots. Three central books (Brass 1997, 2003; Varshney 2002; Wilkinson 2004) emphasize several similar factors, including the rise of Hindu nationalist groups such as the Vishva Hindu Parishad and the Rashtriya Swayamsevak Sangh, and the incentive for political elites to promote violence in the run-up to elections. These books not only have vastly expanded our understanding of ethnic conflict in India, but also have done much to popularize Indian politics to a broader audience across the social sciences. However, two critical factors are missing across these works: a consideration of the deeper historical causes of contemporary violence, and a focus on forms of ethnic conflict other than communalism.

Existing scholarship on Hindu-Muslim riots has focused on proximate causes, highlighting relatively recent factors such as the rise of the Bharatiya Janata Party in the 1980s. Variables such as these are no doubt important, but this book focuses instead on the underlying causes of violence. A major problem with research on Hindu-Muslim riots is the fact that extensive religious violence occurred throughout Indian history, dating as far back as the establishment of the Delhi Sultanate, one of the earliest Islamic empires in South Asia. Therefore, a deeper explanation is needed to understand the root causes of modern violence. By looking at the precolonial, colonial, and postcolonial periods, this book offers a more historically grounded theory of contemporary communal violence.

A second problem of the existing literature is the singular focus on religion. Communal conflict in India has received an enormous amount of scholarly attention, but comparatively little consideration has been given to violence occurring along caste or tribal lines. This is a serious oversight considering that these forms of conflict are prevalent throughout modern India. Thousands of atrocities are committed against members of untouchable castes every year, and the Naxalite rebellion in eastern India was described by Prime Minister Manmohan Singh as the largest security threat in the history of the country. To broaden the scope of existing scholarship on ethnic conflict in India, this book offers a more comprehensive account, examining religious, caste, and tribal conflict together. In doing so, it highlights that most caste and tribal violence in contemporary India descends from the policies of colonial officials who discriminated against low castes and tribal groups. Importantly, this book also shows that religious violence had different causes and was prevalent even before colonialism.

The Puzzle of Ethnic Salience

This book contributes to another social science debate, about why one ethnic identity becomes salient over others. This literature is large but can be crystallized through the work of two scholars. David Laitin (1986) argues that patterns of ethnic identification and conflict stem from history; he finds that despite the existence of a Muslim-Christian divide in Yorubaland in Nigeria, political conflict revolved instead around the ethnic category of ancestral city membership because British colonial officials in the region expunged the salience of religion, believing it to be a dangerous identity that promoted conflict "led by fanatics" (158). In contrast, the work of Daniel Posner (2005) examines ethnic political competition in Zambia. Posner advances a rationalist account, finding that individuals in Zambia will choose to emphasize either their tribal or their linguistic identities on the basis of self-interest as well as existing institutional arrangements.

This book argues that certain ethnic identities became the basis for conflict in India due to historical factors that raised the salience of one category over others. In other words, it finds considerable support for the hegemony argument made by Laitin. Different policies of ethnic stratification in British and princely India created disparate fault lines of conflict. By contrast, Posner's argument about the sizes of particular groups in India does not seem to correspond to patterns of ethnic conflict. The mechanism of individuals using "head counts" (Chandra 2004; Posner 2005) to determine the most instrumental ethnic group is problematic. Numbers alone tell us that counting heads should result in Hindu-Muslim politics in almost every district in India, but in areas such as Malabar—despite the obvious advantage of consolidating the Hindu community—there is instead severe caste fragmentation. Malabar's low castes have steadfastly refused to integrate themselves into a broader notion of Hindu society, even though in that society they would be part of the majority.

This project also investigates the ways in which these patterns of ethnic violence persisted over time, a question often taken for granted in historically oriented political science research (Mahoney 2000). The role of institutions is paramount in answering this crucial question. Formal institutions, such as political parties and education systems, and institutions as informal as an ethnic community's memories of past violence, both reinforced patterns of conflict inherited from the colonial past. Similarly, the salience of particular identities was also maintained by the failure of reform efforts as the postindependence government in India largely embraced rather than altered its varied colonial inheritances (Chatterjee 1986).

On the whole, contrary to a host of recent constructivist accounts that emphasize the epiphenomenal nature of ethnicity (Wilkinson 2004; Posner

2005; Chandra 2004, 2006a, 2012), this book highlights that patterns of ethnic violence in India appear highly durable. Cities such as Jaipur have seen recurrent Hindu-Muslim riots for more than a century while other areas, such as Bastar, have experienced caste and tribal violence over a similarly long duration. As constructivists have argued, ethnic identities around the world are historically constructed. If this is so, then patterns of ethnic violence must also come from the legacies of the past. Too often a historical theory of ethnic conflict has been conflated with a primordialist theory of ethnic conflict. But discussing the history behind contemporary violence does not mean endorsing an "ancient hatreds" thesis; it means only that the roots of modern conflict often lie in the past.

This finding reinforces the fact that the salience of ethnicity cannot be divorced from context. Posner's work vividly highlights the fluid nature of ethnicity in Zambia, but only in the realm of voting and electoral competition. For this purpose, a rationalist account is highly convincing. But Posner (2005: 10) himself notes that the same fluidity in ethnic identification may not apply beyond this realm: "to the extent that the dynamics of ethnic violence are different from the dynamics of nonviolent ethnic politics, the account presented here may be applicable only to explaining the latter." Assuming that the logic of ethnic voting applies to ethnic violence is hazardous; this book shows that violence appears to be one realm in which ethnic identities are not simply instrumental and do not change easily; rather, patterns of violence tend to become hardened over time.

Although the central purpose of this book has been to explain patterns of ethnic conflict, there are some additional implications for the study of ethnic violence more broadly. First, the book aligns with recent institutional explanations for conflict (Cederman, Wimmer, and Min 2010; Lieberman and Singh 2012; Jha 2013). The legacies of British colonial history created patterns of ethnic violence in India, but it was institutions that reinforced and transmitted them over time. Second, studies of ethnicity within political science are currently dominated by the constructivist paradigm. Despite the fact that we are all constructivists now (Van Evera 2001), a constructivist theory of ethnic conflict is still underdeveloped. Most constructivist theories of ethnic conflict place a central focus on the role of elites in fomenting violence.[2] However, in a review of the literature linking constructivism and ethnic violence, James Fearon and David Laitin (2000: 846) note that the major puzzle of these accounts is explaining "why ethnic publics follow leaders down paths that seem to serve elite power interests most of all."

This book offers one answer: ethnic publics have historically inherited views about what kinds of ethnic identities are hegemonic in a particular area and what kinds of ethnic conflict are therefore legitimate. Elites may indeed play a critical role in fomenting conflict, but they may do so only within the dominant ethnic categories of a particular area. Most of the case studies in this book highlight that postindependence elites in India built on the edifice of colonialism rather than trying to reconstruct it. Political leaders in Jaipur who promoted Hindu-Muslim conflict in the city first had to accept that the city's dominant ethnic category was religion. Similarly, the elites of the Communist Party in Kerala did not reorient a colonial legacy that reified castes and tribes. Everywhere, elites were themselves constrained by history.

Colonialism and Ethnic Conflict

To say that colonialism had a major impact on ethnic conflict throughout the world is at this point a truism. The literature linking colonial policies and ethnic violence is enormous and has been referenced at various points in this book. But two often unaddressed problems pertain to this research: determining what kind of violence existed prior to colonialism, and determining whether violence would still have developed despite colonialism. These are naturally difficult questions to answer because they draw on counterfactuals.

India is a unique case in this regard because the princely states were areas that continued the political traditions of precolonial India; studying these areas therefore allows us potentially to answer the first question, about the kind of violence that existed prior to colonialism. The British also had very little impact within these native kingdoms; therefore, by comparing provinces and princely states, it is possible to isolate the effects of colonialism, potentially answering the second question, about whether violence would still have developed despite colonialism. Whereas recent research projects have compared different kinds of European colonialism (Blanton, Mason, and Athow 2001; Lange, Mahoney, and vom Hau 2006; Mahoney 2010; Lee and Schultz 2012), this book takes advantage of the unusual opportunity within the British Raj to compare colonialism in the provinces with its relative absence in the princely states.

Doing so leads to one major insight: British rule was not responsible for an increase in all forms of ethnic violence in India. The British focus on castes and tribes led to an increase in violence centered on these identities, but religious violence was a legacy of brutal precolonial conflicts. During the medieval period—especially the late Mughal period—widespread violence occurred among India's various religious communities, between Hindus and Muslims and between Sikhs and Muslims. The rulers of the princely states continued to emphasize religion, and continued to discriminate against non-coreligionists. The onset of British rule, however, reduced this violence over the long term in the provinces. This book thereby comes to a nuanced conclusion about the effects of colonialism on ethnic conflict in India: it produced an increase in one form of violence but a decrease in another.

Because India served as a model for colonial expansion into parts of Africa and Asia that surrounded the Indian Ocean, this case can serve as a blueprint for disentangling patterns of ethnic conflict in a wide variety of states. Chapter 6 offered a first cut at examining this relationship in the modern cases of Myanmar, Malaysia, and Nigeria, but future research can build further on these insights.

Policy Implications

One final important (and gloomy) question prompted by this book is whether patterns of ethnic violence in India are permanent. In other words, are the historical factors that produced violence patterns deterministic? And if so, what can states do to limit ethnic conflict?

It does seem to be the case that patterns of ethnic violence are extremely difficult to change. The British period was so significant in the construction of ethnic identities because of the strength of the colonial state, which was, as James Scott (1998: 69) notes, "at once more bureaucratized and less tolerant of popular resistance" than contemporary polities. In modern times, nation states may not have the same coercive capacity to construct and reconstruct ethnic identities as happened so often in the past.[3] A key implication of this conclusion is that policymakers should not assume that ethnic identities can easily be changed, which is a general implication of the constructivist paradigm. Rather, they should be aware that violence is one particular realm of ethnic politics in which identities harden and patterns of conflict become difficult to alter. Therefore, policymakers should first and foremost understand how history influenced contemporary conflicts. This is true not only for colonial states, but even for the most consolidated of Western democracies. For instance, among the deepest causes of "the Troubles" in Northern Ireland was the influx of Protestant settlers into the north in the seventeenth century, a historical event that subsequently created a long legacy of discriminatory practices against native Catholics (Terchek 1977).

Another related point is that attempts to change the ethnic cleavage structure of a society, even if successful, may not minimize violence. Chapter 3 showcased that the ethnic cleavage structure of British Malabar—even prior to the colonial period—was based on a rigid caste hierarchy. The widespread conversion of low castes to Islam in the mid-nineteenth century briefly changed the cleavage structure from one based on caste to one based on religion. However, the Mappilla uprisings, culminating in the Mappilla Rebellion of 1921, show that changing the salience of ethnic identities does not necessarily reduce violence; in this case, it vastly increased it. Low levels of caste violence became reformulated as bloody Hindu-Muslim struggle. This outcome may also offer additional evidence that religious mobilization specifically is more violent than other forms of mobilization (Wilkinson 2008).

Nevertheless, despite the overwhelming impact of the past, there are strong reasons to be skeptical of the claim that colonial history alone determines contemporary outcomes. The postcolonial leaders of India and many parts of Africa consciously chose not to alter their colonial inheritance; it should therefore not be surprising that patterns of violence in these particular areas have not changed. But other countries—Malaysia being a quintessential example– have been models for dealing successfully and nonviolently with ethnic diversity. Within India, the state of Kerala offers another important example. The Communist Party in the region has done significant work to reduce overall levels of violence. Both of these cases vividly illustrate the power of human agency and show that history is not destiny.

One potential solution to ethnic conflict in divided societies is to promote the salience of a national identity (Robinson 2013). This approach takes on particular importance in India, a country with strong regional identities but a weak overarching national one. For instance, less than half the population speaks the national language of Hindi, a language that also happens to be widely detested throughout the south because of historic attempts to impose it in schools. A well-known quote from a Member of Parliament in Orissa in the late 1950s highlights the hold that local ethnic

identities had—and still have—on contemporary politics: "My first ambi-
tion is the glory of Mother India. I know in my heart of hearts that I am an
Indian first and an Indian last. But when you say you are a Bihari, I say I am
an Oriya. When you say you are a Bengali, I say I am an Oriya. Otherwise,
I am an Indian."[4] The growth of a salient national identity may be one solution to this problem, although it is unclear if the central government has the
capacity to promote one. But getting the various and diverse ethnic groups
of the country to consider themselves Indians first and foremost may break
the hold on fragmented thinking that still plagues India decades after the
end of colonialism.

Archival Research

All archival material for this book was collected from the following locations: the National Archives of India (NAI), the British Library in London (BL), the Jaipur City Palace Archives (JCP), the Deshbandhu Press Library in Raipur (DPL), the Kerala State Archives (KSA), and the Andhra Pradesh State Archives (APSA).

The following citation formats for archival material are utilized:

NAI: Department, Branch, Year, File Number
BL: Shelfmark, Year
JCP: File Name, Year
DPL: Subject Number, Bin Number, Article Number
KSA: Department, File Number, Year, Bundle Number
APSA: Installment, List, File Number

This is the information required to requisition these documents in the respective archives. Sometimes larger archival files were numbered, so page numbers are included where applicable.

Some archival material directly cited in this book has been lightly edited to enhance clarity, including changes to punctuation, spelling, and grammar. These corrections have not altered the context or meaning of the documents.

Elite Interviews

During the course of researching this project, I conducted elite interviews with dozens of respondents spanning five case studies. Interviewees were selected in a manner that ensured a large cross-section of respondents. For example, I wanted to get a government perspective, but also the perspective of nongovernmental organizations (NGOs). The respondents generally fit into the following categories: local government (district or state) officials, NGO workers, police officers, religious leaders, journalists, and academics. At the end of each interview session I asked respondents for the names of other individuals who might be able to assist me on a particular issue, and the number of respondents snowballed.

Because this project was considered somewhat controversial in India, the identity of all of the interviewees remains confidential. All respondents were told at the outset of the interview that their names would not be used and that any identifying information about them would not be utilized either. This was done to ensure their privacy and candor.

Interviews generally took between thirty minutes and an hour; some longer interviews took almost two hours to complete. They were generally conducted in the respondent's office. Some interviews were conducted over the phone and are labeled as such. Because respondents were often pressed for time, I did not always adhere strictly to the interview questionnaire; in fact, almost all of the interviews became open-ended and conversational. Sometimes I was unable to complete an interview and therefore not all of the questions were asked.

The interviews were—in every state except Kerala—conducted in either Hindi (or what English speakers of Hindi might call "Hinglish") or, less often, English. All interviews in Kerala were conducted entirely in English. I did not utilize a voice or video recorder for interviews (most interviewees would not have consented to being recorded). Instead I took detailed longhand notes during the interview, then typed them up upon returning home. The quotes used in this book, if not taken verbatim, were either very close or based on impressions from the interview.

In addition to the formal elite interviews, I also conducted a number of interviews with everyday people living in each of the five cases studied. For example, I went to local chai stalls and held informal chats with patrons. These interviews were used to provide background information, or simply collect general impressions from citizens of a given area.

The basic questionnaire I used as the prompt for interviews is detailed below:

Questionnaire

1. Can you tell me about your background? What do you do?
2. How long have you worked [with this organization]? What does it do?

[Caste/Tribal Violence]

3. What is the general state of relations between caste groups in this area? Can you tell me about the position of low castes here?
   a. Geographic
   b. Economic
   c. Educational
   d. Political
   e. Historical
   f. How do powerful castes compare to low castes? Is there a large disparity between them? How do they interact?
4. Does this area experience a lot of caste violence?
   a. Can you provide details of recent episodes?
   b. What are its causes?
   c. Who initiates the violence?
   d. Does most of the violence occur around election time?
5. Are there civil society groups that band together low castes and high castes in this area? If so, what are their names?
6. How does this area compare to [other case study] on these issues?
7. What is the state of tribal groups in this area?
8. Does this area experience a lot of tribal violence?
9. How does this area compare to [other case study] on these issues?

[Religious Violence]

10. What is the general state of relations between religious groups in this area?
11. Does this area experience a lot of religious violence?
12. Are there civil society groups that band together different religious groups in this area? If so, what are their names?
13. How does this area compare to [other case study] on these issues?

Notes

Introduction

1. Marx (1852/2008: 15).

2. In this book, the term *low castes* refers to the groups at the lower end of the caste hierarchy, especially those known as the Scheduled Castes (which includes the untouchables, or *dalits*). In India, tribals are often called *adivasis* ("original inhabitants"), and those who have suffered a history of discrimination are known as Scheduled Tribes. This book primarily employs the terms *low castes* and *tribals* to refer to these groups, but the other terms are also used interchangeably.

3. *Frontline,* January 1, 1993.

4. "Gujjars Continue to Block Railway Line", *The Hindu,* May 26, 2008.

5. Multiethnic societies are not more prone to violence than other kinds of states. As Rogers Brubaker and David Laitin (1998: 424) note, most ethnic groups live in peace. But violence is a natural feature of large, modern societies. Therefore, assuming that some level of ethnic conflict will occur, this book is concerned with the specific question of why it revolves around one identity rather than another.

6. See Varshney (2002: 35): "Either there are several master narratives in a country, one hegemonic in some regions and others powerful elsewhere, or some other locally based factors intervene between the potential power of narratives to cleave society and generate violence and the actually observed patterns of violence."

7. The only kind of ethnic violence not analyzed in this book is linguistic violence. However, conflict over language has been shown to be less violent than other forms of ethnic conflict (Laitin 2000). In fact, Steven Wilkinson (2008) finds that linguistic mobilization in India is statistically negatively correlated with deaths and injuries due to ethnic conflict. Other fine scholars, however, have written on linguistic violence in India; see Lacina (2014).

8. The British also referred to these areas as the "native states" or just as "the states." These two terms are utilized at various points throughout the book.

9. An expanded discussion of direct and indirect rule is located in Chapter 1.

10. Castes and tribes are lumped together; see Chapter 1 for an explanation.

11. Kanchan Chandra (2006a) has questioned whether ethnicity is important at all; however, in earlier work (2004: Chapter 2) she shows how ethnic identities may provide informational shortcuts that are useful to individuals. For example, an individual's last name in India provides knowledge about that person's caste, religion, and linguistic group. Information about other identity categories—class, for example—is not nearly as accessible. For arguments that ethnicity relates to deep emotional bonds, see Connor (1993), Kaufman (2001), and Petersen (2002).

12. The terms *ethnic violence* and *ethnic conflict* are used interchangeably.

13. Most of the violence studied in this book occurs between ethnic groups, except for the case study in Chapter 4: tribals in Bastar are rebelling against the Indian government.

14. These are just three of the most well-known works; see also Weiner (1978), Krishna (1985), Engineer (1989a, 1991), Shani (2007), Ollapally (2008), Bohlken and Sergenti (2010), and Mitra and Ray (2014).

15. The term *communalism* in India refers primarily to religious violence, and these two terms are used interchangeably.

16. This is not to say that they are completely unaddressed, though it is historians who have done a lot of the research. On caste conflict, see Gough (1974), Guha (1999), and Urdal (2008). On tribal violence, see Mathur (2004) and Gupta (2007). On linguistic violence, see Lacina (2014). Recently, a number of scholars have begun looking at the Naxalite conflict (a form of tribal violence); see Bohara, Mitchell, and Nepali (2006); Joshi and Mason (2008); Do and Iyer (2010); Vadlamannati (2011); Gawande, Kapur, and Satyanath (2012); and Hoelscher, Miklian, and Vadlamannati (2012).

17. Data from National Crime Records Bureau, Ministry of Home Affairs (2010).

18. See Horowitz (1985: 53): "This concept of ethnicity means that ethnic conflict is one phenomenon and not several. To be sure, that conflict takes different courses . . . [but] the putatively ascriptive character of ethnic identifications imparts to ethnic conflict its intense and permeative qualities."

19. See Lipset and Rokkan (1967), Okamura (1981), and Esteban and Ray (2008).

20. This is a huge interdisciplinary literature, but as good recent examples see Horowitz (1985); Laitin (1986); Peebles (1990); Young (1994); Blanton, Mason, and Athow (2001); Mamdani (1996, 2002); Mason (2003); Posner (2005); and Falola (2009).

21. Quoted in Fisher (1991: 1).

22. I thank James Mahoney for bringing this idea to my attention many years

ago. Almost all studies of ethnic violence in colonial India are either about the entire nation or specific case studies. But this book focuses on *comparing* provinces and princely states. This strategy has been used quite fruitfully, for example, to study contemporary levels of development throughout India. See Wood (1984) and Iyer (2010).

23. See Caporaso (1995), Brady and Collier (2004), and Lieberman (2005).

24. For more information on the project's methodology, see the appendices at the end of this book and online.

25. This concept is also John Stuart Mill's "Method of Difference" (1843). On the value of controlled comparisons, see Slater and Ziblatt (2013).

26. The WITS database also includes some information about religious violence; see its use in Chapter 2 on Jaipur and Ajmer.

Chapter 1

1. Wood (1984: 66).

2. Naturally there is no one correct interpretation of Indian history. I have therefore taken seriously Ian Lustick's (1996) warnings about selection bias in historically oriented political science work and attempted within the text itself and through the use of extensive footnotes to cite authors who have offered historical views that contrast with my own—what Lustick calls the method of "explicit triage" (616)—so that other scholars may compare my arguments with rival explanations and decide for themselves what is more convincing. See an expanded discussion in Appendix 3 (Secondary Source Research) at http://sites.google.com/site/ajayaverghese/home/data).

3. Islamic forces from Arabia had entered South Asia in the eight century.

4. *Mughal* is the Persian word for *Mongol.*

5. Babur was descended from the Mongol ruler Genghis Khan and the Turko-Mongol ruler Timur.

6. See Roy (1984), C. A. Bayly (1985), Nandy (1988), Thapar (1993), Burman (1996), Copland (2005), and Hasan and Roy (2005).

7. Quoted in Ollapally (2008: 26–27).

8. See Ghurye (1968), Baig (1974), Bayly (1985), Gaborieau (1985), Mahmood (1993), and Subrahmanyam (1996).

9. See also Ali (1966).

10. Quoted in Pollock (1993: 284).

11. Quoted in Elliot (2008: 175).

12. The retrenchment of an Islamic political culture began under the reign of Aurangzeb's father, Shah Jahan (1628–58). There is no consensus as to how many temples were destroyed. On this issue, see the work of Goel et al. (1990), Talbot (1995), and Eaton (2000).

13. Quoted in Chandra (1969: 323).

14. In the late seventeenth century, the Marathas created an empire (and later a confederacy of states) that succeeded Mughal rule.

15. Quoted in Gaborieau (1985: 12).

16. Quoted in Ibid. (7).

17. The "latter two classes" refer to the two lower *varna* groups, Vaishyas and Shudras, who probably would have together constituted a majority of the Indian population. The caste system will be discussed at length later in this chapter. Quote is from Ray and Chattopadhyaya (2000: 44).

18. There were tribal rebellions during Mughal rule, however, such as the Bhil rebellion during the seventeenth century.

19. Quoted in Metcalf and Metcalf (2001: 131).

20. "Proclamation by the Queen in Council, to the Princes, Chiefs, and People of India," delivered by Queen Victoria on November 1, 1858.

21. Gun salutes were given by the British to certain princely states (with personal salutes for rulers). The highest salute was twenty-one guns, and generally the higher the salute the more prestigious the kingdom.

22. See Copland (1997) and Ramusack (2004) on indirect rule in India. See Afigbo (1972), Laitin (1986), and Mamdani (1996) on indirect rule in Africa. For broader work, see Newbury (2003); Lange, Mahoney, and vom Hau (2006); and Gerring et al. (2011).

23. Quoted in Assary (2009: 91).

24. This alternative explanation for violence is addressed in the case studies in Chapters 2 through 4.

25. Because India was not a settler colony, and because the overall British presence in the country was so small, the entire colony could perhaps be characterized as indirectly ruled (see Lange, Mahoney, and vom Hau 2006: 1430). In comparison to British colonies like the United States, India certainly featured less colonial interference. But this distinction ignores the important differences between direct rule in the provinces and indirect rule in the princely states, which are detailed in the ensuing chapters.

26. Quoted in Majumdar (1988: 15); see also Fisher (1990) on this period.

27. While some princes were deposed even after 1857, the severity of this threat is unclear. Lakshmi Iyer (2010) notes that from 1858 to 1947, twenty-one princes were deposed (out of her dataset of seventy-one princely states); but relative to the total number of princely states, twenty-one depositions over an eighty-nine-year period is a low figure (697). Furthermore, deposed princes were often replaced with a family member rather than a British administrator, so the princely line generally remained intact. Finally, during the period of "subordinate isolation," a number of princely rulers—even when they governed well—were deposed by the British.

Consider Fisher's (1991: 385) discussion of Awadh in 1856. It seems doubtful that princes were forced to change their practices in order to placate the British.

28. See also Keen (2012).

29. Many historians now working on the princely states have taken them seriously as semiautonomous kingdoms. For a good overview, see Ikegame and Major (2009). For general treatments, see Metcalf (1965), Fisher (1991), Ramusack (2004), and Ikegame (2012).

30. Quoted in Kooiman (2002: 15).

31. Quoted in Majumdar (1988: 646).

32. One lakh is one hundred thousand rupees.

33. British Library (hereafter BL), IOR/R/1/5/66, 1946, 1.

34. Quoted in Kooiman (2002: 15).

35. Quoted in Metcalf (1965: 227).

36. Andhra Pradesh State Archives (hereafter APSA), Installment #47, List #10, File IV, 82.

37. Quoted in Copland (1973: 213).

38. First quote: BL, IOR/R/1/5/66, 1946, 21; second quote: BL, IOR/R/1/1/4203, 1944, 103.

39. Caste and religion can obviously be overlapping categories, as the Introduction noted, but as the following chapters show, one tends to dominate the other. Northern Kerala, for example, is a bastion of caste politics. While the low castes there are technically Hindu, they do not prioritize their religious identity, making caste the hegemonic identity in the region.

40. There is a wealth of opinion on this point. Some scholars argue that the caste system is supported by ancient Hindu texts such as the *Laws of Manu*, whereas others argue that the caste system is not justified by Hinduism or was never intended to be a central facet of Hinduism. See chapter 1 of Bayly (1999) for a good discussion.

41. This view is widespread among scholars of colonial India; for a small sampling of recent literature see Cohn (1996), Bayly (1999), Dirks (2001), and Banerjee-Dube (2008).

42. Naturally the Rebellion of 1857 was a major historical event open to different interpretations. Some British officials perceived it as an army insurrection whereas others saw it as a nationalist uprising. One thread that underlay both of these views, however, was that the 1857 Rebellion was a vast Muslim conspiracy. See Metcalf (1965: 298), Hardy (1972: 62–66), Malik (2008), Wagner (2010), and Padamsee (2014).

43. Quoted in Hardy (1972: 63).

44. Quoted in Majumdar (1991: 300).

45. Quoted in the *Times* (1911: 198).

46. Quoted in Saumarez Smith (2008: 70).

47. Quoted in Dirks (1992: 67).

48. Quoted in Cohn (2008: 30).

49. What happened at the national level of Indian politics often had no relation to the local level. For instance, Varshney (2002: 58) argues that caste did not form the basis of national-level mass politics due to the diversity of castes around the country, whereas religion did not suffer from the same problem.

50. In this instance, they were theocracies ruled by religious kings, not priests.

51. See also Cohn (1996: 65).

52. "Proclamation by the Queen in Council, to the Princes, Chiefs, and People of India," delivered by Queen Victoria on November 1, 1858.

53. Quoted in Metcalf (1965: 237).

54. Quoted in Cohn (2008: 33).

55. Quoted in Ghurye (2008: 43), emphasis added.

56. The term *peasantry* is often used in this book to refer to low castes and tribals. This is because, as Debal K. SinghaRoy (2005: 5505) has argued, "peasants in India broadly represent a vast mass of landless agricultural labourers, sharecroppers, tenants, poor artisans and small and marginal cultivators having a close social interface with the socially deprived, such as the scheduled tribes, scheduled castes, other backward classes and women. The so-called 'outcastes' of the Varna hierarchy in the real sense of the term form the core of the peasantry in rural India." Of course, other groups, such as Muslims, could also be peasants (see Chapter 3).

57. Stokes (1978: 4) also notes that by the mid-nineteenth century most British administrators believed that, prior to colonialism, land in India was jointly managed by village leaders.

58. Quoted in Chandra (1999: 5–6).

59. Quoted in Hasnain (2007: 277).

60. Quoted in Ibid. (237).

61. For excellent overviews, see Gough (1974), Stokes (1978), and Guha (1999); specifically on tribal revolts, see Simhadra (1979), Mathur (2004), Hasnain (2007), and Desai (2007).

62. One crore is ten million rupees.

63. On this view, see Smith (1963), Hardy (1972), Robb (1986), Mallampalli (2004), and Lambert (2013).

64. Quoted in Majumdar (1991: 152).

65. Quoted in Kaura (1977: 202).

66. Some major proponents of this view are Mehta and Patwardhan (1942) and Gopal (1959). Ian Copland (2005: 10) notes, "Among the post-independence generation of Indian historians, it was almost an article of faith that the British actively and consciously cultivated religious divisions and tensions . . . in order to

justify keeping the reins of power firmly in their 'impartial' hands." For a similar view among nationalist leaders, see Rai (1928) and Prasad (1946).

67. See Hardy (1972), Copland (2005: 81–85), and Jaffrelot (2007: 7–10).

68. Quoted in Kooiman (2002: 26).

69. The major studies of communalism in princely India are Kooiman (2002) and Copland (2005).

70. Quoted in Benichou (2000: 250).

71. Quoted in Bose (2005: 16).

72. APSA, Installment #47, List #10, File #82.

73. Ibid.

74. Quoted in Copland (1973: 210).

75. The rajatilaka is a mark of red powder.

76. Quoted in Guha (1996: 2379).

77. See Mahoney (2000) and Page (2006).

78. See also Weiner (1967).

79. From the APSA; the name of the article was missing but it was published in *The Hindu* on December 6, 1947.

80. This comment was made to me by a top Ajmeri police official.

81. National Archives of India (hereafter NAI), Ministry of States, Hyderabad Branch, 1951, #1(16)-H/51, 7.

82. Formed in 1979 to study the state of backward peoples in India and led by B. P. Mandal, the Mandal Commission created institutionalized quotas in education as well as government representation for groups that historically have faced discrimination: Other Backward Classes and Scheduled Castes and Scheduled Tribes.

83. For a good introduction to the Naxalites, see Ray (2002) and Gupta (2007). They are also discussed at length in Chapter 4.

Chapter 2

1. Interview A in Ajmer, January 24, 2011.

2. The names Ajmer and Ajmer-Merwara are used here interchangeably for the British province.

3. *Sawai* means "one and a quarter"—that is, Jai Singh II was more capable than one mere man.

4. Quoted in Sarkar (1920: 96).

5. NAI, Jaipur Residency Records, Short History.

6. NAI, Foreign and Political Department, Internal Branch, 1925, #100-I of 1924.

7. Jaipur had one temple destroyed in 1697–98, although Eaton is not sure who ordered its destruction (2000: 69).

8. NAI, Rajputana Agency, Ajmer-Merwara Files, 1924, #31.

9. NAI, Foreign and Political Department, Internal Branch, 1925, #100-I of 1924.

10. BL, IOR/V/27/249/1, 1925, 6.

11. *Imperial Gazetteer of India* 5 (1909: 149).

12. NAI, Rajputana Agency, Ajmer-Merwara Files, 1924, #31.

13. Ibid.

14. BL, IOR/V/27/249/1, 1925, 5–6.

15. NAI, Jaipur Residency, Jaipur Agency, 1947, #6.

16. The *dargah* in Ajmer is a Muslim shrine to the Sufi saint Mu'in al-din Chishti.

17. Jaipur City Palace Archives (hereafter JCP), Report on the Administration of the Jaipur State, 1934–35 and 1937–38.

18. BL, IOR/R/1/1/3346, 1939.

19. Quoted in Jinnah (1996: 378).

20. Quoted in Ibid (64).

21. BL, IOR/R/1/1/3306, 1939.

22. Ibid.

23. These data are from the Report on the Administration of the Jaipur State for the aforementioned years, and from Jain and Jain (1935: 207).

24. NAI, Jaipur Residency, Part II, 1933, #466.

25. Ibid.

26. Ibid.

27. Ibid.

28. NAI, Jaipur Residency—Part 3, Confidential, 1933, #1134.

29. NAI, Jaipur Residency, Part II, 1937, #278.

30. JCP, Report on the Administration of the Jaipur State, 1942–43, 127.

31. Holi is the Hindu festival of colors.

32. NAI, Jaipur Residency, Part II, 1944, #214.

33. Ibid., emphasis added.

34. NAI, Jaipur Residency, Confidential, 1948, #1-P/48.

35. NAI, Ministry of States, G(R) Branch, 1948, #11(1)-G(R)/48.

36. NAI, Foreign Department, Establishment Branch, 1926, #1–4.

37. Ibid.

38. See, for example, "Hindu Raj at Ajmer," *Muslim Outlook,* August 16, 1925.

39. NAI, Jaipur Residency, Part II, 1939, #315.

40. NAI, Foreign and Political Department, Establishment Branch, 1925, #509-E.

41. Ibid.

42. Ibid.

43. NAI, Foreign Department, Establishment Branch, 1926, #1–4.

44. NAI, Rajputana Agency, Chief Commissioner's Branch, 1923–24, #1195. Ian Copland (2005: 203) has argued that Ajmer was a riot-prone city and that it

"was the first town in Rajputana to blow up, communally speaking." The second statement is true but the first is not. Ajmer had only two minor riots prior to Partition. Similarly, Copland cites only three riots in Jaipur, in 1926, 1932, and 1940. However, the number of incidents found in the National Archives of India and the Fortnightly Reports in the British Library were much higher, and as much supporting documentation as possible for these riots is included in this chapter.

45. Ibid.

46. NAI, Rajputana Agency, Chief Commissioner's Branch, 1923–24, #1195, Confidential Letter, #36C.

47. BL, IOR/L/PJ/7/1079, 1936.

48. BL, IOR/R/1/1/2068, 1931.

49. Ibid.

50. BL, IOR/R/1/1/1362, 1923.

51. BL, IOR/L/PJ/5/283, 1943.

52. *Imperial Gazetteer of India* 5 (1909: 165).

53. *Imperial Gazeteer of India* 13 (1909: 397).

54. Information on how the interview respondents were chosen, what questions they were asked, and so on is included in Appendix 2 (Elite Interviews).

55. Interview in Jaipur, November 30, 2010.

56. Interview in Jaipur, October 27, 2010.

57. Interview in Ajmer, December 22, 2010.

58. Interview in Ajmer, December 25, 2010.

59. Interview in Ajmer, December 9, 2010.

60. Interview in Ajmer, January 15, 2011.

61. See, most notably, Sachar et al. (2006).

62. Interview in Jaipur, November 11, 2010.

63. Interview in Jaipur, November 3, 2010.

64. See Varshney (2001: 372).

65. The Varshney-Wilkinson database probably excludes one other riot in Jaipur in October of 1990. Information on this conflict is contained in a report by the Working Group of National Integration Council to Study Reports of the Commissions of Inquiry on Communal Riots (Ministry of Home Affairs, Government of India 2007).

66. Interview in Jaipur, October 12, 2010.

67. Interview in Jaipur, October 21, 2010.

68. Interview in Jaipur, November 11, 2010; see also Rathore (2013) for more qualitative evidence on the poor state of Hindu-Muslim relations in contemporary Jaipur.

69. Interview A in Ajmer, January 24, 2011.

70. Interview B in Ajmer, January 24, 2011.

71. See Wilkinson (2004: 53–54) for a discussion of this problem.

72. Some interviewees, for example, would claim that they existed but could not provide the names of any actual organizations.

73. *Rajputana Gazetteer* (1879: 141); see also Singh (2003).

74. *Rajputana Gazetteer* (1879: 23).

75. *Imperial Gazetteer of India* 5 (1909: 161).

76. Ibid.

77. *Rajputana Gazetteer* (1879: 90).

78. *Imperial Gazetteer of India* 5 (1909: 153).

79. *Rajputana Gazetteer* (1879: 25).

80. Ibid. B. H. Baden-Powell (1892: 332) notes, "this course [the introduction of the mouzawar system] was afterwards much regretted."

81. *Rajputana Gazetteer* (1879: 31).

82. Ibid. (28).

83. BL, Q/12/9, 1926.

84. *Begar* is bonded (forced) labor.

85. Quoted in Gold and Gujar (2002: 77).

86. *Imperial Gazetteer of India* 5 (1909: 156–57).

87. *Rajputana Gazetteer* (1879: 32).

88. Quoted in Gold and Gujar (2002: 73).

89. NAI, Jaipur Residency, Jaipur Agency, 1947, #6, 9–10.

90. NAI, Home Department, Public Branch, 1935, #31/38/35.

91. BL, IOR/F/4/810/21725, 1824.

92. NAI, Jaipur Residency, Jaipur Agency, 1947, #6.

93. Quoted in Ramusack (2004: 176).

94. NAI, Jaipur Residency—Part 3, Confidential, 1939, 142.

95. Ibid.

96. *Imperial Gazetteer of India* 13 (1909: 393).

97. NAI, Jaipur Residency, Jaipur Agency, 1947, #6.

98. NAI, Jaipur Residency—Part 3, Confidential, 1939, #1442.

99. NAI, Jaipur Agency Part II, Jaipur Residency, 1930, #349.

100. NAI, Jaipur Agency Part II, Jaipur Residency, 1930, #253.

101. Ibid.

102. Interview in Jaipur, September 9, 2010.

103. Kshitiz Gaur, "Ajmer Sees a Change in Caste," *Times of India,* May 7, 2009; see also Kshitiz Gaur, "Pilot Bridges Caste Differences in Ajmer," *Times of India,* June 1, 2009, in which the author notes that "Ajmer was dictated by caste politics."

104. For more on this act, see Sharma (1993: 13–16).

105. Interview in Jaipur, September 16, 2010.

106. See the Ministry of Social Justice and Empowerment's definition of *atrocities,* available at http://socialjustice.nic.in/faqs1.php#q3.

107. Telephone interview from Jaipur, September 14, 2010.

108. Interview in Jaipur, September 16, 2010.

109. Interview in Jaipur, September 29, 2010.

Chapter 3

1. *Imperial Gazetteer of India* 17 (1909: 56).

2. Cochin is not analyzed in this chapter.

3. On Barbosa's account, see Dale (1973).

4. *Imperial Gazetteer of India* 17 (1909: 60).

5. There were also some French settlements in south India, notably at Mahé and Pondicherry. The French retained some of these territories as colonies even after the British established their supremacy over the subcontinent. Certain French areas did not officially merge with the Indian Union until the 1950s.

6. NAI, Madras Government—Travancore and Cochin Residency, Political Dept. (Confidential), 1907, #323.

7. NAI, Madras Government, Political Department (Non-Confidential), 1914, #282–83, 3.

8. Furthermore, Margret Frenz (2003: 5) notes that these two areas have rarely been analyzed together, and that a "comparison between Tiruvitamkur [Travancore] and Malabar in the early modern period is still a desideratum."

9. Quoted in Menon (1956: 274).

10. NAI, Madras Government—Travancore and Cochin Residency, Political Dept. (Confidential), 1907, #323.

11. These wars were of course highly complex historical events. For example, the first Anglo-Mysore War involved the British, the Kingdom of Mysore, the Nawab of the Carnatic (a region of south India), Hyderabad State, and the Maratha Empire. Only brief details on these conflicts are offered here. This discussion is mainly intended to show how Travancore became involved in these wars, and why the British needed their support to defeat Mysore.

12. *Imperial Gazetteer of India* 17 (1909: 57).

13. NAI, Descriptive List of Secret Department Vol. VIII, 1789–90, file dated September 9, 1789, No. 1.

14. *Imperial Gazetteer of India* 24 (1909: 6).

15. A Devasom is a trust used to manage temples.

16. NAI, Madras Government, Political Dept. (Non-Confidential), 1881, #429.

17. Quoted in Logan (1887: 350). This complaint refers to the Sri Padmanabhaswamy Temple in Trivandrum, one of the most famous Hindu temples in India.

18. NAI, Madras Government, Political Department (Non-Confidential), 1914,

#282–83; it is telling that one of the major reasons for British intervention in Travancore (before 1857) was to reduce the religiosity of the kingdom.

19. The Mar Thoma Christians are called Syrian because they claim ancestry from that region and their religious ceremonies are conducted in Syriac.

20. Kerala State Archives (hereafter KSA), Confidential 1944–49, 359, 1945, #158.

21. Quoted in Raghunandan (1995: 159–60).

22. KSA, Confidential 1944–49, 3629, 1944, #174.

23. KSA, Confidential 1944–49, 359, 1945, #158.

24. KSA, Confidential 1913–44, 77, 1940, #52.

25. KSA, Confidential 1944–49, 590, 1946, #187.

26. KSA, General Section 1945–46, 1598, 1946, #409.

27. KSA, Confidential (1913–44), 779, 1930, #21.

28. Ibid.

29. KSA, Confidential 1913–44, 1825, 1944, #80.

30. *Imperial Gazetteer of India* 24 (1909: 8). Population figures for 1901 were utilized for the analysis.

31. *Imperial Gazetteer of India* 17 (1909: 70).

32. Quoted in Kooiman (1995: 2130).

33. The term *Mappilla uprisings* denotes all of the Mappilla conflicts that occurred in the late nineteenth and early twentieth centuries. The major insurrection that occurred in 1921 is referred to as the *Mappilla Rebellion*.

34. Much has been written about the history of the Mappilla Rebellion. See Wood (1987), Panikkar (1989), and other sources cited in this text.

35. NAI, Home Department, Jails Branch, 1927, 293/1927.

36. Interestingly, Varshney (2002: 131) notes that none of the contemporary Muslims he interviewed in Kerala about the Mappilla Rebellion considered it a Hindu-Muslim conflict.

37. Quoted in Hardgrave (1977: 62).

38. Quoted in Ibid. (60).

39. NAI, Legislative Department, Legislative Branch Part A, October 1917, #197–200.

40. Quoted in Hardgrave (1977: 94), emphasis added.

41. BL, IOR/V/26/312/12, 1928.

42. See Dhanagare (1977), Hardgrave (1977), Wood (1976), Panikkar (1989), and Herring (2008).

43. See Bhagavan (2003) on princely state education policies. On the impact of mass schooling in forming distinct identities, see Darden (2015).

44. Interview in Trivandrum, July 22, 2011.

45. Telephone interview from Calicut, April 11, 2014.

46. "Tremors Down South: Ayodhya Sparks Off Trouble in Kerala," *The Week*, August 2, 1992.

47. "One Thousand Communal Clashes, 965 Dead in Last 8 Years," *Times of India*, September 20, 2013.

48. See Appendix 4 (Quantitative Analysis) at http://sites.google.com/site/ajaya verghese/home/data for source information.

49. See also Chiriyankandath (1996) on rioting in Kerala in the post-Babri Masjid period; he notes that most of the violence occurred in Travancore and Co-chin, not Malabar.

50. "One Hundred Fifty Houses Gutted, Several Injured in Clash," *The Hindu*, February 28, 2005.

51. It is difficult to find exact figures; see Appendix 4 (Quantitative Analysis) at http://sites.google.com/site/ajayaverghese/home/data for further information.

52. Interview in Trivandrum, July 22, 2011.

53. Interview in Trivandrum, May 27, 2012.

54. Quoted in Panikkar (1984: 174).

55. Quoted in Somarajan (1983: 132).

56. Quoted in Panikkar (1984: 175).

57. Quoted in Ibid. (176–77).

58. Quoted in Somarajan (1983: 133).

59. BL, IOR/V/26/312/12: 1928, 76.

60. Quoted in Kooiman (1988: 10).

61. *Imperial Gazetteer of India* 17 (1909: 68).

62. Quoted in Panikkar (1984: 162).

63. Quoted in Varghese (1970: 78).

64. Quoted in Guha (2001: 215).

65. KSA, Revenue Department, 16716/F11/56/RD, 09–05–1955, B-1175.

66. Quoted in Assary (2009: 10).

67. NAI, Madras Government, Political Department (Non-Confidential), 1914, #282–83, 15.

68. BL, IOR/V/26/312/12: 1928.

69. NAI, Madras Government, Political Department, 1859, #347.

70. NAI, Madras Government, Political Department (Non-Confidential), 1862, #284.

71. KSA, Cover Files (1728–1903), 15540, 1853, #25.

72. Quoted in Sundar (1997: 191).

73. NAI, Madras Government, Political Department (Non-Confidential), 1862, #284.

74. Quoted in Menon (2001: 27).

75. The communists mobilized along caste lines in Malabar, but an alternative

argument is that the mobilization occurred largely on the basis of *class* (see Herring 2008). But this was not the initial source of communist success. Robin Jeffrey (1978: 82) writes about the 1930s that "there were classes, but there was little class consciousness [in Kerala]. Communal and caste consciousness, however, was intense, and because caste roughly coincided with class, agitation against caste disabilities was to lead the poor towards class consciousness."

76. T. J. Nossiter's (1982) study of communism in Kerala notes that both the Muslim and Christian communities have provided minimal support to the movement in Kerala. He writes, for example, that Christians have so closely aligned with the Congress Party that it has been referred to as "Christian Congress" (22). He also notes that "such limited inroads as the communist movement has made in Muslim areas have been among the depressed landless Moplahs of the interior" (24)—that is, low-caste convert groups. Similarly, Varshney (2002: 164–65) writes that "in areas dominated by Christians and Muslims, the Communists have historically done badly. . . . Communism has made the greatest sense to caste-based Hindu society. Among the Hindus, support for the Communists has been centered among the Ezhavas and other low or scheduled castes."

77. Jeffrey (1978: 83) writes about the comparative weakness of the communists in Travancore: "The big landlord—such a useful focus for class consciousness in Malabar—was largely absent [in Travancore]. These Syrian Christian small holders were more prosperous than the Mappilla tenants and laborers of south Malabar, yet they shared a similarly undisturbed family system and an acute community consciousness reinforced by hundreds of active clergy. They too provided infertile soil for the young leftists of the 1930s."

78. National Crime Records Bureau (2013: Chapter 7, "Crime Against Scheduled Castes & Scheduled Tribes," 111–13).

79. Interview in Trivandrum, July 22, 2011.

80. There was a major insurrection in Travancore in which the communists were involved: the Punnapra-Vayalar uprising of 1946. Like many of the conflicts in Kerala, it garners a wide variety of interpretations. The communists were especially opposed to diwan Ramaswami Iyer's American-style reforms and his intention to keep Kerala an independent state outside the Indian Republic; see Economic and Political Weekly (1977) and Kurup (1988).

Chapter 4

1. NAI, Foreign Department, Secret-I, 1911, #34–40, 4.

2. Parts of this chapter appeared in "British Rule and Tribal Revolts in India: The Curious Case of Bastar." *Modern Asian Studies*, available on CJO2015. doi:10.1017/S0026749X14000687.

3. According to Varshney (2001: 372), Bombay accounts for 15 percent of all Hindu-Muslim riot deaths from 1950 to 1995. Especially considering its small size in comparison to Bombay, Bastar is a much more substantial deviant case.

4. Quoted in Shukla (1988: 13).

5. BL, IOR/R/1/4/26, 1922.

6. NAI, Home Department, Public, April 1855, #47. Note: the name of the author of the report is illegible.

7. NAI, Foreign Department, A-Political-I, January 1884, #117–125, 6–7.

8. Ibid., 13.

9. Ibid., 6–7.

10. Ibid., 16.

11. NAI, Foreign Department, Secret—1, 1911, #34–40, 9.

12. Ibid., 3.

13. BL, IOR/R/1/1/415, 1910.

14. NAI, Foreign Department, Secret–1, 1911, #34–40, emphasis added.

15. Ibid.

16. Ibid.

17. BL, IOR/R/1/1/415, 1910, 15.

18. NAI, Eastern States Agency, F. Files, 1940, #F-6-19/40(M).

19. NAI, Foreign and Political Secretary, Internal, 1922, #319-I.

20. BL, IOR/R/1/1/2703, 1935, 4.

21. Ibid., 2.

22. Ibid., 2.

23. NAI, Eastern States Agency, D. Files, 1936, #D-51-C136.

24. "To Seek Life of a Recluse," *The Statesman,* February 9, 1937.

25. BL, IOR/R/1/1/2973, 1937.

26. BL, IOR/R/1/1/2805, 1936.

27. NAI, Eastern States Agency, D. Files, 1936, #D-51-C136.

28. NAI, Foreign Department, Secret—1, 1911, #34–40.

29. BL, IOR/R/1/1/922, 1919.

30. NAI, Eastern States Agency, D. Files, 1936, #D-51-C136.

31. NAI, Ministry of Home Affairs, Political III, 1961, #5/5/61–Pol. III., Vol. 1, 315.

32. NAI, Ministry of States, Political (B) Section, 1951, F.26(23)-PB/51.

33. Ibid.

34. NAI, Ministry of States, Political Branch, 1953, #18(4)-PB/53 (Secret).

35. Ibid., 136.

36. Quoted in Ernst and Pati (2007: 103).

37. NAI, Foreign and Political Department, Deposit-Internal, 1920, #54.

38. NAI, Ministry of States, Political-B, 1953, #18(4)-PB/53 (Secret).

39. NAI, Ministry of Home Affairs, Political III Branch, 1961, #5/5/61–Poll-III., Vol. 1, 315.

40. See, for example, the *Amrit Sandesh* article from March 25, 2007, entitled "Ambassador of the Revolution and Martyr Pravirchandra Bhanjdev Spilled His Blood in Sacrifice for Bastar," in which the author suggests that "the total number of deaths to this day remains a mystery, as several people claim that hundreds or even thousands died" (my translation from Hindi); Deshbandhu Press Library (hereafter DPL), 24, 1B, un-numbered.

41. "Maharajah Pravirchandra Bhanjdev, Messiah of Tribals" (my translation from Hindi); *Highway Channel,* March 2009—DPL, 24, 1B, un-numbered.

42. "India's Secret War," *Time,* May 29, 2008.

43. Interview in Raipur, April 19, 2011.

44. "Naxalites Meet to Analyse Tribal Revolt Against Them," *Hindustan Times,* June 25, 2005—DPL, 24, IB, 210.

45. Interview in Raipur, April 12, 2011.

46. Interview in Raipur, April 19, 2011.

47. Interview in Raipur, April 12, 2011.

48. Interview in Raipur, April 11, 2011.

49. Interview in Raipur, April 12, 2011.

50. NAI, Ministry of Home Affairs, Political III Branch, 1961, #5/5/61-Poll-III., Vol. 1, 167.

51. NAI, Foreign Department, Secret—1, 1911, #34–40.

52. BL, IOR/R/1/1/922, 1919, 1.

Chapter 5

1. Quoted in Guha (1996: 2379), date unknown.

2. Information on the datasets, analysis, replication files, and additional regression analyses is provided in Appendix 4 (Quantitative Analysis) at http://sites.google .com/site/ajayaverghese/home/data.

3. A government employee in Rajasthan was willing to provide information about castes and tribes and their education levels but stated that when it comes to religious groups, "We do not bifurcate the data like that."

4. This dataset was constructed in collaboration with Emmanuel Teitelbaum.

5. See Cameron and Trivedi (1998) and Hilbe (2007) for more on negative binomial regression analysis. This model has been used often in analyses of conflict; see, for example, Wilkinson (2004), Urdal (2008), Kalyvas (2008), and Bohlken and Sergenti (2010). However, other work on violence uses logistic regression to account for conflict "onset"; see Cederman, Wimmer, and Min (2010).

6. See Appendix 4 (Quantitative Analysis) at http://sites.google.com/site/ajaya verghese/home/data for additional model specifications.

7. The Andaman and Nicobar Islands, Chandigarh, Dadra and Nagar Haveli, and other districts were excluded. However, the Delhi districts, which are substantial in terms of population, are included. The amount of observations in the main regression analyses vary due to missing data, but they never dip below 500. The instrumental variable analysis does not dip below 400.

8. See Appendix 4 (Quantitative Analysis) at http://sites.google.com/site/ajaya verghese/home/data for precise coding procedures.

9. This variable should ideally be continuous. Not all princely states were the same, and though the provinces were generally governed within similar frameworks, they had important differences. However, a simplified dichotomous variable was utilized due to the sheer number of princely states and provinces in India.

10. All control variables are from 2001 unless otherwise noted.

11. Fearon and Laitin (2003: 75) define an insurgency as "a technology of military conflict characterized by small, lightly armed bands practicing guerrilla warfare from rural base areas."

12. A private Indian statistical firm; see http://www.indiastat.com.

13. See Long and Freese (2006: 247–48).

14. Arguments could be made that they wanted to control either violent regions or peaceful regions. Violent regions may have been easier to conquer because the British could come in as a third party against two competing forces. Peaceful regions may have been desired precisely because there was no conflict, and therefore these areas would have required less manpower, arms, and money to annex. However, most of the archival records consulted for this project, many of which included the personal correspondence of British administrators or official minutes from meetings, showcase that these thoughts were not likely on the minds of the men who conquered India.

15. To further illustrate this point, consider that Banerjee and Iyer (2005) find that the most productive land in India today is located in areas that were formerly ryotwari settlements—that is, land where revenue was collected directly from peasants. In other words, they show that productive land today was not rack-rented in the past.

16. For examples on ethnic violence in India, see Iyer (2010) and Bohlken and Sergenti (2010).

17. This analysis was conducted using the *psmatch2* package from Leuven and Sianesi (2012).

18. The results of this analysis (which used the *mhbounds* package) are included in Appendix 4 (Quantitative Analysis) at http://sites.google.com/site/ ajayaverghese/home/data.

19. First-stage regression results are included in Appendix 4 (Quantitative Analysis) at http://sites.google.com/site/ajayaverghese/home/data.

Chapter 6

1. Quoted in Kooiman (2002: 17).

2. It was complicated enough that Gerring et al. (2011: 392) dropped India from their analysis on direct and indirect rule "by virtue of the coding difficulties it poses."

3. Quoted in Assary (2009: 90).

4. These traditional rulers could vary immensely across colonies, and in some cases they were hardly traditional at all. In India, princes could rightly be described as traditional rulers. Throughout the African colonies, however, colonizers may have "invented" traditional rulers (Hobsbawm and Ranger 1983). And Yorubaland in Nigeria may be a kind of middle case in that, as Laitin (1986: 158) argues, the British "resuscitated a declining set of authorities."

5. *Sawbwa* roughly means "king" in Burmese, referring to the leaders of the Shan States. The term *saopha* is also used, which means "lords of the sky" (Tinker 1956: 327).

6. Martin Smith (1994: 36) states that most of these groups find the term *tribe* to be pejorative. In general, the Chin, Kachin, Karen, and so on are known simply as ethnic minorities.

7. This entire section does not pertain to Malaysian Borneo, which was not a part of British Malaya.

8. Kuala Lumpur is the largest city in Malaysia and therefore (like Bombay in India) may not have the highest level of per capita violence in the country.

9. Quoted in Gerring et al. (2011: 399); the original work is Meek (1937).

10. See Afigbo (1967, 1972) for a good overview of the debate.

11. Laitin (1986) notes that the British ruled through local leaders in Yorubaland, which suggests some form of indirect rule; however, a number of scholars suggest that colonial officials were so powerful in the southwest that it was a form of direct rule. This is what Lugard himself believed (Falola and Heaton 2008: 117). See also Meek (1937), Abernathy (1969: 76), and Gerring et al. (2011: 413).

Conclusion

1. Leonard (2003: 364).

2. See Brass (1997), Mueller (2000), Varshney (2002), and Wilkinson (2004).

3. Authoritarian states may be exceptions. Thomas Mullaney (2010) has argued that the Chinese communist state played the key role in classifying the diverse ethnic population of the country into the fifty-six main ethnic nationalities that exist in China today.

4. Quoted in Tambiah (1990: 742).

Bibliography

Abernathy, David B. 1969. *The Political Dilemma of Popular Education: An African Case*. Stanford, CA: Stanford University Press.

Acemoglu, Daron, Simon H. Johnson, and James A. Robinson. 2001. "The Colonial Origins of Comparative Development: An Empirical Investigation." *American Economic Review* 91 (5): 1369–1401.

Adcock, C. S. 2013. *The Limits of Tolerance: Indian Secularism and the Politics of Religious Freedom*. New York: Oxford University Press.

Afigbo, Adiele Eberechukwu. 1967. "The Warrant Chief System in Eastern Nigeria: Direct or Indirect Rule?" *Journal of the Historical Society of Nigeria* 3 (4): 683–770.

———. 1972. *The Warrant Chiefs: Indirect Rule in Southeastern Nigeria, 1891–1929*. London: Longman.

Ali, M. Athar. 1966. *The Mughal Nobility Under Aurangzeb*. New Delhi: Oxford University Press.

Armitage, David. 2000. *The Ideological Origins of the British Empire*. New York: Cambridge University Press.

Asiwaju, I.A. 1970. "The Alaketu of Ketu and the Onimeko of Meko: The Changing Status of Two Yoruba Rulers Under French and British Rule." In *West African Chiefs: Their Changing Status under Colonial Rule in Africa*, edited by Michael Crowder and Obaro Ikime, 134–160. New York, Africana Publishing.

Assary, S. Thulaseedharan. 2009. *Colonialism, Princely States and the Struggle for Liberation: Travancore (1938–1948)*. New Delhi: APH.

Aziz, Azmi, and Shamsul A. B. 2004. "The Religious, the Plural, the Secular and the Modern: A Brief Critical Survey on Islam in Malaysia." *Inter-Asia Cultural Studies* 5 (3): 341–356.

Baden-Powell, B. H. 1892. *The Land Systems of British India*. Oxford: Clarendon Press.

Baig, Mra. 1974. *The Muslim Dilemma in India*. New Delhi: Vikas.

Banerjea, D., ed. 2002. *Criminal Justice India Series*. Vol. 19: *Chhattisgarh*. New Delhi: Allied Publishers.

Banerjee, Abhijit, and Lakshmi Iyer. 2005. "History, Institutions, and Economic Performance: The Legacy of Colonial Land Tenure Systems in India." *American Economic Review* 95 (4): 1190–1213.

Bates, Robert, Rui J. P. De Figueiredo Jr., and Barry R. Weingast. 1998. "The Politics of Interpretation: Rationality, Culture, and Transition." *Politics & Society* 26 (4): 603–642.

Bayly, C. A. 1985. "The Pre-History of 'Communalism'? Religious Conflict in India, 1700–1860." *Modern Asian Studies* 19 (2): 177–203.

Bayly, Susan. 1984. "Hindu Kingship and the Origin of Community: Religion, State and Society in Kerala." *Modern Asian Studies* 18 (2): 177–213.

———. 1989. *Saints, Goddesses and Kings: Muslims and Christians in South Indian Society, 1700–1900*. Cambridge: Cambridge University Press.

———. 1999. *Caste, Society and Politics in India from the Eighteenth Century to the Modern Age*. Cambridge: Cambridge University Press.

Becker, Sascha O., and Marco Caliendo. 2007. "Sensitivity Analysis for Average Treatment Effects." *Stata Journal* 7 (1): 71–83.

Benichou, Lucien D. 2000. *From Autocracy to Integration: Political Developments in Hyderabad State, 1938–1948*. Chennai: Orient Longman.

Besley, Timothy, and Marta Reynal-Querol. 2014. "The Legacy of Historical Conflict: Evidence from Africa." *American Political Science Review* 108 (2): 319–336.

Bhagat, R. B. 2001. "Census and the Construction of Communalism in India." *Economic and Political Weekly* 36 (46/47): 4352–4356.

Bhagavan, Manu. 2003. *Sovereign Spheres: Princes, Education, and Empire in Colonial India*. Oxford: Oxford University Press.

Bienen, Henry. 1986. "Religion, Legitimacy, and Conflict in Nigeria." *Annals of the American Academy of Political and Social Science* 483: 50–60.

Bijoy, C. R., and Ravi Raman. 2003. "*Muthanga*: The Real Story: Adivasi Movement to Recover Land." *Economic and Political Weekly* 38 (20): 1975–1982.

Blanton, Robert, T. David Mason, and Brian Athow. 2001. "Colonial Style and Post-Colonial Ethnic Conflict in Africa." *Journal of Peace Research* 38 (4): 473–491.

Bohara, Alok K., Neil J. Mitchell, and Mani Nepali. 2006. "Opportunity, Democracy, and the Exchange of Political Violence: A Subnational Analysis of Conflict in Nepal." *Journal of Peace Research* 50 (1): 108–128.

Bohlken, Anjali, and Ernest Sergenti. 2010. "Economic Growth and Ethnic Violence: An Empirical Investigation of Hindu–Muslim Riots in India." *Journal of Peace Research* 47 (5): 589–600.

Bose, Sugata. 2006. *A Hundred Horizons: The Indian Ocean in the Age of Global Empire.* Cambridge, MA: Harvard University Press.

Bose, Sumantra. 2005. *Kashmir: Roots of Conflict, Paths to Peace.* Cambridge, MA: Harvard University Press.

Brady, Henry, and David Collier, eds. 2004. *Rethinking Social Inquiry: Diverse Tools, Shared Standards.* Lanham, MD: Rowman & Littlefield.

Brass, Paul R. 1974. *Language, Religion, and Politics in North India.* Cambridge: Cambridge University Press.

———. 1994. *The Politics of India Since Independence.* Cambridge: Cambridge University Press.

———. 1997. *Theft of an Idol: Text and Context in the Representation of Collective Violence.* Princeton, NJ: Princeton University Press.

———. 2003. *The Production of Hindu-Muslim Violence in Contemporary India.* Seattle: Washington University Press.

Brown, David. 1994. *The State and Ethnic Politics in Southeast Asia.* New York: Routledge.

Brubaker, Rogers, and David D. Laitin. 1998. "Ethnic and Nationalist Violence." *Annual Review of Sociology* 24: 423–452.

Brubaker, Rogers, Mara Loveman, and Peter Stamatov. 2004. "Ethnicity as Cognition." *Theory and Society* 33 (1): 31–64.

Bull, Mary. 1963. "Indirect Rule in Northern Nigeria, 1906–1911." In *Imperial Government Essays Presented to Margery Perham,* edited by Kenneth Robinson and Frederick Madden, 47–87. London: Basil Blackwell.

Burman, J. J. Roy. 1996. "Hindu-Muslim Syncretism in India." *Economic and Political Weekly* 31 (20): 1211–1215.

Buultjens, Ralph. 1986. "Religion, Political Legitimacy, and the Secular State." *Annals of the American Academy of Political and Social Science* 483: 93–109.

Byman, Daniel. 2000. "Forever Enemies? The Manipulation of Ethnic Identities to End Ethnic Wars." *Security Studies* 9 (3): 149–190.

Cameron, Adrian Colin, and P. K. Trivedi. 1998. *Regression Analysis of Count Data.* Cambridge: Cambridge University Press.

Caporaso, James A. 1995. "Research Design, Falsification, and the Qualitative-Quantitative Divide." *American Political Science Review* 89 (2): 457–460.

Carland, John M. 1985. *The Colonial Office and Nigeria, 1898–1914.* Stanford, CA: Hoover Press.

Cederman, Lars-Erik, Andreas Wimmer, and Brian Min. 2010. "Why Do Ethnic Groups Rebel? New Data and Analysis." *World Politics* 62 (1): 87–119.

Chand, Tara. 1962. *History of the Freedom Movement in India.* Vol. 1. New Delhi: Publications Division, Ministry of Information and Broadcasting, Government of India.

Chandra, Bipan. 1999. *Essays on Colonialism.* New Delhi: Orient Longman.

Chandra, Kanchan, ed. 2012. *Constructivist Theories of Ethnic Politics.* Cambridge: Cambridge University Press.

Chandra, Kanchan. 2004. *Why Ethnic Parties Succeed: Patronage and Ethnic Head Counts in India.* Cambridge: Cambridge University Press.

―――. 2006a. "What Is Ethnic Identity and Does It Matter?" *Annual Review of Political Science* 9: 397–424.

―――. 2006b. "Review of Brass, Production of Hindu-Muslim Violence." *Journal of Asian Studies* 65 (1): 207–209.

Chandra, Satish. 1969. "Jizyah and the State in India During the 17th Century." *Journal of the Economic and Social History of the Orient* 12 (3): 322–340.

Char, S. V. Desika. 1991. *Caste, Religion and Country: A View of Ancient and Medieval India.* New Delhi: Orient Longman.

Charsley, Simon. 1996. "'Untouchable': What Is in a Name?" *Journal of the Royal Anthropological Institute* 2 (1): 1–23.

Chatterjee, Partha. 1986. *Nationalist Thought and the Colonial World: A Derivative Discourse?* Minneapolis: University of Minnesota Press.

Chaudhary, Latika, and Jared Rubin. 2013. "Religious Identity and the Provision of Public Goods: Evidence from the Indian Princely States." Working paper, Economic Science Institute, Chapman University.

Chhibber, Pradeep K. 1999. *Democracy without Associations: Transformation of the Party System and Social Cleavages in India.* Ann Arbor: University of Michigan Press.

Chhibber, Pradeep K., and John R. Petrocik. 1989. "The Puzzle of Indian Politics: Social Cleavages and the Indian Party System." *British Journal of Political Science* 19 (2): 191–210.

Chiriyankandath, James. 1993. "'Communities at the Polls': Electoral Politics and the Mobilization of Communal Groups in Travancore." *Modern Asian Studies* 27 (3): 643–665.

―――. 1996. "Changing Muslim Politics in Kerala: Identity, Interests and Political Strategies." *Journal of Muslim Minority Affairs* 16 (2): 257–271.

Chopra, P. N., B. N. Puri, M. N. Das, and A. C. Pradhan, eds. 2003. *A Comprehensive History of India.* Volume 3: *Modern India.* New Delhi: Sterling.

Christie, Clive J. 2012. *Ideology and Revolution in Southeast Asia 1900–75.* New York: Routledge.

Cohn, Bernard. 1960. "The Initial British Impact in India: A Case Study of the Benares Region." *Journal of Asian Studies* 19 (4): 418–431.

―――. 1996. *Colonialism and Its Forms of Knowledge: The British in India.* Princeton, NJ: Princeton University Press.

―――. 2008. "The Census, Social Stratification and Objectification in South

Asia." In *Caste in History,* edited by Ishita Banerjee-Dube, 28–39. Oxford: Oxford University Press.

Collier, David, and James Mahoney. 1996. "Insights and Pitfalls: Selection Bias in Qualitative Research." *World Politics* 49 (1): 56–91.

Collins, Alan. 1998. "The Ethnic Security Dilemma: Evidence from Malaysia." *Contemporary Southeast Asia* 20 (3): 261–278.

Connor, Walker. 1993. "Beyond Reason: The Nature of the Ethnonational Bond." *Ethnic and Racial Studies* 16 (3): 373–389.

Copland, Ian. 1973. "The Maharaja of Kolhapur and the Non-Brahmin Movement 1902–10." *Modern Asian Studies* 7 (2): 209–225.

———. 1988. "Communalism in Princely India: The Case of Hyderabad." *Modern Asian Studies* 22 (4): 783–814.

———. 1997. *The Princes of India in the Endgame of Empire, 1917–1947.* Cambridge: Cambridge University Press.

———. 1998. "The Further Shores of Partition: Ethnic Cleansing in Rajasthan 1947." *Past & Present* 160: 203–239.

———. 2002. "The Master and the Maharajas: The Sikh Princes and the East Punjab Massacres of 1947." *Modern Asian Studies* 36 (3): 657–704.

———. 2005. *State, Community and Neighbourhood in Princely North India, c. 1900–1950.* New York: Palgrave Macmillan.

Culshaw, W. J. 1945. "The Santhal Rebellion." *Man in India* 25 (4).

Dale, Stephen F. 1973. "Communal Relations in Pre-Modern India: 16th Century Kerala." *Journal of the Economic and Social History of the Orient* 16 (2): 319–327.

———. 1975. "The Mappilla Outbreaks: Ideology and Social Conflict in Nineteenth-Century Kerala." *Journal of Asian Studies* 35 (1): 85–97.

Darden, Keith. 2015. *Resisting Occupation in Eurasia.* Cambridge: Cambridge University Press.

Datta, Rajat. 2008. *Rethinking a Millennium: Perspectives on Indian History from the Eighth to the Eighteenth Century: Essays for Harbans Mukhia.* New Delhi: Aakar Books.

Desai, Manali. 2005. "Indirect British Rule, State Formation, and Welfarism in Kerala, India, 1860–1957." *Social Science History* 3 (Fall): 457–489.

———. 2007. *State Formation and Radical Democracy in India.* New York: Routledge.

Dhanagare, D. N. 1977. "Agrarian Conflict, Religion and Politics: The Moplah Rebellions in Malabar in the Nineteenth and Early Twentieth Centuries." *Past & Present* 74 (1): 112–141.

Dirks, Nicholas. 1987. *The Hollow Crown: An Ethnohistory of an Indian Kingdom.* New York: Cambridge University Press.

———. 1992. "Castes of Mind." *Representations* 37: 56–78.

———. 2001. *Castes of Mind: Colonialism and the Making of Modern India.* Princeton, NJ: Princeton University Press.

Do, Quy-Toan, and Lakshmi Iyer. 2010. "Geography, Poverty and Conflict in Nepal." *Journal of Peace Research* 47 (6): 735–748.

Dobbin, Frank. 1994. *Forging Industrial Policy: The United States, Britain, and France in the Railway Age.* New York: Cambridge University Press.

Dodwell, H. H., ed. 1932. *The Cambridge History of India.* Vol. 6: *The Indian Empire, 1858–1918.* Cambridge, UK: Cambridge University Press.

Dodwell, H. H. 1934. *The Cambridge Shorter History of India.* Cambridge, UK: Cambridge University Press.

Drèze, Jean, and Amartya Sen. 1995. *India: Economic Development and Social Opportunity.* Oxford: Oxford University Press.

Eaton, Richard. 2000. "Temple Desecration in Pre-modern India." *Frontline* 17 (25).

Economic and Political Weekly. 1977. "Punnapra Vayalar: Rewriting History." *Economic and Political Weekly* 12 (53): 2145.

———. 1989. "Bastar: Development and Democracy." *Economic and Political Weekly* 24 (40): 2237–2241.

Edmunds, David, and Eva Wollenberg, eds. 2003. *Local Forest Management: The Impacts of Devolution Policies.* London: Earthscan.

Elliot, Henry Miers. 2008. *History of India, in Nine Volumes.* Vol. V: *The Mohammedan Period as Described by Its Own Historians.* New York: Cosimo.

Emerson, Rupert. 1937. *Malaysia: A Study in Direct and Indirect Rule.* New York: Macmillan.

Engineer, Asghar Ali, ed. 1991. *Communal Riots in Post-Independence India.* New Delhi: Sangam Books.

Engineer, Asghar Ali. 1989a. *Communalism and Communal Violence in India: An Analytical Approach to Hindu-Muslim Conflict.* New Delhi: Ajanta.

———. 1989b. "Communal Frenzy at Indore." *Economic and Political Weekly* 24 (44/45): 2467–2469.

Ernst, Waltraud, and Biswamoy Pati, eds. 2007. *India's Princely States: People, Princes and Colonialism.* New York: Routledge.

Esteban, Joan, and Debraj Ray. 2008. "On the Salience of Ethnic Conflict." *American Economic Review* 98 (5): 2185–2202.

Falola, Toyin, and Matthew M. Heaton. 2008. *A History of Nigeria.* Cambridge: Cambridge University Press.

Falola, Toyin. 2001. *Culture and Customs of Nigeria.* Westport, CT: Greenwood.

———. 2009. *Colonialism and Violence in Nigeria.* Bloomington: Indiana University Press.

Fawcett, F. 1897. "The *Moplahs* of Malabar." *Imperial and Asiatic Quarterly Review* (October): 288–299.

Fearon, James D., and David D. Laitin. 2000. "Violence and the Social Construction of Ethnic Identity." *International Organization* 54 (4): 845–877.

———. 2003. "Ethnicity, Insurgency, and Civil War." *American Political Science Review* 97 (1): 75–90.

Fernando, Joseph M. 2006. "The Position of Islam in the Constitution of Malaysia." *Journal of Southeast Asian Studies* 37 (2): 249–266.

Fisher, Michael H. 1990. "The Resident in Court Ritual, 1764–1858." *Modern Asian Studies* 24 (3): 419–458.

———. 1991. *Indirect Rule in India: Residents and the Residency System 1764–1858.* New York: Oxford University Press.

Fligstein, Neil. 1990. *The Transformation of Corporate Control.* Cambridge, MA: Harvard University Press.

Freitag, Sandria B. 1989. *Collective Action and Community: Public Arenas and the Emergence of Communalism in North India.* Berkeley: University of California Press.

Frenz, Margret, and George Berkemer. 2006. "Colleges and Kings: Higher Education under Direct and Indirect Rule." *Economic and Political Weekly* 41 (13): 1261–1268.

Frenz, Margret. 2003. *From Contact to Conquest: Transition to British Rule in Malabar, 1790–1805.* Oxford: Oxford University Press.

Furber, Holden. 1951. "The Unification of India, 1947–1951." *Pacific Affairs* 24 (4): 352–371.

Gaborieau, Marc. 1985. "From Al-Beruni to Jinnah: Idiom, Ritual, and Ideology of the Hindu-Muslim Confrontation in South Asia." *Anthropology Today* 1 (3): 7–14.

Gawande, Kishore, Devesh Kapur, and Shanker Satyanath. 2012. "Natural Resource Shocks and Conflict in India's Red Belt." Working paper.

Geddes, Barbara. 1990. "How the Cases You Choose Affect the Answers You Get: Selection Bias in Comparative Politics." *Political Analysis* 2 (1): 131–150.

Gell, Alfred. 1997. "Exalting the King and Obstructing the State: A Political Interpretation of Royal Ritual in Bastar District, Central India." *Journal of the Royal Anthropological Institute* 3 (3): 433–450.

Geoghegan, Patrick M. 2002. *Robert Emmet: A Life.* Kingston, ON: McGill-Queen's University Press.

George, Alexander, and Andrew Bennett. 2005. *Case Studies and Theory Development in the Social Sciences.* Cambridge, MA: MIT Press.

Gerring, John, Daniel Ziblatt, Johan Van Gorp, and Julián Arévalo. 2011. "An Institutional Theory of Direct and Indirect Rule." *World Politics* 63 (3): 377–433.

Ghosh, Parimal. 2000. *Brave Men of the Hills: Resistance and Rebellion in Burma, 1825–1932.* Honolulu: University of Hawaii Press.

Ghurye, G. S. 1968. *Social Tensions in India*. Bombay: Popular Prakashan.

———. 2008. "Excerpt from Caste and British Rule." In *Caste in History*, edited by Ishita Banerjee-Dube, 40–45. Oxford: Oxford University Press.

Goel, Sita Ram, Arun Shourie, Harsh Narain, Jay Dubashi, and Ram Swarup. 1990. *Hindu Temples: What Happened to Them*. New Delhi: Voice of India.

Gold, Ann Grodzins, and Bhoju Ram Gujar. 1997. "Wild Pigs and Kings: Remembering Landscapes in Rajasthan." *American Anthropologist* 99 (1): 70–84.

———. 2002. *In The Time of Trees and Sorrows: Nature, Power, and Memory in Rajasthan*. Durham, NC: Duke University Press.

Gopal, Ram. 1959. *Indian Muslims: A Political History (1858–1947)*. New Delhi: Asia Publishing House.

Gough, Kathleen. 1974. "Indian Peasant Uprisings." *Economic and Political Weekly* 9 (32): 1391–1412.

Gould, William. 2004. *Hindu Nationalism and the Language of Politics in Late Colonial India*. Cambridge, UK: Cambridge University Press.

Grzymala-Busse, Anna. 2012. "Why Comparative Politics Should Take Religion (More) Seriously." *Annual Review of Political Science* 15: 421–442.

Guha, Ramachandra, and Madhav Gadgil. 1989. "State Forestry and Social Conflict in British India." *Past & Present* 123 (1): 141–177.

Guha, Ramachandra. 1983. "Forestry in British and Post-British India." *Economic and Political Weekly* 18 (45/46): 1940–1947.

———. 1996. "Savaging the Civilised: Verrier Elwin and the Tribal Question in Late Colonial India." *Economic and Political Weekly* 31 (35): 2375–2380.

———. 2001. "The Prehistory of Community Forestry in India." *Environmental History* 6 (2): 213–238.

Guha, Ranajit. 1981. *A Rule of Property for Bengal: An Essay on the Idea of the Permanent Settlement*. Durham, NC: Duke University Press.

———. 1999. *Elementary Aspects of Peasant Insurgency in Colonial India*. Durham, NC: Duke University Press.

Gullick, J. M. 1965. *Indigenous Political Systems of Western Malaya*. London: Athlone Press.

Gupta, Dipak K. 2007. "The Naxalites and the Maoist Movement in India: Birth, Demise, and Reincarnation." *Democracy and Security* 3: 157–188.

Habib, Irfan. 1963. *The Agrarian System of Mughal India, 1556–1707*. Oxford: Oxford University Press.

Haeuber, Richard. 1993. "Indian Forestry Policy in Two Eras: Continuity or Change?" *Environmental History Review* 17 (1): 49–76.

Hale, Henry E. 2004. "Explaining Ethnicity." *Comparative Political Studies* 37 (4): 458–485.

———. 2008. *The Foundations of Ethnic Politics: Separatism of States and Nations in Eurasia and the World.* Cambridge: Cambridge University Press.

Hall, Peter A., and Rosemary C. R. Taylor. 1996. "Political Science and the Three New Institutionalisms." *Political Studies* 44: 936–957.

Hardgrave, Robert L., Jr. 1977. "The Mappilla Rebellion, 1921: Peasant Revolt in Malabar." *Modern Asian Studies* 11 (1): 57–99.

Hardiman, David. 1978. "Baroda: The Structure of a 'Progressive' State." In *People, Princes, and Paramount Power: Society and Politics in the Indian Princely States,* edited by Robin Jeffrey, 107–135. New Delhi: Oxford University Press.

Hardy, Peter. 1972. *The Muslims of British India.* Cambridge: Cambridge University Press.

Hasan, Mushirul, and Asim Roy, eds. 2005. *Living Together Separately: Cultural India in History and Politics.* Oxford: Oxford University Press.

Hasnain, Nadeem. 2007. *Tribal India.* Lucknow: New Royal.

Haynes, Edward S. 1990. "Rajput Ceremonial Interactions as a Mirror of a Dying Indian State System." *Modern Asian Studies* 24 (3): 459–492.

Hechter, Michael. 1975. *Internal Colonialism: The Celtic Fringe in British National Development, 1536–1966.* Berkeley: University of California Press.

Heller, Patrick. 1999. *The Labor of Development: Workers and the Transformation of Capitalism in Kerala, India.* Ithaca, NY: Cornell University Press.

Herring, Ronald J. 1983. *Land to the Tiller: The Political Economy of Agrarian Reform in South Asia.* New Haven, CT: Yale University Press.

———. 2008. "From 'Fanaticism' to Power: Deep Roots of Kerala's Agrarian Exceptionalism." In *Speaking of Peasants: Essays on Indian History and Politics in Honor of Walter Hauser,* edited by W. Pinch, 277–319. New Delhi: Manohar.

Hilbe, Joseph M. 2007. *Negative Binomial Regression.* Cambridge: Cambridge University Press.

Hintjens, Helen. 1999. "Explaining the 1994 Genocide in Rwanda." *Journal of Modern African Studies* 37 (2): 241–286.

Hirschman, Charles. 1987. "The Meaning and Measurement of Ethnicity in Malaysia: An Analysis of Census Classifications." *Journal of Asian Studies* 46 (3): 555–582.

Hobsbawm, Eric, and Terence Ranger, eds. 1983. *The Invention of Tradition.* New York: Cambridge University Press.

Hoelscher, Kristian, Jason Miklian, and Krishna Chaitanya Vadlamannati. 2012. "Hearts and Mines: A District-Level Empirical Analysis of Maoist Conflict in India." *International Area Studies Review* 15 (2): 141–160.

Holst, Frederik. 2012. *Ethnicization and Identity Construction in Malaysia.* New York: Routledge.

Horowitz, Donald L. 1985. *Ethnic Groups in Conflict.* Berkeley: University of California Press.

———. 1993. "Democracy in Divided Societies." *Journal of Democracy* 4 (4): 18–38.

Hurd, John, II. 1975. "The Economic Consequences of Indirect Rule in India." *Indian Economic and Social History Review* 12 (2): 169–181.

Hutchins, Francis. 1967. *The Illusion of Permanence: British Imperialism in India.* Princeton, NJ: Princeton University Press.

Ibrahim, Jibrin. 1991. "Religion and Political Turbulence in Nigeria." *Journal of Modern African Studies* 29 (1): 115–136.

Ikegame, Aya. 2012. *Princely India Re-imagined: A Historical Anthropology of Mysore from 1799 to the Present.* Oxon, UK: Routledge.

Ikegame, Aya, and Andrea Major, eds. 2009. "Princely Spaces and Domestic Voices: New Perspectives on the Indian Princely States." Special issue, Indian Economic and Social History Review 46 (3).

Isaac, T., and P. K. Tharakan. 1986. "An Enquiry into the Historical Roots of Industrial Backwardness of Kerala: A Study of Travancore Region." Working paper, Centre for Development Studies, Trivandrum, Kerala.

Isaac, T. M. Thomas. 1985. "From Caste Consciousness to Class Consciousness: Alleppey Coir Workers during Inter-War Period." *Economic and Political Weekly* 20 (4): PE5–PE18.

Iyer, Lakshmi. 2009. "The Bloody Millennium: Internal Conflict in South Asia." Working paper, Harvard Business School.

———. 2010. "Direct versus Indirect Colonial Rule in India: Long-Term Consequences." *Review of Economics and Statistics* 92 (4): 693–713.

Jaffrelot, Christophe. 2000. "The Rise of the Other Backward Classes in the Hindi Belt." *Journal of Asian Studies* 59 (1): 86–108.

———. 2007. *Hindu Nationalism: A Reader.* Princeton, NJ: Princeton University Press.

Jain, Ajmera Kesharlal, and Jawaharlal Jain. 1935. *The Jaipur Album.* Jaipur: Rajasthan Directories Publication House.

Jalal, Ayesha. 1994. *The Sole Spokesman: Jinnah, the Muslim League and the Demand for Pakistan.* Cambridge: Cambridge University Press.

Jeffrey, Robin. 1976. *Decline of Nayar Dominance: Society and Politics in Travancore, 1847–1908.* New York: Holmes & Meier.

———. 1978. "Matriliny, Marxism, and the Birth of the Communist Party in Kerala." *Journal of Asian Studies* 38 (1): 77–98.

———. 1992. *Politics, Women and Well-Being: How Kerala Became a Model.* Oxford: Oxford University Press.

Jha, D. N. 1998. "Against Communalising History." *Social Scientist* 26 (9/10): 52–62.

Jha, Saumitra. 2007. "Trade, Institutions and Religious Tolerance: Evidence from India." Working paper, Harvard University.

———. 2013. "Trade, Institutions, and Ethnic Tolerance: Evidence from South Asia." *American Political Science Review* 107 (4): 806–832.

Jinnah, Mahomed Ali. 1996. *The Nation's Voice, Towards Consolidation: United We Win: Annotated Speeches and Statements April 1940–April 1942*. Karachi: Quaid-i-Azam Academy.

Jones, G. I. 1973. Review of *The Warrant Chiefs: Indirect Rule in Southeastern Nigeria, 1891–1929*, by A.E. Afigbo. *The Journal of African Historical Studies* 6 (4): 716–718.

Jones, Rodney W. 1974. *Urban Politics in India: Area, Power, and Policy in a Penetrated System*. Berkeley: University of California Press.

Joshi, Madhav, and T. David Mason. 2008. "Between Democracy and Revolution: Peasant Support for Insurgency versus Democracy in Nepal." *Journal of Peace Research* 45 (6): 765–782.

Kalyvas, Stathis N. 2003. "The Ontology of 'Political Violence': Action and Identity in Civil Wars." *Perspectives on Politics* 1 (3): 475–494.

———. 2008. "Ethnic Defection in Civil War." *Comparative Political Studies* 41 (8): 1043–1068.

Karat, Prakash. 1973. "Agrarian Relations in Malabar 1925–1948. Part Two: Differentiation Amongst the Peasantry." *Social Scientist* 2 (3): 30–43.

Kareem, C.K. 1977. "The Agrarian Relations of Kerala." *Journal of Kerala Studies* 4 (4).

Kasozi, A.B.K., Nakanyike Musisi, and James Mukooza Sejjengo. 1994. *Social Origins of Violence in Uganda, 1964–1985*. Kingston: McGill-Queen's University Press.

Kaufman, Stuart J. 2001. *Modern Hatreds: The Symbolic Politics of Ethnic War*. Ithaca: Cornell University Press.

Kaufmann, Chaim. 1996. "Possible and Impossible Solutions to Ethnic Wars." *International Security* 20 (4) 136–175.

Kaura, Uma. 1977. *Muslims and Indian Nationalism: The Emergence of the Demand for India's Partition, 1928–40*. New Delhi: Manohar Press.

Kawashima, Koji. 1998. *Missionaries and a Hindu State: Travancore, 1858–1936*. Oxford: Oxford University Press.

Keen, Caroline. 2012. *Princely India and the British: Political Development and the Operation of Empire*. New York: I.B. Tauris & Co. Ltd.

Keltie, J. Scott, ed. 1903. *The Statesman's Year-Book: Statistical and Historical Annual of the States of the World for the Year 1903*. London: Macmillan and Co.

Kocher, Matthew Adam. 2004. *Human Ecology and Civil War*. PhD. diss., University of Chicago.

Kooiman, Dick, Adrian Koster, Peter Smets, and Bernhard Venema, eds. 2002. *Conflict in a Globalising World: Studies in Honour of Peter Kloos*. Assen: Royal Van Gorcum, BV.

Kooiman, Dick. 1988. "State Formation in Travancore." *Journal of Kerala Studies* 15 (1–4).

———. 1993. "Political Rivalry among Religious Communities: A Case-Study of Communal Reservations in India." *Economic and Political Weekly* 28 (7): 287–294.

———. 1995. "Communalism and Indian Princely States." *Economic and Political Weekly* 30 (34): 2123–2133.

———. 2002. *Communalism and Indian Princely States: Travancore, Baroda, and Hyderabad in the 1930s*. New Delhi: Manohar Press.

Korieh, Chima Jacob, and G. Ugo Nwokeji. 2005. *Religion, History, and Politics in Nigeria: Essays in Honor of Ogbu U. Kalu*. Lanham, MD: University Press of America.

Koya, S.M. Mohamed. 1975. "Commercial Interests in the Making of British Policy in Malabar." *Journal of Kerala Studies* 2 (4).

Krishna, Gopal. 1985. "Communal Violence in India: A Study of Communal Disturbance in Delhi." *Economic and Political Weekly* 20 (2): 61–74.

Kulkarni, Sharad. 1983. "Towards a Social Forest Policy." *Economic and Political Weekly* 18 (6): 191–196.

Kumar. A. 2001. *Indian Agriculture: Issues and Prospects*. New Delhi: Sarup & Sons.

Kunhaman, M. 1985. "The Tribal Economy of Kerala: An Intra-Regional Analysis." *Economic and Political Weekly* 20 (11): 466–474.

Kurup, K.K.N. 1976. "British Colonial Policy in Malabar." *Journal of Kerala Studies* 3 (3/4).

———. 1988. "Peasantry and the Anti-Imperialist Struggles in Kerala." *Social Scientist* 16 (9): 35–45.

Kusuman, K.K. 2003. *Issues in Kerala Historiography*. Thiruvananthapuram: Kerala University Co-operative Press.

Lacina, Bethany. 2014. *Governance and Violence in Indian Federalism, 1950–2009*. Rochester University, *Book Manuscript*.

Laitin, David D. 1986. *Hegemony and Culture: Politics and Religious Change Among the Yoruba*. Chicago: University of Chicago Press.

———. 2000. "Language Conflict and Violence: The Straw That Strengthens the Camel's Back." *European Journal of Sociology* 41 (1): 97–137.

Lambert, Richard D. 2013. *Hindu-Muslim Riots*. Oxford: Oxford University Press.

Lange, Matthew, James Mahoney, and Matthias vom Hau. 2006. "Colonialism and Development: A Comparative Analysis of Spanish and British Colonies." *American Journal of Sociology* 111 (5): 1412–1462.

Lange, Matthew. 2009. *Lineages of Despotism and Development: British Colonialism and State Power*. Chicago: University of Chicago Press.

Lee, Alexander, and Kenneth A. Schultz. 2012. "Comparing British and French

Colonial Legacies: A Discontinuity Analysis of Cameroon." *Quarterly Journal of Political Science* 7 (4): 365–410.

Lee-Warner, William. 1910. *The Native States of India*. London: Macmillan.

Leifer, Michael. 1964. "Communal Violence in Singapore." *Asian Survey* 4 (10): 1115–1121.

Leonard, Karen. 2003. "Reassessing Indirect Rule in Hyderabad: Rule, Ruler, or Sons-in-Law of the State?" *Modern Asian Studies* 37 (2): 363–379.

Lieberman, Evan, and Prerna Singh. 2012. "The Institutional Origins of Ethnic Violence." *Comparative Politics* 45 (1): 1–24.

Lieberman, Evan. 2005. "Nested Analysis as a Mixed-Method Strategy for Comparative Research." *American Political Science Review* 99 (3): 435–452.

Lieberman, Victor. 1984. *Burmese Administrative Cycles: Anarchy and Conquest, 1580–1760*. Princeton, NJ: Princeton University Press.

Lieten, George Kristoffel. 1975. "The Economic Structure of Kerala in the Mid-Fifties." *Journal of Kerala Studies* 2 (4).

Lintner, Bertil. 1984. "The Shans and the Shan State of Burma." *Contemporary Southeast Asia* 5 (4): 403–450.

Lipset, Seymour M., and Stein Rokkan. 1967. *Party Systems and Voter Alignments: Cross-National Perspectives*. New York: Free Press.

Logan, William. 1887/1989. *Malabar Manual*. New Delhi: Asian Educational Services.

Long, J. Scott, and Jeremy Freese. 2006. *Regression Models for Categorical Dependent Variables Using Stata*. College Station, TX: Stata Press.

Ludden, David. 1999. *An Agrarian History of South Asia*. Cambridge: Cambridge University Press.

Leuven, Edwin, and Barbara Sianesi. 2012. "PSMATCH2: Stata Module to Perform Full Mahalanobis and Propensity Score Matching." Boston College: Statistical Software Components. Available at https://ideas.repec.org/c/boc/bocode/s432001.html.

Lustick, Ian S. 1996. "History, Historiography, and Political Science: Multiple Historical Records and the Problem of Selection Bias." *American Political Science Review* 90 (3): 605–618.

Madan, T. N. 1987. "Secularism in Its Place." *Journal of Asian Studies* 46 (4): 747–759.

Maddison, Angus. 2006. *The World Economy*. Paris: Organisation for Economic Co-operation and Development.

Mahmood, Cynthia Keppley. 1993. "Rethinking Indian Communalism." *Asian Survey* 33 (7): 722–737.

Mahoney, James. 2000. "Path Dependence in Historical Sociology." *Theory and Society* 29 (4): 507–548.

———. 2010. *Colonialism and Postcolonial Development: Spanish America in Comparative Perspective.* Cambridge: Cambridge University Press.

Majumdar, R. C., ed. 1988. *The History and Culture of the Indian People.* Vol. 9: *British Paramountcy and Indian Renaissance, Part I,* 3rd ed. Bombay: Bharatiya Vidya Bhavan.

———. 1991. *The History and Culture of the Indian People.* Vol. 10: *British Paramountcy and Indian Renaissance, Part II,* 3rd ed. Bombay: Bharatiya Vidya Bhavan.

Malik, Salahuddin. 2008. *1857: War of Independence or a Clash of Civilizations?: British Public Reactions.* Oxford: Oxford University Press.

Mallampalli, Chandra. 2004. *Christians and Public Life in Colonial South India, 1863–1937: Contending with Marginality.* New York: Routledge.

Malleson, G. B. 1875. *An Historical Sketch of the Native States of India.* London: Longmans, Green.

Mamdani, Mahmood. 1996. *Citizen and Subject: Contemporary Africa and the Legacy of Late Colonialism.* Princeton, NJ: Princeton University Press.

———. 2002. *When Victims Become Killers: Colonialism, Nativism, and the Genocide in Rwanda.* Princeton, NJ: Princeton University Press.

Mankekar, D. R. 1965. *Red Riddle of Kerala.* Bombay: Manaktalas.

Mann, Michael. 2001. "Timber Trade on the Malabar Coast, c. 1780–1840." *Environment and History* 7 (4): 403–425.

Marshall, P. J. 2005. *The Making and Unmaking of Empires: Britain, India, and America, c. 1750–1783.* New York: Oxford University Press.

Marx, Karl. 1852/2008. *The 18th Brumaire of Louis Bonaparte.* Rockville, MD: Wildside Press.

Mason, Philip. 1985. *The Men Who Ruled India.* New York: Norton.

Mason, T. David. 2003. "Structures of Ethnic Conflict: Revolution versus Succession in Rwanda and Sri Lanka." *Terrorism and Political Violence* 15 (4): 83–113.

Mathew, George. 1989. *Communal Road to a Secular Kerala.* Delhi: South Asia Books.

Mathur, L. P. 2004. *Tribal Revolts in India Under British 'Raj.'* New Delhi: Aavishkar.

Mayaram, Shail. 1993. "Communal Violence in Jaipur." *Economic and Political Weekly* 28 (46): 2524–2541.

———. 1997. *Resisting Regimes: Myth, Memory, and the Shaping of a Muslim Identity.* Oxford: Oxford University Press.

———. 2005. "Living Together: Ajmer as a Paradigm for the (South) Asian City." In *Living Together Separately: Cultural India in History and Politics,* edited by Mushirul Hasan and Asim Roy, 145–171. Oxford: Oxford University Press.

———. 2008. "The Shudra Right to Rule: Caste, Clan, Community and State."

In *Caste in History,* edited by Ishita Banerjee-Dube, 109–135. Oxford: Oxford University Press.

Meek, C. K. 1937. *Law and Authority in a Nigerian Tribe.* Oxford: Oxford University Press.

Mehta, Asoka, and Achyut Patwardhan. 1942. *The Communal Triangle in India.* Allahabad: Kitabistan.

Mendelsohn, Oliver, and Marika Vicziany. 1998. *The Untouchables: Subordination, Poverty, and the State in Modern India.* Cambridge: Cambridge University Press.

Menon, A. Sreedhara. 2001. *Triumph and Tragedy in Travancore: Annals of Sir CP's Sixteen Years.* Kottayam: Current Books.

Menon, Dilip M. 1992. "Communism in Malabar, 1934–1948." *Economic and Political Weekly* 27 (51/52): 2705–2715.

———. 2007. *Caste, Nationalism and Communism in South India: Malabar 1900–1948.* Cambridge: Cambridge University Press.

Menon, Krishna. 1995. "Politics in Kerala." *India International Centre Quarterly* 22 (2/3): 16–26.

Menon, Meena. 2011. *Riots and After in Mumbai: Chronicles of Truth and Reconciliation.* New Delhi: Sage.

Menon, Shungoony P. 1878. *History of Travancore.* Madras: Higginbottom.

Menon, V. P. 1956. *The Story of the Integration of the Indian States.* New York: Macmillan.

Metcalf, Barbara Daly. 1982. *Islamic Revival in British India: Deoband, 1860–1900.* Princeton, NJ: Princeton University Press.

Metcalf, Barbara, and Thomas Metcalf. 2001. *A Concise History of Modern India.* Cambridge: Cambridge University Press.

Metcalf, Thomas. 1965. *The Aftermath of Revolt: India, 1857–1870.* Princeton, NJ: Princeton University Press.

———. 2007. *Imperial Connections: India in the Indian Ocean Arena, 1860–1920.* Berkeley: University of California Press.

Michaels, Axel. 2004. *Hinduism: Past and Present.* Princeton, NJ: Princeton University Press.

Miklian, Jason, and Scott Carney. 2010. "Fire in the Hole: How India's Economic Rise Turned an Obscure Communist Revolt into a Raging Resource War." *Foreign Affairs,* Sept./Oct.

Mill, James. 1817. *The History of British India.* London: Baldwin, Cradock and Joy.

Mill, John Stuart. 1843. *A System of Logic, Ratiocinative and Inductive: Being a Connected View of the Principles of Evidence and the Methods of Scientific Investigation.* Volume 1. London: John W. Parker, West Strand.

Miller, Michael K. 2013. "The Case Against Matching." Working paper, George Washington University.

Miller, Roland E. 1976. *Mappila Muslims of Kerala: A Study in Islamic Trends.* Bombay: Orient Longman.

Milner, Anthony. 1982. *Kerajaan: Malay Political Culture on the Eve of Colonial Rule.* Tucson: University of Arizona Press.

————. 2011. *Malaysian Monarchy and the Bonding of the Nation.* Eighth Pok Rafeah Chair Public Lecture, Institute of Malaysian and International Studies.

Ministry of Home Affairs, Government of India. 2007. Report of Working Group of National Integration Council to Study Reports of the Commissions of Inquiry on Communal Riots. New Delhi: Ministry of Home Affairs, Government of India.

Mishra, Narayan. 2001. *Scheduled Castes Education: Issues and Aspects.* New Delhi: Kalpaz Publications.

Mitra, Anirban, and Debraj Ray. 2014. "Implications of an Economic Theory of Conflict: Hindu-Muslim Violence in India." *Journal of Political Economy* 122 (4): 719–765.

Mohamad, Maznah. 2010. "The Ascendance of Bureaucratic Islam and the Secularization of the Sharia in Malaysia." *Pacific Affairs* 83 (3): 505–524.

Mohammed, U. 2007. *Educational Empowerment of Kerala Muslims: A Socio-Historical Perspective.* Calicut: Other Books.

Mohanty, P. K. 2006. *Encyclopaedia of Scheduled Tribes in India.* New Delhi: Gyan Publishing.

Moore, Barrington, Jr. 1966. *Social Origins of Dictatorship and Democracy: Lord and Peasant in the Making of the Modern World.* Boston: Beacon Press.

More, J.B.P. 1997. *The Political Evolution of Muslims in Tamilnadu and Madras, 1930–1947.* Hyderabad: Orient Longman.

More, Leena. 2003. *English East India Company and the Local Rulers in Kerala: A Case Study of Attingal and Travancore.* Pondicherry: Mission Press.

Mueller, John. 2000. "The Banality of Ethnic War." *International Security* 25 (1): 43–71.

Mukhia, Harbans. 1972. "Communalism: A Study in its Socio-Historical Perspective" *Social Scientist* 1 (1): 45–57.

Mullaney, Thomas. 2010. *Coming to Terms with the Nation: Ethnic Classification in Modern China.* Berkeley: University of California Press.

Naipaul, V. S. 1971. "The Election in Ajmer." *Sunday Times Magazine* 8: 17.

Nair, Shanti. 1997. *Islam in Malaysian Foreign Policy.* New York: Routledge.

Nairn, Tom. 1977. *The Break-up of Britain: Crisis and Neo-nationalism.* London: New Left Books.

Nandy, Ashis. 1988. "The Politics of Secularism and the Recovery of Religious Tolerance." *Alternatives: Global, Local, Political* 13 (2): 177–194.

Narayanan, Yamini. 2014. *Religion, Heritage and the Sustainable City: Hinduism and Urbanisation in Jaipur.* Oxon, UK: Routledge.

Nath, Devindar. 1972. "Of Logs and Men." In *New Challenges in Administration,* Committee on Case Studies. New Delhi: Indian Institute of Public Administration.

Navlakha, Gautam. 2010. "Days and Nights in the Maoist Heartland." *Economic and Political Weekly* 45 (16): 38–47.

Newbury, Colin. 2003. *Patrons, Clients, and Empire: Chieftaincy and Over-Rule in Asia, Africa, and the Pacific.* Oxford: Oxford University Press.

Nicholson, Andrew J. 2014. *Unifying Hinduism: Philosophy and Identity in Indian Intellectual History.* New York: Columbia University Press.

Nossiter, T. J. 1982. *Communism in Kerala: A Study in Political Adaptation.* Berkeley: University of California Press.

———. 1988. *Marxist State Governments in India: Politics, Economics and Society.* London: Pinter.

O. J. 1983. "Political Backdrop to Trivandrum Riots." *Economic and Political Weekly* 18 (7): 209–211.

Okamura, J. Y. 1981. "Situational Ethnicity." *Ethnic and Racial Studies* 4: 452–465.

Ollapally, Deepa M. 2008. *The Politics of Extremism in South Asia.* Cambridge: Cambridge University Press.

Oommen, John. 1995. "Politics of Communalism in Kerala." *Economic and Political Weekly* 30 (11): 544–547.

Osella, Filippo, and Caroline Osella. 2008. "Islamism and Social Reform in Kerala, South India." *Modern Asian Studies* 42 (2–3): 317–346.

Padamsee, Alex. 2014. "Ideology and Paradox in British Civil Service Accounts of Muslim 'Conspiracy' in 1857–59." In *Mutiny at the Margins: New Perspectives on the Indian Uprising of 1857,* edited by Crispin Bates, 63–81. London: Sage.

Paden, John N. 1973. *Religion and Political Culture in Kano.* Berkeley: University of California Press.

Page, Scott E. 2006. "Path Dependence." *Quarterly Journal of Political Science* 1 (1): 87–115.

Pandey, Gyanendra. 1990. *The Construction of Communalism in Colonial North India.* Oxford: Oxford University Press.

Panikkar, K. N. 1984. "Peasant Exploitation in Malabar in the Nineteenth Century." *Journal of Kerala Studies* 11 (1–4).

———. 1989. *Against Lord and State: Religion and Peasant Uprisings in Malabar, 1836–1921.* Oxford: Oxford University Press.

Peebles, Patrick. 1990. "Colonization and Ethnic Conflict in the Dry Zone of Sri Lanka." *Journal of Asian Studies* 49 (1): 30–55.

Petersen, Roger. 2002. *Understanding Ethnic Violence.* New York: Cambridge University Press.

———. 2012. "Identity, Rationality, and Emotion in State Disintegration and Reconstruction." In *Constructivist Theories of Ethnic Politics,* edited by Kanchan Chandra, 387–421. Cambridge: Cambridge University Press.

Pillai, T. K. Velu. 1940. *The Travancore State Manual,* Volume I. Cochin: Kerala Books and Publication Society.

Pollock, Sheldon. 1993. "Ramayana and Political Imagination in India." *Journal of Asian Studies* 52 (2): 261–297.

Pope, G. U. 1880. *Text-book of Indian History: Geographical Notes, Genealogical Tables, Examination Questions.* London: Allen.

Posner, Daniel. 2005. *Institutions and Ethnic Politics in Africa.* Cambridge: Cambridge University Press.

Prakash, B. A. 1988. "Agricultural Backwardness of Malabar During the Colonial Period: An Analysis of Economic Causes." *Social Scientist* 16 (6/7): 51–76.

Prasad, Kedar Nath. 1998. *Dimensions of Development: Agriculture.* New Delhi: Concept Publishing.

Prasad, Rajendra. 1946. *India Divided.* New Delhi: Hind Kitabs.

Price, Pamela. 1993. "Democracy and Ethnic Conflict in India: Precolonial Legacies in Tamil Nadu." *Asian Survey* 33 (5): 493–506.

Putnam, Robert. 1993. *Making Democracy Work: Civic Traditions in Modern Italy.* Princeton, NJ: Princeton University Press.

Radhakrishna, Meena. 2001. *Dishonoured by History: Criminal Tribes and British Colonial Policy.* New Delhi: Orient Longman.

Radhakrishnan, P. 1989. *Peasant Struggles, Land Reforms and Social Change: Malabar 1836–1982.* New Delhi: Sage.

Raghunandan, Lakshmi. 1995. *At the Turn of the Tide: The Life and Times of Maharani Setu Lakshmi Bayi, The Last Queen of Travancore.* Bangalore: Maharani Setu Lakshmi Bayi Memorial Charitable Trust.

Rai, Lala Lajpat. 1928. *Unhappy India.* Calcutta: Banna.

Rai, Mridu. 2004. *Hindu Rulers, Muslim Subjects: Islam, Rights, and the History of Kashmir.* Princeton, NJ: Princeton University Press.

Ramusack, Barbara. 2004. *The Indian Princes and Their States.* Cambridge: Cambridge University Press.

Ranger, Terence. 1988. "Missionaries, Migrants and the Manyika: The Invention of Ethnicity in Zimbabwe." In *The Creation of Tribalism in Southern Africa,* edited by Leroy Vail, 118–150. London: James Currey.

Rathore, Gayatri Jai Singh. 2013. "Ramganj, Jaipur: From Occupation-Based to

'Communal' Neighborhood?" In *Muslims in Indian Cities: Trajectories of Marginalisation,* edited by Laurent Gayer and Christophe Jaffrelot, 81–104. Noida: Harper Collins India.

Ravindran, T. K. 1978. *Institutions and Movements in Kerala History.* Trivandrum: Charithram Publications.

Ray, Niharranjan, and Brajadulal Chattopadhyaya. 2000. *A Sourcebook of Indian Civilization.* New Delhi: Orient Blackswan.

Ray, Rabindra. 2002. *The Naxalites and Their Ideology.* Oxford: Oxford University Press.

Regani, Sarojini. 1963. *Nizam-British Relations, 1724–1857.* Hyderabad: Booklovers.

Reid, Richard. 2007. *War in Pre-Colonial Eastern Africa.* Athens: University of Ohio Press.

Richards, John F. 1976. "The Imperial Crisis in the Deccan." *Journal of Asian Studies* 35 (2): 237–256.

———. 1993. *The Mughal Empire.* New York: Cambridge University Press.

———. 2003. *The Unending Frontier: An Environmental History of the Early Modern World.* Berkeley: University of California Press.

Richter, William. 1971. "Princes in Indian Politics." *Economic and Political Weekly* 6 (9): 535–542.

Risley, Herbert Hope. 1892. *The Tribes and Castes of Bengal,* Vol. 1. Calcutta: Bengal Secretariat Press.

Robb, Peter. 1986. "The Challenge of Gau Mata: British Policy and Religious Change in India, 1880–1916." *Modern Asian Studies* 20 (2): 285–319.

Robinson, Amanda Lea. 2013. *Trust Amid Diversity: Nationalism and Interethnic Trust in Africa.* PhD diss., Stanford University.

Robinson, Francis. 1974. *Separatism Among Indian Muslims: The Politics of the United Provinces' Muslims 1860–1923.* Cambridge: Cambridge University Press.

———. 1998. "The British Empire and Muslim Identity in South Asia." *Transactions of the Royal Historical Society* 8: 271–289.

Rosenbaum, Paul R. 2002. *Observational Studies,* 2nd ed. New York: Springer.

Rosin, Thomas R. 1978. "Peasant Adaptation as Process in Land Reform." In *American Studies in the Anthropology of India,* edited by Sylvia Vatuk, 460–495. New Delhi: Manohar Press.

———. 2010. "Touring Ajmer-Marwara: The Tripartite Drainage at the Ajmer Saddle." Working Paper.

Roy, Asim Kumar. 1978. *History of the Jaipur City.* New Delhi: Manohar.

Roy, Asim. 1984. *The Islamic Syncretistic Tradition in Bengal.* Princeton, NJ: Princeton University Press.

Rubin, Barnett. 1983. *Feudal Revolt and State-Building: The 1938 Sikar Agitation in Jaipur.* New Delhi: South Asian Publishers.

Rudolph, Lloyd I., and Susanne Hoeber Rudolph. 1960. "The Political Role of India's Caste Associations." *Pacific Affairs* 33 (1): 5–22.

————. 1966. "Rajputana under British Paramountcy: The Failure of Indirect Rule." *Journal of Modern History* 38 (2): 138–160.

————. 1987. *In Pursuit of Lakshmi: The Political Economy of the Indian State.* Chicago: University of Chicago Press.

Rudolph, Susanne Hoeber, and Lloyd I. Rudolph. 1984. *Essays on Rajputana.* New Delhi: Concept Publishing.

Sarkar, Jadunath. 1920. *Studies in Mughal India.* London: Longman, Green.

————. 1932. *Fall of the Mughal Empire,* Volume 1. Calcutta: Orient BlackSwan.

————. 1984. *A History of Jaipur.* New Delhi: Orient Longman.

Sarkar, Sumit. 2007. "Christian Conversions, Hindutva, and Secularism." In *The Crisis of Secularism in India,* edited by Rajeswari Sunder Rajan and Anuradha Dingwaney Needham, 356–368. Durham, NC: Duke University Press.

Sartori, Giovanni. 1970. "Concept Misinformation in Comparative Politics." *American Political Science Review* 64 (4): 1033–1053.

Saumarez Smith, Richard. 2008. "From Village to Community." In *Caste in History,* edited by Ishita Banerjee-Dube, 67–69. Oxford: Oxford University Press.

Scott, James. 1998. *Seeing Like a State: How Certain Schemes to Improve the Human Condition Have Failed.* New Haven, CT: Yale University Press.

————. 2009. *The Art of Not Being Governed: An Anarchist History of Upland Southeast Asia.* New Haven, CT: Yale University Press.

Selth, Andrew. 1986. "Race and Resistance in Burma, 1942–1945." *Modern Asian Studies* 20 (3): 483–507.

Shani, Ornit. 2007. *Communalism, Caste and Hindu Nationalism: The Violence in Gujarat.* Cambridge: Cambridge University Press.

Sharma, C. L. 1993. *Ruling Elites of Rajasthan.* New Delhi: M.D. Publications.

Shoup, Brian. 2008. *Conflict and Cooperation in Multi-Ethnic States: Institutional Incentives, Myths, and Counter-Balancing.* New York: Routledge.

Shukla, H. L. 1988. *Tribal History: A New Interpretation, with Special Reference to Bastar.* New Delhi: Allied.

Sikand, Yoginder, and Manjari Katju. 1994. "Mass Conversions to Hinduism among Indian Muslims." *Economic and Political Weekly* 29 (34): 2214–2219.

Simhadra, V. C. 1979. *Ex-Criminal Tribes of India.* New Delhi: National Publishing.

Singh, Godwin R. 1985. *In Search of Communal Harmony.* New Delhi: I.S.P.C.K..

Singh, Hira. 2003. "Princely States, Peasant Protests, and Nation Building in India: The Colonial Mode of Historiography and Subaltern Studies." *Social Movement Studies* 2 (2): 213–228.

Singh, Prerna. 2010. "We-ness and Welfare : A Longitudinal Analysis of Social Development in Kerala, India." *World Development* 39 (22): 282–293.

SinghaRoy, Debal K. 2005. "Peasant Movements in Contemporary India: Emerging Forms of Domination and Resistance." *Economic and Political Weekly* 40 (52): 5505–5513.

Sisson, Richard. 1969. "Peasant Movements and Political Mobilization: The Jats of Rajasthan." *Asian Survey* 9 (12): 946–963.

———. 1971. *The Congress Party in Rajasthan: Political Integration and Institution-Building in an Indian State.* Berkeley: University of California Press.

Sivaramakrishnan, Kalyanakrishnan. 1999. *Modern Forests: Statemaking and Environmental Change in Colonial Eastern India.* Stanford, CA: Stanford University Press.

Skaria, Ajay. 1999. *Hybrid Histories: Forests, Frontiers, and Wildness in Western India.* New York: Oxford University Press.

Slater, Dan, and Daniel Ziblatt. 2013. "The Enduring Indispensability of the Controlled Comparison." *Comparative Political Studies* 46 (10): 1301–1327.

Smith, Donald Eugene. 1963. *India as a Secular State.* Princeton, NJ: Princeton University Press.

Smith, Martin. 1994. *Ethnic Groups in Burma: Development, Democracy and Human Rights.* London: Anti-Slavery International.

Snider, Nancy L. 1968. "What Happened in Penang?" *Asian Survey* 8 (12): 960–975.

Snyder, Richard. 2001. "Scaling Down: The Subnational Comparative Method." *Studies in Comparative International Development* 36 (1): 93–110.

Somarajan, C. N. 1983. "A Survey of Land Reforms in Kerala Up To 1956." *Journal of Kerala Studies* 10 (1–4).

Srinivas, M. N. 1957. "Caste in Modern India." *Journal of Asian Studies* 16 (4): 529–548.

Sriskandarajah, Dhananjayan. 2005. "Development, Inequality and Ethnic Accommodation: Clues from Malaysia, Mauritius and Trinidad and Tobago." *Oxford Development Studies* 33 (1): 63–79.

Stark, Rodney. 2001. *One True God: The Historical Consequences of Monotheism.* Princeton, NJ: Princeton University Press.

Stern, Robert W. 1988. *The Cat and the Lion: Jaipur State in the British Raj.* Leiden: Brill.

Stevenson, H.N.C. 1945. "The Case for Applied Anthropology in the Reconstruction of Burma." *Man* 45 (Jan.-Feb.): 2–5.

Stokes, Eric. 1978. *The Peasant and the Raj: Studies in Agrarian Society and Peasant Rebellion in Colonial India.* Cambridge: Cambridge University Press.

Subrahmanyam, Sanjay. 1996. "Before the Leviathan: Sectarian Violence and the State in Pre-Colonial India." In *Unravelling the Nation: Sectarian Conflict and India's Secular Identity,* edited by K. Basu and S. Subrahmanyam, 44–80. New Delhi: Penguin Books.

———. 2001. *Penumbral Visions: Making Polities in Early Modern South India*. Ann Arbor: University of Michigan Press.

Sundar, Nandini. 1997. *Subalterns and Sovereigns: An Anthropological History of Bastar, 1854–2006*. Delhi: Oxford University Press.

———. 2001. "Debating Dussehra and Reinterpreting Rebellion in Bastar District." *Journal of the Royal Anthropological Institute* 7 (1): 19–35.

Talbot, Cynthia. 1995. "Inscribing the Other, Inscribing the Self: Hindu-Muslim Identities in Pre-Colonial India." *Comparative Studies in Society and History* 37 (4): 692–722.

Tambiah, Stanley J. 1990. "Presidential Address: Reflections on Communal Violence in South Asia." *Journal of Asian Studies* 49 (4): 741–760.

Tandor, Rajeshwari, ed. 2005. *A Case for Conservation of Tribal Heritage & Environment of Tribal Areas*. New Delhi: INTACH Press.

Taylor, Robert H. 2009. *The State in Myanmar*. Singapore: National University of Singapore Press.

Terchek, Ronald J. 1977. "Conflict and Cleavage in Northern Ireland." *Annals of the American Academy of Political and Social Science* 433: 47–59.

Thapar, Romila. 1993. *Interpreting Early India*. Oxford: Oxford University Press.

Thurston, Edgar. 1909. *Castes and Tribes of Southern India*. Madras: Government Press.

Times. 1911. *India and the Durbar: A Reprint of the Indian Articles in the "Empire Day" Edition of the Times, May 24, 1911*. London: Macmillan.

Tinker, Hugh. 1956. "Burma's Northeast Borderland Problems." *Pacific Affairs* 29 (4): 324–346.

Tod, James. 1829/1920. *Annals and Antiquities of Rajasthan or the Central and Western Rajpoot States of India*. London: Oxford University Press.

Ukiwo, Ukoha. 2003. "Politics, Ethno-Religious Conflicts and Democratic Consolidation in Nigeria." *Journal of Modern African Studies* 41 (1): 115–138.

Urdal, Henrik. 2008. "Population, Resources, and Political Violence: A Subnational Study of India, 1956–2002." *Journal of Conflict Resolution* 52 (4): 590–617.

Vadlamannati, Krishna Chaitanya. 2011. "Why Indian Men Rebel? Explaining Armed Rebellion in the Northeastern States of India, 1970–2007." *Journal of Peace Research* 48 (5): 605–619.

Vanaik, Achin. 2007. "The Paradoxes of Indian Politics." *History Compass* 5/4: 1078–1090.

van der Veer, Peter. 1994. *Religious Nationalism: Hindus and Muslims in India*. Berkeley: University of California Press.

———. 2001. *Imperial Encounters: Religion and Modernity in India and Britain*. Princeton, NJ: Princeton University Press.

Van Evera, Stephen. 2001. "Primordialism Lives!" *APSA-CP* 12 (1): 20–22.

Varghese, T. C. 1970. *Agrarian Change and Economic Consequences*. Calcutta: Allied Publishers.

Varma, S. C. 1978. *The Bhil Kills*. New Delhi: Kunj Publishing.

Varshney, Ashutosh. 2001. "Ethnic Conflict and Civil Society: India and Beyond." *World Politics* 53 (3): 362–398.

———. 2002. *Ethnic Conflict and Civic Life: Hindus and Muslims in India*. New Haven, CT: Yale University Press.

Varshney, Ashutosh, and Steven Wilkinson. 2006. *Varshney-Wilkinson Dataset on Hindu-Muslim Violence in India, 1950–1995, Version 2*. ICPSR04342–v1. Ann Arbor, MI: Inter-university Consortium for Political and Social Research [distributor], 2006-02-17. http://doi.org/10.3886/ICPSR04342.v1.

Vergara, Benito M. 1995. *Displaying Filipinos: Photography and Colonialism in Early Twentieth Century Philippines*. Quezon City: University of the Philippines Press.

Von Der Mehden, Fred. 1961. "Buddhism and Politics in Burma." *Antioch Review* 21 (2): 166–175.

von Fürer-Haimendorf, Christoph. 1982. *Tribes of India: The Struggle for Survival*. Berkeley: University of California Press.

———. 1985. *Tribal Populations and Cultures of the Indian Subcontinent*. Leiden: Brill.

Wagner, Kim A. 2010. *The Great Fear of 1857: Rumours, Conspiracies and the Making of the Indian Uprising*. Oxfordshire: Peter Lang.

Wal, S., ed. 2006. *Child Labour in Various Industries*. New Delhi: Sarup.

Wald, Kenneth D., Adam L. Silverman, and Kevin S. Fridy. 2005. "Making Sense of Religion in Political Life." *Annual Review of Political Science* 8: 121–143.

Walton, Matthew J. 2008. "Ethnicity, Conflict, and History in Burma: The Myths of Panglong." *Asian Survey* 48 (6): 889–910.

Washbrook, D. A. 1976. *The Emergence of Provincial Politics: The Madras Presidency, 1870–1920*. Cambridge: Cambridge University Press.

Weiner, Myron. 1967. *Party Building in a New Nation: The Indian National Congress*. Chicago: University of Chicago Press.

———. 1978. *Sons of the Soil: Migration and Ethnic Conflict in India*. Princeton, NJ: Princeton University Press.

Wigle, John. 2010. "Introducing the Worldwide Incidents Tracking System (WITS)." *Perspectives on Terrorism* 4 (1): 3–23. Available at http://www.terrorismanalysts.com/pt/index.php/pot/article/view/88/html.

Wilkinson, Steven I. 2004. *Votes and Violence: Electoral Competition and Ethnic Riots in India*. Cambridge: Cambridge University Press.

———. 2008. "Which Group Identities Lead to Most Violence? Evidence from India." In *Order, Conflict, and Violence,* edited by Stathis N. Kalyvas, Ian Shapiro, and Tarek Masoud, 271–300. Cambridge: Cambridge University Press.

————. 2012. "A Constructivist Model of Ethnic Riots." In *Constructivist Theories of Ethnic Politics,* edited by Kanchan Chandra, 359–386. Oxford: Oxford University Press.

Wolpert, Stanley. 2009. *A New History of India,* 8th ed. Oxford: Oxford University Press.

Wood, Conrad. 1974. "Historical Background of the Moplah Rebellion: Outbreaks, 1836–1919." *Social Scientist* 3 (1): 5–33.

————. 1976. "First Moplah Rebellion against British Rule in Malabar." *Modern Asian Studies* 10 (4): 543–556.

————. 1978. "Peasant Revolt: An Interpretation of Moplah Violence in the Nineteenth and Twentieth Centuries." In *The Imperial Impact: Studies in the Economic History of Africa and India,* edited by Clive Dewey, and A. G. Hopkins, 132–151. London: Athlone Press.

————. 1987. *The Moplah Rebellion and its Genesis.* Delhi: South Asia Books.

Wood, John R. 1984. "British versus Princely Legacies and the Political Integration of Gujarat." *Journal of Asian Studies* 44 (1): 65–99.

Young, Crawford. 1994. *The African State in Colonial Perspective.* New Haven, CT: Yale University Press.

Zagoria, Donald S. 1971. "The Ecology of Peasant Communism in India." *American Political Science Review* 65 (1): 144–160.

Zainal, Abdul bin Abdul Mahid, ed. 1970. *Glimpses of Malaysian History.* Kuala Lumpur: Dewan Bahasa Dan Pustaka.

Zakaria, Rafiq. 1970. *Rise of Muslims in Indian Politics: An Analysis of Development from 1885 to 1906.* Bombay: Samaiya Publications.

Zaman, Muhammad Qasim. 1999. "Religious Education and the Rhetoric of Reform: The Madrasa in British India and Pakistan." *Comparative Studies in Society and History* 41 (2): 294–323.

Newspapers Consulted

Frontline
Hindustan Times
Muslim Outlook
The Hindu
The Muslim
The Statesman
The Week
Time
Times of India

Government Reports and Other Sources

5th Report from the Select Committee on the Affairs of the East India Company. 1786. Appendix No. 13: Political Survey of the Northern Circars—James Grant, Esq. to Warren Hastings, Esq.

Archives Treasury. 2010. Rejikumar, ed. Trivandrum: State Archives Department.

National Crime Records Bureau, Ministry of Home Affairs. 2010. *Crime in India.* New Delhi: National Crime Records Bureau, Ministry of Home Affairs.

National Crime Records Bureau, Ministry of Home Affairs. 2013. *Crime in India.* New Delhi: National Crime Records Bureau, Ministry of Home Affairs.

Indian Department of Statistics (IDS), Commercial Intelligence Department. 1908. *Statistics of British India: Part 3.* New Delhi: Superintendent Government Printing.

India Planning Commission. 2007. Kerala Development Report. New Delhi: India Planning Commission.

Sachar, Rajindar, Sayyid Hamid, T. K. Oomen, M. A. Basith, Akhtar Majeed, Abu Saleh Shariff, Rakesh Basant, and Mohammad Alamgir Ansari. 2006. Social, Economic and Educational Status of the Muslim Community of India: A Report. New Delhi: Prime Minister's High Level Committee, Cabinet Secretariat, Government of India.

Imperial Gazetteer of India. 1909. Oxford: Clarendon Press.

Rajputana Gazetteer, Volume II. 1879. Calcutta: Office of the Superintendent of Government Printing.

Index

Adivasis: British policies regarding, 35, 39–40; definition of, 5, 31–32; demography of, 83, 131–132, 150; precolonial conflict involving, 19–20; princely policies regarding, 35, 49–50; policies regarding in Ajmer, 87–88, 204; policies regarding in Bastar, 153–154, 157–159; policies regarding in Jaipur, 91, 205; policies regarding in Malabar, 136–137, 144, 204; policies regarding in Travancore, 141–142, 144, 205; relationship with caste system, 31–32; reservation policies regarding, 1–2, 54; violence involving, 8, 13, 145–146, 154–156, 162–165, 168, 171–174, 177–179

Ajmer Province (also Ajmer-Merwara Province, Ajmer District): 5, 57, 58, 83; British rule in, 61, 62–63; caste and tribal violence in, 1–2, 3, 92–95; caste- and tribe-based discrimination in, 83–84, 85–88; communal representation in, 70; communal violence in, 72–73, 79–80; geography and demography of,

12, 57–59, 62; Hindu nationalist organizations in, 75; landholding system of, 38, 84–85, 85–87; precolonial history of, 60–61; religious neutrality in, 63, 70–72, 75, 82; similarities with Malabar, 125, 132, 136, 137, 142, 147

Akbar: 16, 17, 18, 59, 62

Al-Biruni: views on caste relations, 19; views on Hindu-Muslim relations, 17

Ali, Hyder: 104–105, 118. *See also* Tipu Sultan

Aligarh movement: 42, 43–44, 124

Alwar State: 52; ethnic cleansing in, 45, 47

Andhra Pradesh: 24, 97, 143, 164, 169

Anglo-Mysore Wars: 101, 104–107, 132; effect on landholding system of Malabar, 122, 124, 133

Aurangzeb: 20, 59, 60, 64; agricultural policies of, 38; religious discrimination during reign of, 18

Ayodhya: *See* Babri Masjid

Babri Masjid: 1, 74, 80, 127, 174, 206